First World War
and Army of Occupation
War Diary
France, Belgium and Germany

23 DIVISION
69 Infantry Brigade
Duke of Wellington's (West Riding Regiment)
10th Battalion
23 August 1915 - 31 October 1917

WO95/2184/1

The Naval & Military Press Ltd
www.nmarchive.com
Published in association with The National Archives

Published by

The Naval & Military Press Ltd

Unit 10 Ridgewood Industrial Park,
Uckfield, East Sussex,
TN22 5QE England
Tel: +44 (0) 1825 749494

www.naval-military-press.com

www.nmarchive.com

This diary has been reprinted in facsimile from the original. Any imperfections are inevitably reproduced and the quality may fall short of modern type and cartographic standards.

© **Crown Copyright**
Images reproduced by permission of The National Archives, London, England, 2015.

Contents

Document type	Place/Title	Date From	Date To
Heading	WO95/2184/1 23 Div 69 Inf. 1915 Aug-1917 Oct 10th Btn Duke Of Welling.		
Heading	23rd Division 69th Infy Bde 10th Bn Duke Of Wellington's Regt Aug 1915-1917 Oct To Italy.		
War Diary	Bramshott	23/08/1915	31/08/1915
War Diary	Nortleulinghem	01/09/1915	11/09/1915
War Diary	Outersteen	12/09/1915	13/09/1915
War Diary	Erquinghem	14/09/1915	30/09/1915
Operation(al) Order(s)	Extracts from 69th Infantry Brigade Order No. 1	14/09/1915	14/09/1915
Operation(al) Order(s)	69th Ht Bde Operation Order No. 2	22/09/1915	22/09/1915
Operation(al) Order(s)	69th Infantry Bde Orders No. 3	23/09/1915	23/09/1915
Operation(al) Order(s)	10th West Riding Order No. 3	24/09/1915	24/09/1915
Operation(al) Order(s)	10th. West Riding Regt. Order No. 4	24/09/1915	24/09/1915
Operation(al) Order(s)	10th West Riding Regiment. Order No. 5	24/09/1915	24/09/1915
Miscellaneous	25th September 1915	25/09/1915	25/09/1915
Miscellaneous	3rd Corps report Meerut Div. got in pretty easily Enemy reported to be surrending fairly freely Two battalions 8th Division reported to be in German 3rd line trenches.	25/09/1916	25/09/1916
Heading	23rd Division 10th W. Riding Vol. 3 Oct 15		
War Diary	Bois Grenier Line	01/10/1915	03/10/1915
War Diary	Jesus Farm	04/10/1915	14/10/1915
War Diary	T. 63.64.65.66	15/10/1915	31/10/1915
Heading	23rd Division 10th W. Riding. Vol. 4 Nov. 15		
War Diary	Wangerie	01/11/1915	11/11/1915
War Diary	Laventie	12/11/1915	14/11/1915
War Diary	Rue Marle	15/11/1915	18/11/1915
War Diary	Trenches	19/11/1915	22/11/1915
War Diary	Rue Marle	23/11/1915	24/11/1915
War Diary	Jesus Farm	25/11/1915	30/11/1915
Operation(al) Order(s)	10th (S) Battn. Duke Of Wellington's (West Riding) Regiment. Operation Order No. 1	21/11/1915	21/11/1915
Operation(al) Order(s)	69th Infantry Brigade. Operation Order No. 19		
Heading	23rd Div 10th W. Ridings Vol. 5		
War Diary	Jesus Farm Near Erquinghem	01/12/1915	06/12/1915
War Diary	Trenches	07/12/1915	13/12/1915
War Diary	Reserve Billets at La Rolanderie Farm Morning	14/12/1915	14/12/1915
War Diary	Trenches Afternoon	15/12/1915	16/12/1915
War Diary	Trenches	17/12/1915	17/12/1915
War Diary	Trenches Morning & Afternoon Reserve Billets Area Relief In Me Evening At La Rolanderie Farm.	18/12/1915	21/12/1915
War Diary	Reserve Billets Morning & Afternoon Div reserve Evening at Dormoire.	22/12/1915	28/12/1915
War Diary	DW Reserve Billets Morning Afternoon Trench Volume Evening	29/12/1915	31/12/1915
Operation(al) Order(s)	10th (S) Bn. Duke Of Wellington's (West Riding) Regt. Operation Order No. 2	04/12/1915	04/12/1915
Operation(al) Order(s)	10th (S) Bn. Duke Of Wellington's (West Riding) Regiment. Operation Order No. 3	09/12/1915	09/12/1915
Operation(al) Order(s)	10th (S) Battn. Duke Of Wellington's (West Riding) Regiment. Operation Order No. 4	13/12/1915	13/12/1915

Operation(al) Order(s)	10th (S) Bn. Duke Of Wellington's (West Riding) Regiment. Operation Order No. 6	17/12/1915	17/12/1915
Operation(al) Order(s)	10th (S) Bn. Duke Of Wellington's (West Riding) Regiment. Operation Order No. 7	21/12/1915	21/12/1915
Miscellaneous	Programme Of Battalion Concert, 25th December 1915. To Be Held In Recreation Room, Headquarters.	25/12/1915	25/12/1915
Operation(al) Order(s)	10th. Battalion, West Riding Regt. Operation Order No. 8	28/12/1915	28/12/1915
Miscellaneous	Defence Orders.	28/12/1915	28/12/1915
Heading	10th West Riding Vol 6 Jan 16		
War Diary	Rue Marle (Bde Reserve)	01/01/1916	01/01/1916
War Diary	Rue Marle Morning A Afternoon Trenches Evening	02/01/1916	14/01/1916
War Diary	Trenches Morning And Afternoon Divisional Reserve at Hallobeau Evening	15/01/1916	22/01/1916
War Diary	Divisional Reserve Morning & Afternoon Bde Reserve Evening	23/01/1916	31/01/1916
Operation(al) Order(s)	Operation Orders No. 9	01/01/1916	01/01/1916
Miscellaneous	Move Orders	01/01/1916	01/01/1916
Operation(al) Order(s)	Operation Orders. No. 10	05/01/1916	05/01/1916
Operation(al) Order(s)	Operation Order No. 11	05/01/1916	05/01/1916
Operation(al) Order(s)	10th (S) Battn. Duke Of Wellington's (West Riding) Regiment. Operation Order No. 12	09/01/1916	09/01/1916
Operation(al) Order(s)	10th (S) Battn. Duke Of Wellington's (West Riding) Regiment. Operation Order No. 13	14/01/1916	14/01/1916
Operation(al) Order(s)	10th (S) Battn. Duke Of Wellington's (West Riding) Regiment. Operation Order No. 14	22/01/1916	22/01/1916
Operation(al) Order(s)	After Operation Order No. 14 10th (S) Battn. Duke Of Wellington's (West Riding) Regiment.	23/01/1916	23/01/1916
Operation(al) Order(s)	10th (S) Battn. Duke Of Wellington's (West Riding) Regiment. Operation Order No. 16	26/01/1916	26/01/1916
Miscellaneous	10th (S) Battn. Duke Of Wellington's (West Riding) Regiment. Attachments.	26/01/1916	26/01/1916
Operation(al) Order(s)	10th (S) Battn. Duke Of Wellington's (West Riding) Regiment. Operation Order No. 17	30/01/1916	30/01/1916
Operation(al) Order(s)	10th (S) Battn. Duke Of Wellington's (West Riding) Regiment. Operation Order No. 18	30/01/1916	30/01/1916
Miscellaneous	Action In Case Of Attack		
War Diary	La Rolanderie Farm (Brigade) Reserve	01/02/1916	03/02/1916
War Diary	Bde Reserve Morning & Afternoon Trenches evening	04/02/1916	07/02/1916
War Diary	Trenches & Morning Afternoon Divisional Reserve Evening.	08/02/1916	29/02/1916
Operation(al) Order(s)	10th (S) Battn. Duke Of Wellington's (West Riding) Regiment. Operation Order. No. 19	03/02/1916	03/02/1916
Operation(al) Order(s)	10th (S) Battn. Duke Of Wellington's (West Riding) Regiment. Operation Order. No. 29	07/02/1916	07/02/1916
Operation(al) Order(s)	10th (S) Battn. Duke Of Wellington's (West Riding) Regiment. Operation Order No. 22	13/02/1916	13/02/1916
Operation(al) Order(s)	10th (S) Battn. Duke Of Wellington's (West Riding) Regiment. Operation Order No. 23	26/02/1916	26/02/1916
Heading	10 August Riding Vol 8 March 1916		
Operation(al) Order(s)	10th (S) Battn. Duke Of Wellington's (West Riding) Regiment. Operation Order No. 25	29/02/1916	29/02/1916
War Diary	Hesdigneul	01/03/1916	31/03/1916
Operation(al) Order(s)	10th (Ser) Battn. Duke Of Wellington's (West Riding) Regiment. Operation Orders, No. 27	06/03/1916	06/03/1916

Operation(al) Order(s)	10th (S) Battn. Duke Of Wellington's (West Riding) Regiment. Operation Orders, No. 28	12/03/1916	12/03/1916
Operation(al) Order(s)	10th (S) Battn. Duke Of Wellington's (West Riding) Regiment. Operation Orders, No. 29	17/03/1916	17/03/1916
Operation(al) Order(s)	10th (S) Battn. Duke Of Wellington's (West Riding) Regiment. Operation Orders, No. 30		
Operation(al) Order(s)	10th (S) Battn. Duke Of Wellington's (West Riding) Regiment. Operation Orders, No. 32	18/03/1916	18/03/1916
War Diary	Trenches	01/04/1916	04/04/1916
War Diary	Reserve Billets Fosse 10	05/04/1916	09/04/1916
War Diary	Billets Morning & Afternoon Trenches Evening	10/04/1916	10/04/1916
War Diary	Trenches	11/04/1916	26/04/1916
War Diary	Hersin	27/04/1916	30/04/1916
Miscellaneous	Operations Orders	04/04/1916	04/04/1916
Operation(al) Order(s)	10th (S) Battn. Duke Of Wellington's (West Riding) Regiment. Operation Orders. No. 34	09/04/1916	09/04/1916
Operation(al) Order(s)	10th (S) Battn. Duke Of Wellington's (West Riding) Regiment. Operation Order. No. 36	14/04/1916	14/04/1916
Operation(al) Order(s)	10th (S) Battn. Duke Of Wellington's (West Riding) Regiment. Operation Order. No. 36	15/04/1916	15/04/1916
Miscellaneous	Orders By Lieut. Colonel S.S. Haynes, Commdg. 10th (S) Battn. Duke Of Wellington's (West Riding) Regiment.	16/04/1916	16/04/1916
Operation(al) Order(s)	Operation Order No. 2 By Lieut. Colonel S.S. Haynes, Commdg. 10th (S) Battn. Duke Of Wellington's (west Riding) Regiment.	18/04/1916	18/04/1916
Operation(al) Order(s)	Operation Orders. No. 3, By Lieut. Colonel S.S. Hayne, Commanding, 10th (S) Battn. Duke Of Wellington's (West Riding) Regiment.	25/04/1916	25/04/1916
War Diary	Hersin	01/05/1916	04/05/1916
War Diary	Pernes	05/05/1916	12/05/1916
War Diary	Trenches	12/05/1916	17/05/1916
War Diary	Reserve Billets	18/05/1916	30/05/1916
War Diary	Bouvigny Huts	30/05/1916	31/05/1916
Operation(al) Order(s)	Operation Orders, No. 4, By Lieut. Colonel, S.S Hayne, Commanding, 10th (S) Battalion, Duke Of Wellington's (West Riding) Regiment.	04/05/1916	04/05/1916
Operation(al) Order(s)	Operation Orders No. 5, By Lieut. Colonel S.S Hayne, Commdg. 10th (S) Battalion, Duke Of Wellington's (West Riding) Regiment.	10/05/1916	10/05/1916
Operation(al) Order(s)	Operation Orders No. 7, By Lieut. Colonel S.S Hayne, Commdg. 10th (S) Battalion, Duke Of Wellington's (West Riding) Regiment.	11/05/1916	11/05/1916
Operation(al) Order(s)	Operation Orders, No. 8, By Major C.G. Buckle, Commanding, 10th (S) Battalion, Duke Of Wellington's (West Riding) Regiment.	21/05/1916	21/05/1916
Miscellaneous	Operation Orders By Major C.G. Buckle	26/05/1916	26/05/1916
Operation(al) Order(s)	Operation Orders No. 9 By Major C.G. Buckle, Commanding, 10th (S) Battalion, Duke Of Wellington's (West Riding) Regiment.	29/05/1916	29/05/1916
War Diary	Bouvigny Huts	01/06/1916	09/06/1916
War Diary	Trenches (Late Evening)	09/06/1916	09/06/1916
War Diary	Trenches	10/06/1916	13/06/1916
War Diary	Billets	14/06/1916	23/06/1916
War Diary	Enquin Les Mines	23/06/1916	25/06/1916
War Diary	Fremont	26/06/1916	30/06/1916

Operation(al) Order(s)	Operation Order No. 12, By Lieut. Colonel S.S. Hayne, Commanding, 10th Battalion, Duke Of Wellington's Regiment.	09/06/1916	09/06/1916
Operation(al) Order(s)	Operation Order, No. 15, By Lieut, Colonel S.S Hayne Commanding, 10th Bn. Duke Of Wellington's Rgt.	15/06/1916	15/06/1916
Operation(al) Order(s)	March Orders No. 16, By Lieut, Colonel S.S. Hayne, Commanding, 10th Bn. Duke Of Wellington's Regiment.	23/06/1916	23/06/1916
Operation(al) Order(s)	Operation Orders, No. 17, By Lieut, Colonel S.S. Hayne, Commanding, 10th Battalion, Duke Of Wellington's Regiment.	28/06/1916	28/06/1916
Heading	69th Inf. Bde 23rd Div. 10th Battn. The Duke Of Wellington's (West Riding Regiment). July 1916. Attached: Appendices "A" to "E" (Reports On Operations).		
Heading	War Diary.		
War Diary	Coisy	01/07/1916	01/07/1916
War Diary	Baizieux	02/07/1916	02/07/1916
War Diary	Becourt	03/07/1916	04/07/1916
War Diary	Trenches	05/07/1916	05/07/1916
War Diary	Becourt	05/07/1916	06/07/1916
War Diary	Lozenge	07/07/1916	08/07/1916
War Diary	Trenches	09/07/1916	09/07/1916
War Diary	Contalmaison	10/07/1916	11/07/1916
War Diary	Franvillers	12/07/1916	12/07/1916
War Diary	Molliens Au Bois	13/07/1916	25/07/1916
War Diary	Millencourt	25/07/1916	25/07/1916
War Diary	Becourt	26/07/1916	29/07/1916
War Diary	Trenches	30/07/1916	31/07/1916
Heading	Appendices "A", "B", "C", "D", & "E". Reports On Operations.		
Miscellaneous	Headquarters, 69th Infantry Brigade.		
Miscellaneous	Headquarters, 69th Infantry Brigade.	14/07/1916	14/07/1916
Miscellaneous	Captain James Christopher Bull.		
Miscellaneous	Movement Orders By Lieut. Colonel S.S. Hayne, Commanding, 10th Battalion, Duke Of Wellington's Regiment.	25/07/1916	25/07/1916
Miscellaneous	Report On Operations Carried Out By 10th Battalion, Duke Of Wellington's Regiment. On The Night Of 28/29th July 1916	28/07/1916	28/07/1916
Heading	69th Brigade. 23rd Division. 1/10th Battalion The Duke Of Wellington's Regiment. August 1916		
War Diary	Scots Redoubt	01/08/1916	01/08/1916
War Diary	Albert	02/08/1916	02/08/1916
War Diary	Scots Redoubt	03/08/1916	05/08/1916
War Diary	Peake Wood	05/08/1916	08/08/1916
War Diary	Bresle	09/08/1916	12/08/1916
War Diary	Buigny L'Abbe	12/08/1916	16/08/1916
War Diary	Metrien	16/08/1916	20/08/1916
War Diary	Ploegsteert	21/08/1916	22/08/1916
War Diary	Rue Du Sac	23/08/1916	25/08/1916
War Diary	New Trench	25/08/1916	26/08/1916
War Diary	Trenches Ploegsteert	27/08/1916	31/08/1916
War Diary	Trenches	31/08/1916	31/08/1916

Miscellaneous	Movement Order By Lieut. Colonel S.S. Hayne, Commanding, 10th Battalion, Duke Of Wellington's Regiment.	03/08/1916	03/08/1916
Operation(al) Order(s)	69th Infantry Brigade. Order No. 73	07/08/1916	07/08/1916
Miscellaneous	March Table.		
Miscellaneous	Movement Order By Lieut Colonel S.S. Hayne Commanding, 10th Battalion, Duke Of Wellington's Regiment.	09/06/1916	09/06/1916
Miscellaneous	Movement Order By Lieut Colonel S.S. Hayne Commanding, 10th Battalion, Duke Of Wellington's Regiment.	13/08/1916	13/08/1916
Miscellaneous	March Orders By Lieut. Colonel S.S. Hayne Commanding, 10th Battalion, Duke Of Wellington's Regiment.	16/08/1916	16/08/1916
Heading	Major R.H Gill.		
Miscellaneous	March Orders By Lt. Col. S.S. Hayne Commanding 10th Duke Of Wellington's Rgt.	17/08/1916	17/08/1916
Miscellaneous	With reference to working party for tomorrow night consisting of 350 men, it will be supplied and officered as follows.	20/08/1916	20/08/1916
Miscellaneous	March Orders By Lieut, Colonel S.S. Hayne, Commdg., 10th Battalion, Duke Of Wellington's Regiment.	22/08/1916	22/08/1916
Miscellaneous	Operation Orders By Lieut. Colonel S.S. Hayne, Commanding, 10th Battn. Duke Of Wellington's Regiment.	24/08/1916	24/08/1916
Miscellaneous	Operation Orders By Lt. Colonel S.S. Hayne, Commanding, 10th Battalion, Duke Of Wellington's Regiment.	29/08/1916	29/08/1916
War Diary	Front Line Trenches	01/09/1916	02/09/1916
War Diary	Reserve Trenches	03/09/1916	30/09/1916
Miscellaneous	Movement Order By Lieut. Colonel S.S. Hayne, Commanding, 10th Battalion, Duke Of Wellington's Regiment.	01/09/1916	01/09/1916
Miscellaneous	March Orders By Lieut. Colonel S.S. Hayne, Commanding, 10th Battalion, Duke Of Wellington's Regiment.	03/09/1916	03/09/1916
Miscellaneous	March Orders By Lieut. Colonel S.S. Hayne, Commanding, 10th Battalion, Duke Of Wellington's Regiment.	05/09/1916	05/09/1916
Miscellaneous	March Orders By Lieut. Colonel S.S. Hayne, Commanding, 10th Battalion, Duke Of Wellington's Regiment.	09/09/1916	09/09/1916
Miscellaneous	March Orders By Lieut. Colonel S.S. Hayne, Commanding, 10th Battalion, Duke Of Wellington's Regiment.	11/09/1916	11/09/1916
Heading	War Diary		
Miscellaneous	A Form. Messages And Signals.		
Miscellaneous	Operation Orders & Lt Col S.S. Hayne Commdg. 10th Duke Of Wellington In The Field.	26/09/1916	26/09/1916
Miscellaneous	Operation Orders & Lt. Col S.S Hayne Commanding 10th (S) Battn West Riding Regt. In the field.	30/09/1916	30/09/1916
Miscellaneous	To Headquarters, 69th. Infantry Brigade.	00/11/1916	00/11/1916
War Diary	Gourley Trench	01/10/1916	06/10/1916
War Diary	Le Sars	06/10/1916	08/10/1916
War Diary	Round Wood	08/10/1916	08/10/1916
War Diary	Albert	09/10/1916	12/10/1916

War Diary	Longpre	12/10/1916	12/10/1916
War Diary	Yvrench	14/10/1916	14/10/1916
War Diary	Poperinghe	15/10/1916	22/10/1916
War Diary	Trenches (Ypres Salient)	23/10/1916	25/10/1916
War Diary	Trenches Ypres	26/10/1916	29/10/1916
War Diary	Barracks Ypres	30/10/1916	31/10/1916
Miscellaneous	Operations Orders By Lt. Col. S.S Hayne Commg. 10th West Riding Regt.	02/10/1916	02/10/1916
Miscellaneous	In The Field, 4.10.1916	04/10/1916	04/10/1916
Miscellaneous	B Operation Orders By Lieut-Colonel Hayne, Commanding 10th. Battalion Duke Of Wellington's Regiment.	05/10/1916	05/10/1916
Miscellaneous	Report On Operations Carried Out By 10th Battalion Duke Of Wellington's Regiment From 4th To The 8th October 1916	08/10/1916	08/10/1916
Miscellaneous	Report On Operations S.W. & W Of Le Sars From 4th To 9th October, 1916 By Major R.H. Gill, 10th Bn. W. Riding Regt.	11/10/1916	11/10/1916
Miscellaneous	Movement Orders By Lt Col. S.S Hayne Commanding 10th Duke Of Wellington Regt.	12/10/1916	12/10/1916
Miscellaneous	Movement Orders By Lieut-Colonel S.S Hayne, Commanding 10th. Battalion Duke Of Wellington's Regt.	14/10/1916	14/10/1916
Miscellaneous	Operation Orders By Lieut-Colonel S.S Hayne Commanding. 10th Battalion Duke Of Wellington's Regiment.	23/10/1916	23/10/1916
War Diary	Ypres	01/11/1916	04/11/1916
War Diary	Winnipeg Camp I. 19. B. 2.3 Map 1/20000	05/11/1916	10/11/1916
War Diary	Trenches Ypres Salient I. 24. D. 8.9 1/2 To I. 24. D. 7.2 Map 1/1000	11/11/1916	13/11/1916
War Diary	Zillebeke Bund I. 15.d. 1.2 to I. 21. B. 1.2 1/2 Map 1/1000	14/11/1916	20/11/1916
War Diary	Trenches Ypres Salient	20/11/1916	20/11/1916
War Diary	Zillebeke Bund	22/11/1916	22/11/1916
War Diary	Winnipeg Camp I. 19.b 2.3	23/11/1916	29/11/1916
War Diary	Trenches Ypres Salient I. 18a. 5.7 To I. 18.c. 4.7 Map 1/1000 Sheet 28 NW. 4.9 NE 3	29/11/1916	30/11/1916
Operation(al) Order(s)	Operation Orders No. 51 By Lieut.-Colonel R.R. Raymer, D.S.O. Commanding 10th. Battn. Duke Of Wellington's Regt.	19/11/1916	19/11/1916
Miscellaneous	Secret Code For Use Between Credit And Cast		
Miscellaneous	Report On Operations Against Enemy Sap At J. 19.c. 00.35 On Night Of 20th./21st. November, 1916	20/11/1916	20/11/1916
War Diary	Ypres Salient I. 18.a. 5.7 To I. 18.c. 4.7 Map 1/1000 23 NW 4 & NE3	01/12/1916	03/12/1916
War Diary	Infantry Barracks Ypres	04/12/1916	06/12/1916
War Diary	Trenches I. 18.a. 5.7 To I. 18.c. 4.7	07/12/1916	11/12/1916
War Diary	Infantry Barracks Ypres Winnipeg Camp H. 19. B. 2.3 Map 1/20000	12/12/1916	17/12/1916
War Diary	Ypres Salient I. 24. D. 6.0 To I. 30.c 2.8	23/12/1916	26/12/1916
War Diary	The Hospice Ypres	27/12/1916	31/12/1916
Heading	Headquarters 69th Infantry Brigade Enclosed please find War Diary of this Battalion for the month of January 1917		
War Diary	Trenches Ypres Salient I. 24. D. 7.11/2 To I. 30. A. 4.0 Map 1/5000	01/01/1917	01/01/1917

Type	Description	From	To
War Diary	Ypres Billets	04/01/1917	05/01/1917
War Diary	Winnipeg Camp H. 19.b. 2.3 Map 1/20000	09/01/1917	10/01/1917
War Diary	Ypres Infantry Barracks	16/01/1917	20/01/1917
War Diary	Ypres Salient Trenches I 24.b, 21/2.81/2 To I 24.b. 81/2. 31/2 Map 1/5000	20/01/1917	23/01/1917
War Diary	Barracks Ypres	24/01/1917	27/01/1917
War Diary	Trenches I. 24. B. 21/2. 81/2 To I. 24.b. 81/2. 31/2 Map 1/5000	28/01/1917	31/01/1917
War Diary	Ypres Salient Trenches I. 24.b. 21/2. 81/2 To I. 24b. 81/2. 31/2 Map 1/5000	01/02/1917	01/02/1917
War Diary	Winnipeg Camp H. 19.b. 2.3 Map 1/20000	02/02/1917	09/02/1917
War Diary	Ypres Salient Trenches. I. 24.c. 7.1 To I. 24.c. 8.6 Map 1/5000	09/02/1917	13/02/1917
War Diary	Zillebeke Bund I. 21.a. 1.5 Map 1/50000	13/02/1917	17/02/1917
War Diary	Trenches I. 24.c. 7.1 To I. 24.c 8.6 Map 1/50000	17/02/1917	20/02/1917
War Diary	Zillebeke Bund I. 21.a. 1.5 Map 1/50000	21/02/1917	25/02/1917
War Diary	Winnipeg Camp H. 19.b. 2.3	25/02/1917	26/02/1917
War Diary	Camp. Z. F. 25.c Sheet 27	27/02/1917	28/02/1917
War Diary	Bollezeele Eperlecque Bollezeele	01/03/1917	19/03/1917
War Diary	Houtkerque	20/03/1917	20/03/1917
War Diary	Camp Z L. 3.c Sheet 27 1/40000	21/03/1917	31/03/1917
War Diary	L. Camp. Poperinghe L. 3.c Sheet 27 1/40000	01/04/1917	06/04/1917
War Diary	Scottish Camp G. 23.c. O.8 Sheet 28. N.W.	07/04/1917	12/04/1917
War Diary	Hill. 60 (Sub. Sector) I. 34.b & 35.a. Sheet 28 N.W.	14/04/1917	14/04/1917
War Diary	Scottish Camp G. 23.c. 0.8 Sheet 28 NW	22/04/1917	29/04/1917
War Diary	Steenvoorde K. 31.d. 3.4 Sheet. 27. 1/40,000	29/04/1917	30/04/1917
War Diary	Steenvoorde (K.31.d 27 N.E. 1:20,000).	01/05/1917	05/05/1917
War Diary	Halifax Camp (H. 14.c. 3.5 28 N.W. 1.20000)	06/05/1917	06/05/1917
War Diary	Chippewa Camp. M. 6.a. Central	08/05/1917	12/05/1917
War Diary	Scottish Camp (G. 23.b.0.5 28 N.W. 1.20000)	12/05/1917	17/05/1917
War Diary	Hill 60 Sub Sector (Verbrandenmolen I. 28.d. 7.5 28 NW 1.20000)	18/05/1917	24/05/1917
War Diary	Boeschepe Training Area H.Q. At K. 5.d.c. 27. N.E 1.20000	25/05/1917	31/05/1917
Miscellaneous	Left Front. Right Front		
Miscellaneous	Advance Movement Orders By Lieut-Colonel H.H. Hayne, Commanding 10th. Battalion Duke Of Wellington's Regiment.	11/10/1916	11/10/1916
Miscellaneous	Operation Instructions By Lieut-Colonel F.W. Lethbridge, Commanding 10th. Battalion Duke Of Wellington's Regiment.	18/09/1917	18/09/1917
War Diary	Boschepe Area Camp At L.35a. 9.2	01/06/1917	02/06/1917
War Diary	Q Camp G 18.c. 9.2	03/06/1917	03/06/1917
War Diary	Railway Dugouts I. 35.c.	04/06/1917	05/06/1917
War Diary	Front Line I. 34.b	05/06/1917	07/06/1917
War Diary	Battle Wood I. 35.c. 6.7 I. 35.d. 8.7	07/06/1917	10/06/1917
War Diary	Zillebeke Bund	11/06/1917	12/06/1917
War Diary	Halifax Camp. H. 14.b. 1.5 Map 28 N.W.	12/06/1917	13/06/1917
War Diary	Berthen Area	14/06/1917	28/06/1917
War Diary	Chippewa Area	28/06/1917	28/06/1917
War Diary	Support To Front Line (Sheet 28 N.W)	29/06/1917	29/06/1917
Miscellaneous	10th. Battalion Duke Of Wellington's West Riding Regiment.	28/05/1917	28/05/1917
Miscellaneous	10th. Battalion Duke Of Wellington's West Riding Regiment. Instruction No. 2		
Miscellaneous			

War Diary	Ypres Salient	01/07/1917	01/07/1917
War Diary	Trench Map Hill 60 Fast Of Sheet 28 1/5000	02/07/1917	02/07/1917
War Diary	Camp. H. 31b. 2.2 Map 28. N.W. 1/2000	03/07/1917	03/07/1917
War Diary	Steenvoorde Area	04/07/1917	11/07/1917
War Diary	Camp H. 31.b. 2.2 Map 2.2 NW 1/2000	12/07/1917	12/07/1917
War Diary	Ypres Salient	13/07/1917	13/07/1917
War Diary	Trench Map Hill 60 Fast Of Sheet 28 1/5000	13/07/1917	19/07/1917
War Diary	Camp. H. 32b. 2.5.7 Map 27 NW 1/2000	23/07/1917	23/07/1917
War Diary	Berthen Area R. 28. C Map 27 1/40000	23/07/1917	23/07/1917
War Diary	Berthen Area	25/07/1917	25/07/1917
War Diary	Boisdinghem Area Sheet 27th S.E 1/20000	26/07/1917	07/08/1917
War Diary	Boisdinghem Area Map Sheet 27 NE 1/20000	01/08/1917	07/08/1917
War Diary	Moulle Map Sheet 27th NE 1/2000	09/08/1917	19/08/1917
War Diary	Patricia Camp K 29.b. 1.8 Map Sheet 27 1/4000	24/08/1917	24/08/1917
War Diary	Camp H. 33. 9.8.3. Map Sheet 28 NW 1/2000	25/08/1917	25/08/1917
War Diary	Chateau Segard H. 30 Central	27/08/1917	31/08/1917
Miscellaneous	Report On Attack Of Village Of Veldhoek And German Lines Immediately East Of It And The Subsequent Holding Of The Green Line By The 10th Duke Of Wellington's Regiment And 8th Yorkshire Regiment.		
War Diary	Chateau Segard H. 30 Central Belgium Sheet 28 RW	01/09/1917	01/09/1917
War Diary	Steenvoorde Area About K 33 Central Belgium France Sheet 27	02/09/1917	02/09/1917
War Diary	Lederzeele G 27d. 6.8 Sheet 27	03/09/1917	12/09/1917
War Diary	Steenvoorde Area K 25c 93 Sheet 27	13/09/1917	13/09/1917
War Diary	Wood Camp M 5 D 55 Sheet 28 SW	14/09/1917	14/09/1917
War Diary	Middle East Camp Mid 35 Sheet 28	16/09/1917	16/09/1917
War Diary	Ypres Salient	19/09/1917	19/09/1917
War Diary	Rif N of Zillebeke Sheet 28d N.W. 4 North East 3	20/09/1917	23/09/1917
War Diary	Wood Camp M S D 5.5	24/09/1917	25/09/1917
War Diary	Canal Bank Dug Outs. Sheet 28 N. Absent I 25b 7.7	27/09/1917	30/09/1917
War Diary	Ridgewood Camp Sheet 28 Absent N 5b 1.4	01/10/1917	01/10/1917
War Diary	Berthen Area Sheet 27 Central R. 21.c & D	02/10/1917	04/10/1917
War Diary	Ypres Sheet 28 H 6 C Central	04/10/1917	10/10/1917
War Diary	Camp Sheet 28 H 35c Central	11/10/1917	11/10/1917
War Diary	Brewery Camp H 28 A 4.2	12/10/1917	15/10/1917
War Diary	Railway Dugouts Zillebeke Bund	16/10/1917	16/10/1917
War Diary	The Butte J 10a 70 90	17/10/1917	19/10/1917
War Diary	The Butte J 10a 70.90 (Gheluvelt Sheet 28 NW)	19/10/1917	19/10/1917
War Diary	C. Camp H 30 C. 4.2 (Ref Sheet 28 1/40000)	20/10/1917	20/10/1917
War Diary	Micmac Camp	21/10/1917	21/10/1917
War Diary	Zudausques Area Sheet 27a S.E	22/10/1917	31/10/1917

WO 95
2184/1

23 Div
69 Inf.

1915 Aug - 1917 Oct

10th Bttn Duke of Welling

23RD DIVISION
69TH INFY BDE

10TH BN DUKE OF WELLINGTON'S REGT

AUG 1915 — FEB 1919
1917 OCT

TO ITALY

WAR DIARY or INTELLIGENCE SUMMARY

Army Form C. 2118.

10 W.O.SC.
69/23
23
Aug '15
7 & 19
1/5th (sic) Battn Duke of Wellington's Regt

1.7.
23 sheets

Place	Date	Hour	Summary of Events and Information	Remarks and references to Appendices
BRAMSHOTT	23/8/15		Received definite orders to move abroad. The Battn is to move in sections. The 1st Echelon of Transport - M.T. section, and some men of A Coy under 2nd Lt. J Reid to assist in loading the Echo party, numbering 110 all ranks and it acc drivers entrain at LIPHOOK STATION at 10.30 p.m. 24-8-15 under Command of Major Anderson.	
	24/8/15		The other parties consisting of the remainder of the Battalion are divided as follows :- 1st Party "C" & "D" Companies under Capt. Eill second party H.Qrs "A" "B" Companies. These parties to entrain at LIPHOOK in the afternoon of at 4-45 p.m. and 5-20 p.m. respectively. The 2nd and 3rd Parties cross from Folkstone to BOULOGNE The 1st Party from Southampton to HAVRE	
	27/8/15		The 2nd and 3rd parties met on the boat at Folkestone. They reached BOULOGNE at 11-15 p.m. and were guided to the rest camp about 3½ miles from the district. At 5 am they were on the move again and at 10 a.m. left PONT d'ABRIQUES which is some 2 miles from BOULOGNE. At about 4 pm they arrived at	

WAR DIARY
or
INTELLIGENCE SUMMARY.
(Erase heading not required.)

Army Form C. 2118.

Place	Date	Hour	Summary of Events and Information	Remarks and references to Appendices
	28.8.15		WATTEAU where they detrained and marched to billets at NORTLEULINGHEM, where the transport arrived soon after. Attached is nominal roll of Officers with the Battn at this time	
	29.8.15 to 6		Nothing of any note happened this day. The men were given a rest and settled down in billets which consisted of Barns & Farm Houses during this period the Battn remained in Billets at	
	31.8.15		NORTLEULINGHEM A few route marches were taken.	

Willoughby C??all Capt
for O.C. 10/W Redcars Regt

WAR DIARY
or
INTELLIGENCE SUMMARY.
(Erase heading not required.)

Army Form C. 2118.

Place	Date	Hour	Summary of Events and Information	Remarks and references to Appendices
HORTLEUL- INGHEM	1/9/15 to 5.9.15		whilst at this place training carried principally of short route marches. 5 men were admitted to hospital with minor complaints. On the 6th we had orders to prepare to move with the Brigade each next morning	
	6/9/15	6.45 A.m	the Battn marched out from NORTLEULINGHEM turning due day the Brigade performed a march of about 20 miles As the day advanced the heat became great. Three continued with we had under 100 the Canal of the minimum men who fell out.	
		3.15 P.m.	we marched into Billets at WALLON CAPPE 14.	
		7.9.15	At 9 A.m we marched out of Billets and proceeded to Billets between VIEUX BERQUIN and OUTERSTEEN. The billets were very inefficient The Batt. was inspected by General Pulteney Comdg 3rd Corps to whom	
		8.9.15	the 2.2?? Divinion belongs.	
	9.9.15 to 14.9.15		Nothing of any note. The Batta carried out a short route march on the 9th inst	

WAR DIARY or INTELLIGENCE SUMMARY

Army Form C. 2118.

Place	Date	Hour	Summary of Events and Information	Remarks and references to Appendices
OUTERSTEEN	12-9-15	about 1.0am	The Battn received written orders to move next day. The orders arrived about 1.0am. At 9 am the Battn quitted billets and marched about seven miles to ERQUINGHEM. There it was met by the Staff Captain of the 81st Brigade who conducted it to bivouac about 1½ miles South of the town. At the same time the landlord of a copy of the Battalion programme for a period of preparation for the Battalion. For this preparation the Batt. was attached to the 27th Divn.	
	13-9-15	9 am	The C.O., 2nd in Command, Adjutant, Company Commanders and my S. Officers proceeded to the trenches and reported to the Headquarters 1st Argyle & Sutherland Highlanders for instruction in the routine etc. in the Trench.	
		11 am	The Officers and Sergeants reported H.Q. 3rd Gloucestershire Regt for instruction in billets. At the same time warrant officers and sergeants of the same Regt proceeded to our HQ to instruct the Corporals and men of the Battn in Billets.	
		6 pm	"C" Company marched off to the trenches for 24 hours instruction in the trenches under the Argyle & Sutherland Highlanders. The instruction consisted of the officers, N.C.O.'s and men performing the same duties as the instructors	

WAR DIARY
or
INTELLIGENCE SUMMARY.

Army Form C. 2118.

Place	Date	Hour	Summary of Events and Information	Remarks and references to Appendices
ERQUINGHEM	14.9.15		During the day A & B Companies were instructed in the Billets of the 9/Argyll & Suthd Regt.	
		6.30pm	A & B Companies proceeded to the trenches for instruction under the Argyll & Sutherland for 24 hrs. C & D Coys returned to Bivouac	
		8pm	Orders were received under Secret heading for the Bath to enter over the trenches as shown in the order, what is attached	
	15.9.15	7pm	Relieved 9/Argyle & Sutherland, 9th Royal Scots, 2nd Gloucester Regt of parts of their trenches. The Battn now occupy 752. 753. 754 & part of the BOIS GRENIER line from MOAT FARM to the N.E. The night was quiet. During inspection of trenches many improvements to be carried out were noticed, several places where parapets and dug-outs were destroyed were noted. Several German snipers annoyed the sentries during the night. No Casualties. Amount of S.A.A. expended was 5060 rounds.	

WAR DIARY
or
INTELLIGENCE SUMMARY.
(Erase heading not required.)

Army Form C. 2118.

Place	Date	Hour	Summary of Events and Information	Remarks and references to Appendices
	16/9/15		All quiet. Artillery duel over our heads German Artillery dropped on our trenches, but did no damage. We suffered one 1st Casualty No. 13664 Pte Arthur Hargreaves A Coy (was sniped) whilst cooking his dinner. He died instantaneously. In the evening the dumping ground was swept by M.G. fire by the enemy, during his time Lt Col (Oatt R.D. Tullibardine of A Company was shot (through the head, Both Casualties were buried in the BOIS GRENIER Church Yard. Cross were erected over their bodies.	
	17/9/15		During the night, an alarm was given that the Germans were attacking our trenches. The artillery was turned on, but no attack took place both the the location of much sniping nothing of any note occurred. The weather up to now has been all that could be desired. The early mornings were clear, for observation much work was done on improving the positions of the present	
	18/9/15		morning dug-outs that had been destroyed. Situation normal. No casualties weather fine + clear	
	19.9.15		Situation normal. All quiet - except for a few snipers. Our Artillery	

T2134. Wt. W708—776. 500000. 4/15. Sir J.C.&S.

WAR DIARY
or
INTELLIGENCE SUMMARY.

Army Form C. 2118.

Place	Date	Hour	Summary of Events and Information	Remarks and references to Appendices
			were registering most of the day the German retaliated on our trench. Several hostile aeroplanes passed over during the day, much anti aeroplane ammunition was wasted on them. None were hit. The enemy sniping received somewhat, & one or two Europeans reported that they had hit several men out. At night the German started rockets to our line, but what they said was harmle, audible as we are 400ˣ from his trenches	
	30 April		heard fire rebel all quiet, heavy firing heard to the south. Our Artillery continued to register to which the German retaliate on our trenches with whizz bangs. No Casualties first shots of a big bombardment fired. Our guns both heavy slightly pounded at the enemy trench all day and most of the night. Bombardment sounds general all along the line, little or no retaliation. The enemy shot fell in the WATER FARM, proving a tank. This is serious, as with two turns it was difficult to keep a big supply of water. No Casualties enemy parapet badly damaged, but not yet not so badly.	

Army Form C. 2118.

WAR DIARY
or
INTELLIGENCE SUMMARY.
(Erase heading not required.)

Instructions regarding War Diaries and Intelligence Summaries are contained in F. S. Regs., Part II. and the Staff Manual respectively. Title pages will be prepared in manuscript.

Place	Date	Hour	Summary of Events and Information	Remarks and references to Appendices
	30.9.15		Bombardment continues only heavier. Mu true enemy retaliate. Most of their shells however fell behind our trenches, nevertheless they damaged our parapet in places and blew in a communication trench. Three men were wounded two severely 13685 Pte William Burley A Coy. 13789 Pte Ernest Franklin seriously, 13729 " Arthur Stubbs A.Coy. One shell burst about 8 yds from our front store and the men in guard received severe injury the night and the guns were trotting stopped in the enemy wire, but did not cut it very much. Observation is difficult from our trenches owing to the long grass. At night working parties repaired our damage and endeavoured to surround the remaining wapes trail with sand-bags but were shelled out. During the day preliminary order for an attack on Wednesday were received. Copy marked X attached hereby to the bombardment (para 2 was not able to be carried out	

WAR DIARY or INTELLIGENCE SUMMARY

Army Form C. 2118.

Place	Date	Hour	Summary of Events and Information	Remarks and references to Appendices
	28-9-15		Bombardment continues heavier. Enemy proper treated in many places. No artillery firing 8" shells. The attack other marked O was arrived and duly carried out. As there was a thunderstorm in progress at the time it was impossible to judge to what extent the wire succeeded. At 1 Am the attacked others marked P were received and others marked Q were carried to Carpanic. At 4 Am all were in position and at 4.35 am the bombardment commenced, all guns of all calibre and rifles were firing upon the German salts up many places but did not retaliate until our bombardment had ceased. They then sent several heavy shells roaring bangs into us without however doing any harm to the trenches. During this affair 5 men were wounded, none seriously. After this all was quiet for some hours. At about 9 am our guns commenced a steady bombardment of the enemy's lines doing much damage to their parapets but very little otherwise	

The enemy retaliated with heavy shells (4.5 Howitzers & 77 m/m) which damaged our Communication trenches in parts. During the morning we suffered 2 Casualties No.11454 Pte A Fletcher "D" Company. He was shot through the head by a sniper. In the afternoon one man was wounded. In the evening we got the attached Order numbered Q to cut gaps through our wire. The attached operation orders numbered R were issued to Companies. In the evening hostile aircraft was active but owing to the wet and a stiff breeze did not remain in the air long. During the night all was quiet looking parties from each Company went outside our parapet and cut openings in our wire. Though which we could pass if the order to advance was given.

9.30 & 9.40 p.m. Punctually to the minute a most terrific bombardment by our Artillery on the German line commenced. This was the commencement of a forward movement by the 3rd Army Corps which on its own was a small part of a large advance by the French English troops

WAR DIARY
or
INTELLIGENCE SUMMARY.
(Erase heading not required.)

Army Form C. 2118.

Place	Date	Hour	Summary of Events and Information	Remarks and references to Appendices
Cont'd	29th		Almost simultaneously the enemy started and a terrible artillery fire was kept up for several hours and did not quieten until 9pm for the most part, the German shells burst on firing trench and in crossway little material damage was done. The moral effect however was great. Our men were splendid, especially covering it was their first real action. During the morning we only suffered 14 casualties of which only two were serious. One proved fatal the man dying shortly after being admitted to the field ambulance. At 4.30 am the 8th Division crossed the German trenches (over) by small bodies and took the trenches with no opposition. They feared our musketry till the 69th Brigade approached. 10 rds of volleys fire and 1st Gords Regt being in the fire trenches kept up a bombardment will rifle and by fire which had the effect of driving a great portion of the enemy fire for the troops which were actually attacking during the morning. No orders were received during the day which show the attached orders will till further orders during the morning. A very exhaustion	

WAR DIARY
or
INTELLIGENCE SUMMARY

Army Form C. 2118.

Place	Date	Hour	Summary of Events and Information	Remarks and references to Appendices

advance by the Allies.

The message with reference to the German movement westward from LILLE gave warnings of a heavy counter attack by the enemy. The men were by now completely worn out having been 12 nights in succession in the trenches, followed up by the Castle bombardment. In the morning of 25th a Brigade order was received pointing to the effect that the Battn. would be relieved by the 11th Leicesters, that we were to take over new billets about 1½ miles north of BOIS GRENIER. During the day all was exceptionally quiet. Preparatory bulletins were received from H.Q. showing good progress in the part of our allies the French as well as on the part of the British troops. At 7.20 p.m. relief commenced and by 9.20 was complete. By 10.30 pm the Battn. were settled in its new billets, which consisted of small huts specially built for the purpose. Serving the last two days in the trenches, owing to the mud which was ankle deep, matters were rather uncomfortable for the men.

WAR DIARY
or
INTELLIGENCE SUMMARY.

(Erase heading not required.)

Army Form C. 2118.

Place	Date	Hour	Summary of Events and Information	Remarks and references to Appendices
	27 Apl to 30 Apl		Nothing to report. Good news continues to arrive from all sides. On the evening of 30th 2 Companies relieved the 8th Yorks in the BOIS GRENIER line. Weather colder and some rain.	

Arthur Croad
Lt Col.
O.C. 10th Duke [?]

Extracts from 69th Infantry Brigade Order No. 2.

14.9.15.

Ref. Sheet 36 ___1___
             40,000

The 69th Infantry Brigade will relieve the 81st. Infantry Brigade in trenches 52-58 inclusive and the night 15/16th Sept. as in attached table.

Transport will be billetted as follows :-

<u>Battalions in trenches</u>. All transport in Brigade 1st line Transport Lines.
                           All requirements of Officers and other ranks to be brought up at night with the rations.
                           No more movement from front to rear or vice versa other than is absolutely necessary.

After relief is complete reports will be sent to 69th Brigade H.Q. situated in advance Divisional H.Q. Dug Outs in La ROLANDERIE FARM square H.11.c.

sd. D.H. Hanney, Capt.
Brigade Major.

Preliminary ✗ Copy No. 3

69th Inf Bde Operation Order No 2

Ref 36. NW Sheet 4
1:10000
22-9-15

1. On the morning of Saturday 25th Sept the 69th Inf Bde will be prepared to attack if ordered. Objectives will be given verbally to OC units

2. The following will be rehearsed by Btns in trenches ~~in trenches~~ this afternoon & again on Thursday morning when the GOC Bde will be present (10th W Rid Rgt 11 am, 8th Yorks 12 noon). A GHQ pamphlet is issued with these orders & attention is drawn to the following points

Each man will carry   1 W P Sheet
                     1 Cardigan Jacket
                     3 Sandbags

He will be provided with a 4th Sandbag for his spare kit. Each Btn in the trenches will be provided with ~~40~~ 100 ladders. The men will be drawn up in the trenches, the position of the ladders will be indicated and all men will be shown how they will pass the parapet either by ladder or by the Saps, & by which openings they will pass our wire (Later they will be told where the enemy's wire has been breached) Bombing & bayonet parties will be told off & these will pass the parapet first. Every other man will carry a Shovel slung over the right shoulder. All men will be informed how the further advance will be made & exactly what is required of each man when the enemy's trenches are reached. Men not carrying shovels will carry their entrenching tools ready in their belts.

Filled Water Bottles ⎫
Days Ration & Iron Ration ⎬ to be carried.
200 rds per man ⎭

Ammunition ⎫ ~~carrying~~ parties to be detailed
Bombs ⎭

3. M.G. officers will take their orders direct from Bde M.G. officer

4. During the next 4 days, units must be prepared for a possible gas attack with asphyxiating shells.

D.R. Hannay, Capt.
Bde Major 69 IB

5. Behind each Coy 1000 filled Sandbags to be ready to repair parapet immediately if necessary

DRH

SECRET

69th Infantry Bde Orders No 3.
23/9/15:

1. There will be a false alarm tonight as follows:—

At 8 p.m. The Brigade Grenadier Officer will fire rockets in the front trenches. The men will cheer and wave their bayonets as if about to attack. Having got the enemy to man the parapets there will be one round of "Gun fire" throughout the Corps against the hostile parapet.

Acknowledge

T R Hannay
Captain
Brigade Major
69th Infantry Brigade

10th Inf. Brigade Order No. 3   Copy No.
W.R. 81   24.9.15

1. The following programme will be carried out on Saturday morning 25th inst.

2. The 8th Division time table is as follows:—
   4.20 a.m. Beginning of Bombardment. single guns, smoke, catapults and demonstrations on each flank.
   5.50 a.m. Assault.

3. The 69th Brigade throw smoke bombs from 4.50 to 5.30 a.m.

4. The 69th I.B. will bombard with Infantry and M.G. fire the trenches to our front from 4.25 a.m. till smoke commences, or as long as the advance of the 8th Division permits.

5. The 8th Div. will mark the position of their bombers and advanced Infantry with red flags.

6. The programme as far as the 69th Brigade is concerned will be rehearsed this morning with the following exceptions:—
   1. There will be no smoke.
   2. The M.G's will be manned in the Battle Emplacements, but will not fire, and the loopholes will remain screened.

(3) All fire will cease at 4.32 a.m. and the normal programme taken up for the remainder of the day.

Acknowledge & return copy to me.
C Bathurst Capt
D Unit

Copy

By runner 1.15 a.m.

Watches will be set on receipt of this.
CB.

Recieved at [Paranade?]/W
2.0 a.m.
24/Sept/15

10th. West Riding Regt.   Order No. 4.   Copy No.

1. Companies will remain in trenches occupied at present until orders orders are received to take up "Attack" formation, dispositions will be issued later.

2. Dress – Marching order, but the pack will only contain the following :– Three sandbags,
    Jersey, if not worn on person.
    Waterproof sheet.
    200 rounds of ammunition per man will be carried

3. The remainder of each mans kit will be put into an empty sandbag, carefully marked with the mans Regtl. No. rank, name and and Regiment, in indelible pencil. The whole of these kits will be stacked by Companies in the vicinity of Company Headquarters and will be left in charge of a Guard consisting of two cooks and two officers servants. 50% of each Company will carry a shovel slung over the left shoulder. The remainder will carry entrenching tools assembled in their belts.

4. Company Commanders will see that all wire-cutters are carried by the leading half companies, each man carrying a wire-cutter must be marked by white-tape or some clear mark on his shoulders, if any one of these men is "knocked out", his wire-cutters are to be taken by the man nearest to him.

5. Every man is to see that his rifle is perfectly clean, and that the bolt action works easily. It should be impressed upon every man how important this is.

6. Company Officers will set their watches with the Brigade time tonight by telephone from Battalion Headquarters.

7. Water duty men, Sergt. Chitty and two Sanitary men per Company, Pioneers will report to the Sergeant Major at JOCK'S JOY at 5 p.m. tonight. These men will act as ammunition carriers and at 4 a.m. tomorrow will assemble in JOCK'S JOY under the Sergeant Major.
The Orderly Room Sergeant and clerk, Headquarter Officers servants, Headquarters Cook, will remain at Headquarters and guard Headquarter baggage, &c.
Sergeant Carrodus will be given special instructions.
Stretcher Bearers will follow behind their companies with stretchers.
Medical Officers Orderlies remain with M.O. at "first aid" station, the position of which will be notified later.
Signallers receive special instructions from Signalling Officer.
Bombers.– Instructions issued later.
All other N.C.O's. and men are to be with their Companies.

8. The Battalion will bombard with rifle fire and machine gun fire the trenches to our front from 4-25 a.m. till smoke commences, or as long as the advance of the 8th Division permits. The 8th Division will mark the position of their bombers and advanced infantry with red flags. At 4-30 a.m. the 8th Division assaults the enemy's trenches. The 69th Brigade must give all the support in its power.
At 4-56 a.m. the 69th I.B. throw smoke bombs and continue to do so until 5-30 a.m. Company Commanders are warned that in the event of Gas being used by our own troops or those of the enemy, Gas helmets will be put on. Men are to be warned only to breathe out of the mouth valve and not to suck in.

9. As no orders have been received from Headquarters no further information can be given, but this will be done as soon as possible.

Capt.& Adjt.
D. Unit.

24.9.15

10th West Riding Regiment.   Order No. 5.   Copy No. _____

Ref. 36 N.W. Sheet 4.

1. Instructions for possible assault tomorrow :-

   (a). Bombers of "A" and "B" Companies will accompany the first line, and receive their orders from 2/Lieut. Lavarack.
   (b). Six Bombers each of "C" and "D" Companies will fire the smoke balls under the direction of 2/Lieut. Kerridge. They will afterwards be employed in carrying up spare bombs to our first line.
   (c). On orders being received to prepare for attack "B" Company will move to the living trench in rear of T.52. "A" Company will extend to its left as far as the centre of T.53. "D" Company will move to the right, joining hands with "A" Company, its left being on the unmetalled road S.E. from I.26.c.5.6½. "C" Company will move into the Living trench in rear of "D" Company.

Each Company will advance in two lines 50 yards between lines and 200 yards between Companies.

The objective for each Company and the signal to advance will be communicated later.

Any additional shovels, or as many as are available must be obtained from JOCK'S JOY this afternoon.

Companies will ensure that all water bottles are filled and that each man is in possession of his day's rations and his Iron Rations.

Company Runners will remain with the C.O.

24.9.15.
                                                        Capt. & Adjt.
                                                        D Unit.

Routine Orders by Lt.Col. J.J. Bartholomew, D.S.O.

1. Company Commanders will ensure that all rifles in his company are inspected daily by an officer before 9 a.m.

                                                        Capt. & Adjt.
24.9.15.   D. Unit.

25th September 1915.

French have broken through German lines near RHEIMS on a front of 35 Kilometers aaa First Army report LOOS and PUIRS have been taken and advance is being continued aaa 1st Division have taken HULLUCK 7th Division GOTE ST ELDI aaa 9th Division FOSSE No. 8 and reserve Brigades directed on HAISNES aaa MEERUR Div. have taken 120 prisoners and 8th have taken 100.

from 69th Brigade.

25.9.15

3rd Corps report MEERUT Div. got in pretty easily

Enemy reported to be surrending fairly freely

Two battalions 8th Division reported to be in

German 3rd line trenches.

from 69th Brigade.

2.y.
7 sheets

121/7595

23rd Return

Representing at Ort

to the W. Redwig
Vol: 3

Oct 15

WAR DIARY
or
INTELLIGENCE SUMMARY

(Erase heading not required.)

Army Form C. 2118.

Instructions regarding War Diaries and Intelligence Summaries are contained in F. S. Regs., Part II. and the Staff Manual respectively. Title pages will be prepared in manuscript.

Place	Date	Hour	Summary of Events and Information	Remarks and references to Appendices
BOIS GRENIER LINE	1st Oct.		2 Coys. (C & D) under Major Buchanan moved to the BOIS GRENIER Line, and relieved the 8th Yorks. Ryt. The same day our H.Q. was ordered to proceed to the Advance Brigade H.Q. & the Colonel took command of BOIS GRENIER LINE behind trenches 52 – 59 inclusive. The orders in the event of a hostile attack were to immediately organize a counter attack. Major Buchanan returned to the Billets and took over Command of right half Battalion.	
	2nd		On this day we lost one killed and one wounded. The deceased was 12710 Pte. A. Hiley, D Company.	
	3rd		Nothing to report. Whole Battalion found working parties. One man was wounded.	
	4th		Nothing to report. Left half Battn. was relieved by 10th Northumberland Fusiliers, and moved into billets at JESUS FARM, ERQUINGHAM, where they were joined by the right half Battn.	
JESUS FARM	5th to 10th		The Battn. was then in Divisional Reserve, relieving the 8th Yorks. Ryt. The 11th West Yorks. & 9th Yorks were in Reserve to 20th Div., at ESTAIRES. Battn. remained in Reserve, finding large working parties each evening. Weather, from 1st inst. to now very fair.	† See supplementary page

Army Form C. 2118.

WAR DIARY
or
INTELLIGENCE SUMMARY.

(Erase heading not required.)

Place	Date	Hour	Summary of Events and Information	Remarks and references to Appendices
JESUS FARM	9th		Supplementary. Draft of 60 N.C.O and men received from 11th Battn. Physique of men very good. Draft contained many men who had served out in the 2nd Battn. in FLANDERS and with the 8th Battn. in GALLIPOLI. This draft brings strength of Battn. up to 29 Officers and 982 O.R.	

WAR DIARY
or
INTELLIGENCE SUMMARY.
(Erase heading not required.)

Army Form C. 2118.

Place	Date	Hour	Summary of Events and Information	Remarks and references to Appendices
	10th		The Battalion was ordered to proceed that same evening to relieve the 8th Battn York & Lancs in the BOIS GRENIER LINE in support of trenches 59 - 64 inclusive. The relief was duly carried out.	
	11th		Nothing to report. Weather fine. Heavy fighting South, in direction of LA BASSÉE.	
	12th 13th 14th 15th		Weather fine. No casualties. Nothing to report.	
T.63.64.65 .66.			On the night of 15th, orders were received to relieve the 11th WEST YORKS in the fire trenches T.63.64.65.66 on the following day.	
	16.		The Battn. relieved 11th West Yorks at dusk in the evening. Our H.Q. was the FARM DU BIEZ. The trenches in this part of the line were good, some of the dug outs being made of cement and there were several communication trenches to the BOIS GRENIER LINE.	
	17th		Two men were wounded by rifle fire. Nothing further. The usual patrols sent out. All was quiet, weather fine, but colder in early morning & cold at night. Dawn broke very foggy.	
	18th		Two men wounded. Nothing to report. Some rain, but very little. Orders received that 8th York would relieve us the	
	19th		[illegible]	

WAR DIARY
or
INTELLIGENCE SUMMARY

Army Form C. 2118.

Place	Date	Hour	Summary of Events and Information	Remarks and references to Appendices
Trenches 63.64.65.66	19th		following day. One man wounded. One man wounded yesterday, died of wounds.	
	20th		2nd the enemy. 8th Yorks relieved us, and we went to billets at RUE MARLE.	
	21st		Orders received at night that the Battn. was to stand our billets the following day to 2/EAST LANCS REGT, and proceed for the night to FORT ROMPU, en route to ESTAIRES where we would become part of 20th Divisional Reserve. During this period in Reserve we were to amalgamate with 1/WORCESTERSHIRE REGT, but this order was afterwards cancelled.	
	22nd		Weather fine. Moved to billets at FORT ROMPU.	
	23rd		Moved to billets at ESTAIRES.	
	24,25,26,27		Rest of the Battn. employed as working parties for R.E. The same as for 22nd. Weather still before fine.	
	28		The Battalion remained in ESTAIRES, found working parties daily for the R.E's Weather bad, much rain.	
	29.		Received orders for the Battn. to move into 5qth Brigade Reserve and relieve 1/Worcester, Working parties found for R.E's. Arrangements made for relief of the Battalion	

WAR DIARY
or
INTELLIGENCE SUMMARY

(Erase heading not required.)

Army Form C. 2118.

Place	Date	Hour	Summary of Events and Information	Remarks and references to Appendices
	30th		Relieved 1/Worcesters in DEAD END, MASSELOT, WANGERIE, HOUGEMONT, FORT DESQUIN, LONELY, ROAD BEND posts, and WHITE HOUSE billets. One Company remained at the 1/Worcesters under the Command of 1 O/ west Riding, in place of "C" Coy, who remained at the 173rd Coy. R.E. Tunnelling. ※ C Company lost two men at this work, one killed by a shell, the other being buried in a dug-out knocked down by a shell. Since the arrival the Battalion has undergone the transport has proved the difficulty. If each Battalion was given four motor lorries, the whole of the work would be done more easily and quicker. Although the initial outlay would be heavy, in the end it would be cheaper than the present system being it would save forage for some 50 animals. Also it would relieve about 40 men for the fire trenches.	※ 14528 Pte. T. BEARDSLEY 15918. Pte. E. GILL
	31st		One man wounded whilst on sentry duty. Weather much colder. Trenches very muddy and dirty.	

69/
23 not Known

10 W. Riding
Vol: 4

121/
7656

Nov. 15.

3.Y.
10 sheets

Lt Bolland M.C
gazed
4/11/15

Army Form C. 2118.

WAR DIARY
or
INTELLIGENCE SUMMARY
(Erase heading not required.)

Place	Date	Hour	Summary of Events and Information	Remarks and references to Appendices
WANGERIE	1/11/15		Received orders from 59th I.B. to relieve 11th K.R.R. in front line trenches M.24.5. M.24.6. M.24.7. Found large R.E. working parties. Weather bad, much rain. Enemy did not shell very much during the day. No casualties.	
	2/11/15	1pm	Commenced relief in daylight. This was rather risky as the communication trenches were impassible owing to rain, & fallen in revetments. The relief was done by sections up the main road, & was carried out without casualties. The trenches were in an exceedingly bad state of repair, owing to the rain and water and loose sandbags. The parapet and dug outs fell down badly. At night a dug out fell & buried 8 men of D Coy. 2 were killed. In spite of an order to the contrary these men had entered the dug out.	13328 A/Cpl S. HOLROYD. 13559 Pte. H. WOODHOUSE
	3/11/15		Rain still continued. Trenches very bad. In places water came up to the knees, & the mud was over the ankles. No casualties.	
	4/11/15		Still raining. Much work on trenches was impossible owing to state of the ground, & scarceness of R.E. material. Working party under Lt. BOLLAND was harassed by the enemy, & the covering party was nearly cut off. Two men were killed. Lieut BOLLAND with great coolness & courage got the covering party safely back, himself carrying one of the let men in on his	X See next page matter ⓧ

Army Form C. 2118.

WAR DIARY
or
INTELLIGENCE SUMMARY

(Erase heading not required.)

Instructions regarding War Diaries and Intelligence
Summaries are contained in F. S. Regs., Part II.
and the Staff Manual respectively. Title pages
will be prepared in manuscript.

Place	Date	Hour	Summary of Events and Information	Remarks and references to Appendices
			shoulder. He received 2 bullets through his coat during the feat. He was recommended for the Military Cross.	⊙ 14760. Pte. F. FORD. 11737. Pte. J. BRADLEY.
	5/11/15		Weather bad. Trenches fell in almost as fast as they can be rebuilt. Both sides very quiet.	
	6/11/15		Weather cleared, though morning very foggy which necessitated extra sentries and patrols. No. 15202 Pte SUTCLIFFE, was wounded accidentally by discharging his own rifle. He was tried by F.G.C.M. & was awarded 1 month Imprisonment which was commuted to 1 month F.P. No. 1. No. 13529 Pte. TURNER was wounded in the fire trench	
	7/11/15 8/11/15		Nothing to report. Weather fine but much colder. Both sides very quiet except for M.G.s which traversed the parapets.	
	9/11/15		Received orders from 59th I.B. to proceed to LAVENTIE.	
	10/11/15		Relieved by the 10th (S) K.R.R. The relief took place during daylight which was a hazardous proceeding. The enemy shelled us during the relief, but we were lucky enough to lose only one man No. 14783 Pte. YOUNG. W.L. The Battalion proceeded to billets in LAVENTIE.	
	11/11/15		Orders received from 20th Division to proceed to 20th Divisional reserve in ESTAIRES	

Army Form C. 2118.

WAR DIARY
or
INTELLIGENCE SUMMARY.

(Erase heading not required.)

Instructions regarding War Diaries and Intelligence Summaries are contained in F.S. Regs., Part II. and the Staff Manual respectively. Title pages will be prepared in manuscript.

Place	Date	Hour	Summary of Events and Information	Remarks and references to Appendices
LAVENTIE	12/11/15	11 a.m.	LAVENTIE was heavily shelled by the Germans. The Battalion quitted billets and went into shelter trench. One man was wounded, 13545 Pte. WALKER, R.P.	
		By 1 p.m.	the shelling had ceased, & at 3pm the Battn marched by Platoon to ESTAIRES, where the we took over billets from the 10th R.13.S.	
	13/11/15		Received orders from 20th Division to rejoin 23rd Division the following day.	
	14/11/15		The Battn marched to RUE MARLE and joined the 69th I.B. The weather for this march was fine, but owing to recent rain, the roads were in a very bad condition.	
RUE MARLE	15/11/15		Lieut L.G. BOLLAND was presented with the ribbon of the Military Cross by Major-General BABINGTON, G.O.C. 23rd Division. His act of gallantry for which the M.C. was presented is recorded in this diary on the 4th day of this month.	
	17/11/15		Received orders from 69th I.B. to proceed to front line trench of left sub-sector.	
	18/11/15		RUE MARLE and South side of ARMENTIERS heavily shelled by the enemy. A great number of the shells failed to explode.	
		5 p.m.	Relieved the 8th Yorks in the left sub-sector trenches. Head quarters were situated at FME du BIEZ.	

Army Form C. 2118.

WAR DIARY
or
INTELLIGENCE SUMMARY.
(Erase heading not required.)

Instructions regarding War Diaries and Intelligence Summaries are contained in F. S. Regs., Part II. and the Staff Manual respectively. Title pages will be prepared in manuscript.

Place	Date	Hour	Summary of Events and Information	Remarks and references to Appendices
TRENCHES	19th		With the exception that enemy M.G.'s traversed our parapet frequently, the day was quiet. 16563 Pte. CARDWELL J. was killed whilst sniping. 15220 L/Cpl KENNETT went out to bring in Pte CARDWELL and in so doing was shot through the head and killed.	
	20th		Weather began to get very cold. The trenches were in a very muddy condition, but considering the bad weather, were in an exceedingly good state of repair. The danger of 'frost bite' and 'trench foot' has been brought out. Many precautions such as change of socks, application of whale oil are insisted upon, and have very satisfactory results.	
		11am	During the morning, a splendid shell burst over one of the bays in "C" "B" Coy. trench. Several casualties were sustained, as follows:— 19469 Pte HOLLAND E. Killed 12462 Sgt. ELLIS I. Wounded, since died of wounds. 6 men wounded.	
	21st		Received orders from H.Q. 69th I.B. to move the following day to RUE MARLE. This day the 3rd Corps had a readjustment of the whole line.	

WAR DIARY
or
INTELLIGENCE SUMMARY

Army Form C. 2118.

Place	Date	Hour	Summary of Events and Information	Remarks and references to Appendices
	22"		A Copy of the orders as far as the 69th I.B. was concerned are attached, marked A. The new distribution meant that the Battalion held a front of over 1000 yards.	
		5 p.m.	Relieved in the trenches by the 8th Yorkshire Regt. The Battalion was distributed as follows after the relief:- A Company in BOIS GRENIER line in immediate support to the Battn. in the right sub-sector trenches. B. Company in billets in CHAPELLE d'ARMENTIERS in direct an immediate support to the Battn. in the left sub-sector. C & D Coys. and H.Q. in billets in RUE MARLE.	
RUE MARLE	23"		The weather had now turned very cold, several degrees of frost were registered during the night. 14755 Pte WAKEFIELD, S. was awarded the D.C.M. The ribbon was pinned on him by G.O.C. 23rd Division. For this, C & D Companies paraded.	

Army Form C. 2118.

WAR DIARY
or
INTELLIGENCE SUMMARY.
(Erase heading not required.)

Instructions regarding War Diaries and Intelligence Summaries are contained in F. S. Regs., Part II. and the Staff Manual respectively. Title pages will be prepared in manuscript.

Place	Date	Hour	Summary of Events and Information	Remarks and references to Appendices
	23.		Received orders to proceed to Divisional Reserve at JESUS FARM.	
	24th	6pm	Left RUE MARLE for JESUS FARM. The Battn. was relieved in RUE MARLE by the 11th Northumberland Fusiliers.	
JESUS FARM	25} 30}		Remained in Divisional Reserve at JESUS FARM. The cold for the first 3 days was severe, 20 degrees of frost being registered. By now each man had been provided by a fur jacket. During these 5 days, special attention was given to training of specialists such as Machine Gunners, Signallers, Grenadiers. Each man in the Battn. was instructed in the mechanism and use of the Mills Bomb, which is the only bomb in use at present.	

2353 Wt. W2514/1454 700,000 5/15 D. D. & L. A.D.S.S./Forms/C. 2118.

COPY.

10TH (S) BATTN. DUKE OF WELLINGTON'S (WEST RIDING) REGIMENT.
Operation Order No.1.

1. A redistribution of the line will take place on the 22nd. Inst.

2. B.Battalion (10th West Ridings) will take over Trench 62.
   2 platoons of the left Coy. will be withdrawn as local support, and be accommodated at the Farm du BIEZ.

   The line will then be held as follows with 3½ Coys.:-

   D.Coy.- Whole of T.62 and up to and including No.11 bay of 63 (I.21.4)

   A.Coy.- Thence to end of bay 25. T.64. (I.15.1.) inclusive.

   B.Coy.- Thence to bay No.3 of T.66 (I.16) inclusive.

   C.Coy.- (less 2 platoons). - Thence to extreme left of I.16.

3. Coy.Hd.Qrs. and Signalling Stations remain in their present positions.

4. After the relief by the 8th Yorks on the 22nd, the Hd.Qrs. of B.Battn. will be at the ORCHARD POST (I.16.c.9.3½.).

5. The Brigade Signal Officer is reponsible for the opening communications between Hd.Qrs. and Companies.

6. O.C. D.Coy. will take over all trench stores, including S.A.A. and bombs, now on charge of I.21.3. (T.62.) and will hand these over, in addition to those remaining in the bays 1-11 inclusive of I.21.4., to the relieving unit. This list should be compiled with care.
   A.Coy. will take over from O.C. D.Coy. the trench stores now in bays 12-22 inclusive of I.21.4.
   B.Coy. will take over trench stores in bays 1-4 inclusive Trench I.16.

7. This redistribution is to be completed by 10-30 a.m. on the 22nd Inst. and Coys. will report to Farm Du BIEZ when they have completed.

8. A duplicate of the return of trench stores to be handed over to the relieving unit, will reach Battn.Hd.Qrs. for inclusion in the log book by 4 p.m. 22nd. Inst. This return is to be rendered in accordance with alphabetical specimen copy sent to Coys. before entering the trenches.

9. M.Guns. remain in their present emplacements.
   The location of the two M.Guns 9th Yorks which are moving from the S.Line to the fire trenches will be detailed by the Brigade M.G.Officer.

                                        sd. C.Bathurst. Capt. & Adjt.

21.11.15.

Note- The two platoons of "C" Coy., detailed for the local support, will not retire to Farm Du BIEZ until ordered to do so, and accommodation can be provided.

COPY.

SECRET.   A

69th Infantry Brigade.   Copy No. 5.

OPERATION ORDER No. 19.

Ref. Map
1/10,000.

1. On the 22nd November the Brigade will extend to its right and take over trenches I.20.1., and I.26.5.
2. The 10th West Riding Regiment will take over trench I.21.3., together with all trench stores for same, from the 11th West Yorkshire Regiment. Relief to be complete by 11 a.m. 22nd November.
3. One Company 11th West Yorkshire Regiment will take over trenches I.20.1, and I.26.5. from 1st Sherwood Foresters at at 1 p.m. 22nd. November. They will form the Garrison of the trench, but are not responsible for taking over trench stores.
4. The O.C. 9th Yorkshire Regiment will send to trenches I.20.1., I.26.5., at 12 noon 22nd.
   Representatives to take over trench stores.
   Signallers   " "   "   stations.
   Machine Gun detachments " " Machine Gun Emplacements.
   also a representative and signallers to take over Battn. Hd.Qr. at BURNT FARM at 1 p.m. from 1st Sherwood Foresters.
5. All trench Stores, less rockets and Vermoral sprayers, for trenches I.20.1, I.26.5. will be taken over.
   Log books for the above trenches and for the battalion Hd.Qrs. will also be taken over by the 9th Yorkshire Regiment.
6. The Brigade Grenadier Officer will issue four additional GREEN rockets to the O.C. 8th Yorkshire Regiment for use in trench I.21.3 and eight RED rockets for use in trenches I.20.1., I.26.5., to the O.C. 9th Yorkshire Regiment. The O.C. 11th West Yorkshire Regiment will send four RED rockets to Headquarters, BURNT FARM by 4 p.m., 22nd November.
7. After trench reliefs on the night of 22nd the Headquarters of Battalions will be as follows :-
   "A" Battalion.   near BURNT FARM.
   "B" Battalion.   The ORCHARD.
   "C" Battalion.   Advanced Brigade Headquarters unless otherwise ordered.

sd. A.J. Fraser. Capt.
Brigade Major.
69th Infantry Brigade.

16th W. Riding.
vol: 5

121/7936

23

Army Form C. 2118.

WAR DIARY
or
INTELLIGENCE SUMMARY
(Erase heading not required.)

10th (Ser) Battn. Duke of Wellington's (West Riding) Regiment

Place	Date	Hour	Summary of Events and Information	Remarks and references to Appendices
Jews Farm Rest Brigenham	1/4/15 to 5/4/15		Billets (Divisional reserve.) We found working parties during this period and carried out training in accordance with Divisional programme. The weather very cold, much snow and wet weather. Civilians apparent. The interned N.C.Os & men were employed as a result of accident whilst filling in bombs used as bomb course. Cont of Injury has been received. 13580 Sergt No 9 Williams (since died of wounds) 17384 Pte J. Holden. On the 4th inst we received orders to take over the left sub sector of Bois Grenier line from the 2nd Northants the 24th Inf Brigade being relieved by the 69th Inf Bde. in the night 4-12-15 marked A attached regarding relief. Battn orders dated 4-12-15 marked A attached regarding relief.	
	6/4/15		Weather rainy, above relief carried out. The trenches are in a bad state owing to bad weather of late, the water being very high in places. Casualties nil.	

WAR DIARY
or
INTELLIGENCE SUMMARY.

(Erase heading not required.)

Army Form C. 2118.

Place	Date	Hour	Summary of Events and Information	Remarks and references to Appendices
Vimden	7/10/15	10.30	R.F.A. told that they would shell M.G. enemy trenches at 11.30 am assisted by the heavy guns. much good work was done, the detonation satisfactory and very effective. The enemy retaliated feebly, about 40 shells 4-5" and 10" being ably. An enemy plane passed our line flying at a great height, night considerably quiet.	
	8/10/15		Great improvement in the weather, quiet generally prevailed. During the afternoon our artillery shelled the German trenches. The shells fell with accuracy were very effective. The Germans retaliated by shelling the town of Armentières feebly, would weapons were very active during the day, night was generally quiet, no following casualties occurred. (1 man killed 1 man wounded)	
	9/10/15		Morning troops quiet, light rain fell and 10 Entrenching Coys were reported that the enemy had built a dam and that they were prepared to let out their [trench?] to shell into the same. About 10 Am information received that the howitzers were to shell the dam in question, this was passed to all corps and head 22.00 that they could take advantage of cover in the event of premature [bursting?]. The bombardment was effected and the desired result obtained, the enemy retaliated, sending a large number of shells without doing much damage. Relief orders received today. During the night the enemy very active with [copy marked B attached]. Machine guns continually sweeping out parapets.	

Army Form C. 2118.

WAR DIARY
or
INTELLIGENCE SUMMARY.
(Erase heading not required.)

Instructions regarding War Diaries and Intelligence Summaries are contained in F. S. Regs., Part II. and the Staff Manual respectively. Title pages will be prepared in manuscript.

Place	Date	Hour	Summary of Events and Information	Remarks and references to Appendices
Tunnels	10/7/15		Another dull, heavy morning, small rain. About 9 a.m. the enemy opened fire with Artillery; this became intense and continued with unabated fury until 11 a.m. All men sought cover as in trenches. The Battn headquarters was evidently the main object also support & communication trenches. One wing passed through the A.Q Signal station, one of the signallers having a miraculous escape. The damage caused to parapets etc was exceedingly small. The casualties very light only 6 wounded, one of which was returned to duty after being hardly scratched. Relief was carried out with some apparently owing to the bad state of the weather and trenches, no further casualties. Battn relieved by 8th Lancs.	
11/7/15		In reserve billets at La Rolanderie Farm. We are instructed to find working parties as follows. 40 other ranks morning 40 other ranks afternoon to assist in general improvement to trenches. Weather bad.	
12/7/15		Weather improved but much colder, nothing to report, found working parties as above date.	
13/7/15		Weather much improved, though cold. Nothing to report. Operation order for taking over trenches, issued copies one attached numbered "C". Found working parties as for 11th & 12th inst.	

WAR DIARY
or
INTELLIGENCE SUMMARY

Army Form C. 2118.

Instructions regarding War Diaries and Intelligence Summaries are contained in F. S. Regs., Part II. and the Staff Manual respectively. Title pages will be prepared in manuscript.

(Erase heading not required.)

Place	Date	Hour	Summary of Events and Information	Remarks and references to Appendices
Reserve Billets at La Rolanderie Farm	14/9/15 morning		Weather dull, but little seen. Reliefs carried out and completed about 6.30 p.m. Casualties nil. Our Artillery sent over a few shells during the late evening and night. The enemy did not reply the night passed off without incident the enemy very quiet.	
"	15/9/15 Afternoon		Weather dull, enemy parapet mostly at 2 am. nothing unusual happened. One of our men claimed to have shot a German who was passing a gap which to flanders mostly in the enemy lines.	
	15/9/15		Weather continues very dull, morning passed off quietly, one or two of our guns sending a few shells at enemy wire and parapet. At 2 p.m. the Germans opened a very heavy bombardment, shells of all calibre coming over, our front line and headquarters seemed the major portion. It is pleasing to relate that not a single casualty occurred. The men were all in dug-outs. Crossing the trenches, except and making notes where the shells had fallen so that the rose cups could be procured. Our artillery did not send quite so many in reply but what did go appeared to have the desired results. One of our guns fired at irregular intervals from 9 p.m to 3 a.m it is thought that a relief was taking place. The German bombardment closed about 4 p.m.	

WAR DIARY or INTELLIGENCE SUMMARY

Army Form C. 2118.

Instructions regarding War Diaries and Intelligence Summaries are contained in F.S. Regs., Part II. and the Staff Manual respectively. Title pages will be prepared in manuscript.

(Erase heading not required.)

Place	Date	Hour	Summary of Events and Information	Remarks and references to Appendices
Trenches	17/10/15		Weather dull, some rain, in the afternoon evenings, on our front nothing. All is quiet. An artillery duel is taking place on our right. During the night the enemy were very active with rifle fire. Our artillery sent 3 salvoes into their trenches which seemed to quieten them. Move orders for relief received and issued to all concerned. Copy marked D attached.	
Trenches morning & afternoon. Reserve billets after relief in the evening at La Rolanche Farm.	18/10/15		All was particularly quiet during the morning, about 2 pm the Germans sent about 6 shells and a number of trench mortars which resulted in slightly wounding a man in A Coy. The relief was carried out without mishap and it is pleasing to relate that the above mentioned was the only casualty during the past 4 days in the trenches.	
	19/10/15		An improvement in the weather. Aeroplanes all along the line very active. Heavy bombardment on both sides. Ammunition appears to be in receipt of a good share from the enemy. Nothing further to report.	
	20/10/15		All quiet, we found working parties in the Bois Grenier line 65 N.C.O.s & men afternoon and evening, nothing further to report.	
	21/10/15		Poured with rain all day, found working parties as above, quiet all along the front. Instructions received issued to all concerned for move of Batln into Divisional reserve. Copy marked E attached.	

WAR DIARY
or
INTELLIGENCE SUMMARY

Army Form C. 2118.

Place	Date	Hour	Summary of Events and Information	Remarks and references to Appendices
Reserve Billets morning & afternoon	22/12/15		Weather continued very rainy, nothing to report beyond the fact that Reliefs in personal reserve are in a bad state owing to the continued wet weather	
We were moving at DORMOIRE	23/12/15		All very much the same as preceding day, weather still bad. Nothing to report.	
	24/12/15		Still very rainy, to water about to approach, our heavy artillery has been at work all day, nothing further to report. CHRISTMAS EVE Artillery duels in progress, rats so striking some very heavy shells over. A plentiful supply of useful presents has arrived for the Battn. and all are making as merry as possible under the circumstances.	
	25/12/15		The weather continues rainy. Artillery duels are still in progress, our trenches being particularly active. A concert for the Batn. has been arranged for. The above mentioned took place in a large barn close to Billets which was prettily decorated. The programme which is attached was gone through and greatly enjoyed. Our heavy Artillery is very active again. The rain came on very heavily and continued through the night.	

Place	Date	Hour	Summary of Events and Information	Remarks and references to Appendices
	26/7/15		Weather continues hot, a lot of rain is still downing, nothing further to report.	Our Artillery
	27/7/15		Still raining, indictor to yesterday in all respects during the night a heavy gale was blowing.	
	28/7/15		The weather very much better, the wind of the night having a good drying effect upon the ground. Our Artillery (Craonne) that the Batln will proceed to RUE MARLE to relieve Bills, the 69th Inf Bde is to relieve the 2nd It Inf Bde in the trenches. Copy marked F attached. Also issued defence scheme to all concerned. Copy marked G attached.	
Bis Ricard Billets morning afternoon trench reserve evening	29/7/15		Weather continues much better. Move from Billets to RUE MARLE carried out without incident; all relief completed about 6 pm nothing further to report	D.O.R MOIRE

Army Form C. 2118.

WAR DIARY
or
INTELLIGENCE SUMMARY.
(Erase heading not required.)

Instructions regarding War Diaries and Intelligence Summaries are contained in F. S. Regs., Part II. and the Staff Manual respectively. Title pages will be prepared in manuscript.

Place	Date	Hour	Summary of Events and Information	Remarks and references to Appendices
	30/9/15		Weather dull. Found working party of bomen early morning nothing further.	
	31/9/15		Dull morning no news, found working party as above nothing further	

J A Ballantine Lieut Colonel
Commanding 10th (Sv.) Batt.
Duke of Wellington's
(West Riding Regt)

10th.(S) Bn. Duke of Wellington's (West Riding) Regt.

Operation Order. No. 2.

Copy No. 9

Reference Map
1/40,000.

4th December 1915.

1... The 69th I.Bde. will relieve the 24th I.Bde. in the Right Section on the night of 6/7th December.

2... The 10th Duke of Wellington's will relieve the 2nd/Northants Regt. in the left sub-sector.

3... The Battalion will be termed B.Unit whilst in this sub-sector.

4... Companies will take over trenches as follows :-

        A, B, & D. Coys. in front line.
        A.Coy. on the right.
        B.Coy. in the centre.
        D.Coy. on the left.

C.Coy. will be in the BOIS GRENIER Line (on either side of SHAFTESBURY AVENUE)

5... Company Commdrs. will visit the trenches to be taken over on Sunday morning, the 5th Inst.
Guides will be met at Battn. Hd.Qrs. I.25.d.2.2. at 11 a.m. in the case of A, B, D, & M.Gun.
C.Coy. Commdr. will meet a guide at North End of SHAFTESBURY AVENUE at the same hour.

6... At least one officer per Company and one representative of each platoon will be at Battn. Trench Hd.Qrs. at 2 p.m. on Monday, the 6th Inst., (except C. Coy. who will be at North end of SHAFTESBURY AVENUE) where guides will be met.
These parties will take over all trench stores as laid down in "Lists of articles to be treated as trench stores" issued to Coys. on the 29th November.

7.. M.Gun Detachment will take over their emplacements by daylight on the afternoon of the 6th Inst.
The detachment will proceed via SHAFTESBURY AVENUE to Battn. Trench Hd.Qrs. where guides will be met at 3-30 p.m.
M.Gun Limbers at M.Gun billets 11-30 a.m., and will not proceed further than GRIS POT whence the guns will be man-handled to the trenches.

8... The Signalling Officer will arrange to take over all lines at 2-30 p.m. on the 6th Inst.

9... The Battn.Sergt.Major will proceed to the trenches on Monday 6th Inst., and will take over from the Sergt.Major of the 2nd Northants at 2 p.m. that day.

10... Transport is allotted as follows :-

No.	Type of Wagon.	Coy.	Time.
1	G.S. Blankets.	A.Coy.	9 a.m.
1	ditto	B. & M.G.	9 "
1	ditto	C. & H.Q.	9 "
1	ditto	D. & Sigs.	9 "

Blankets rolled in 10's. need not be labelled as they are to be

taken to STEENWERCK to be fumigated.
Signallers blankets will be rolled and loaded with the Coy. to which they are attached for duty.

No.	Type of wagon.	Coy.	Time.
1	G.S.Baggage.	A. & D. & M.G.	11-30 a.m.
1	G.S. "	C. & B.Sigs.H.Qs.	11-30 a.m.

At the time named the wagon will call at the 1st named Coy. proceeding thence to the others in succession. These wagons are for surplus stores and kits which will be taken to the Qr.Mr. Stores and stored.

1	G.S.Limber.	A. & D. Coys.	2-30 p.m.
1	ditto	B. & C. Coys.	"
1	ditto	Hd.Qrs. & Sigs.	"
1	Maltese Cart	M.O.Inspection R.	"
1	Mess Cart.	Hd.Qrs.	2 p.m.

Coy.Messes will be carried on the Coy.Limbers.
All Cookers will be ready to move to the transport lines by 2 p.m.
Instructions for Watercarts will be issued later.

11.. O.C.Coys. will ensure that all precautions are taken against frostbite before troops proceed to the trenches.

12.. The battalion will move as follows :-
Starting point - B.Coy.Hd.Qrs. B.26. d.6.5. Time of starting 3-20 p.m.
An interval of 10 minutes will be maintained between companies.
An interval will be maintained of 100 yards between platoons after clearing the cross roads N.18.c.3½.5½.
Route - ERQUINGHEM_LA ROLANDERIE_GRIS POT_LA VESEE_SHAFTESBURY AVENUE.
The leading platoon will not pass the Railway Crossing H.10.b.10.7 until 4 p.m.
Order of march :-
       A.Coy. & Hd.Qr. Party.
       B.Coy.
       D.Coy
       C.Coy.

13.. Companies and M.Gun Section will telegraph to Battn.Trench Hd.Qrs. when relief is completed.

4.12.15.　　　　　　　　　　　　sd. C.Bathurst. Capt. & Adjt.

Copy No 2 Major L.E.Buchanan.
      1 Capt.C.Bathurst.
      3 Medical Officer.
      4 O.C. A.Coy.
      5   " B. "
      6   " C. "
      7   " D. "
      8 Capt.A. P.Harrison.
      9 Lt.A.K.Lavarack.
    10 2/Lt.R.C.Perks.
    11 Transport Officer.
    12 Quartermaster.
    13 Batth.Sergt.Major.
    14 War Diary.

10TH (S) BN. DUKE OF WELLINGTON'S (WEST RIDING) REGIMENT.

Operation Order No. 3.   Copy No. 13

1... The battalion will be relieved by 8th Yorks tomorrow, 10th Inst..

2... The battalion will proceed to billets of which Battalion Hd.Qrs. is at LA ROLANDERIE Farm. (H.11.c.5.5.).

3... Whilst in these billets the battalion will be known as "D" Unit.

4... Companies will be distributed as follows :-
   Hd.Qrs. & 2 M.Guns at LA ROLANDERIE Farm.
   D.Coy. at LA ROLANDERIE Farm. (H.11.d.0.4.)
   A.Coy. at H.18.c.3.5.
   B.Coy. at H.17.c.9.1.
   C.Coy. & 2 M.Guns holding BOIS GRENIER POST & occupying billets in RUE des CHARLES.

5... Coys. will send one officer per Coy. and 1 representative from each platoon to take over billets during the morning.
   Representatives of 8th Yorks will proceed to trenches tomorrow to take over. Guides will be sent to meet them as follows:
   1 from each Coy, M.Gun, & Bombing Officer to be at N. end of SHAFTESBURY AVENUE at 10 a.m.
   Guides will meet the incoming Unit as follows :-
   1 from Signallers N. end of SHAFTESBURY AVENUE 12 noon.
   6 guides for guards (C.Coy.)   "   "   "   3-30 p.m.
   1 guide for Hd.Qrs.   "   "   "   3-30 p.m.
   1 guide from each platoon (A,B,D,Coys). " " 4-15 p.m.
   1 guide C.Coy.   "   "   4-30 p.m.
   These guides must have definite platoons allotted to them.

6... All baggage will be taken down by daylight & stacked at Farm at N. end of SHAFTESBURY AVENUE by 2-30 p.m.

   Transport will be allotted as follows :-

   1 Limber for B. & C. Coys.   )N. end of
   1   "   "   A. & D. Coys.   )SHAFTESBURY
   1 Limber & Officers Mess Cart for all Hd.Qr. baggage.)AVENUE 4-30 p.m.

   1. M.Gun Limber to be at H.24.a.10.8. at 4-30 p.m.

7... Copy of alphabetical list of Trench Stores to be handed over to incoming unit to be in Orderly Room by 12 noon tomorrow.

   sd. C.Bathurst. Capt.& Adjt.

9.12.15.

   Copy No. 1 Major L. E. Buchanan.
         2 Capt. C. Bathurst.
         3 O.C. A. Coy.
         4   B. "
         5   C. "
         6   D. "
         7 M.Gun Officer.
         8 Lt. A.K. Lavarack.
         9 Quartermaster.
         10 Transport Officer.
         11 Regt. Sergt. Major.
         12 Signalling Sergt.
         13 War Diary.

10TH (S) BATTN. DUKE OF WELLINGTON'S (WEST RIDING) REGIMENT.

Operation Order No. 4.   Copy No. 13

1...   The 10th Duke of Wellington's Regt. will relieve the 8th Yorks in the Left Sub Sector on the night of 14/15th December.

2...   The battalion will be termed "B" Unit whilst in this Sub Sector.

3...   Coys. will take over trenches I.32.1 to I.26.4. as follows :-
         "A" Coy. will be on the right.
         One platoon of "C" Coy. in the centre.
         "D" Coy. on the left.
"B" Coy. and 3 platoons "C" Coy. will be in the BOIS GRENIER LINE on either side of SHAFTESBURY AVENUE.

4...   Coy. Commdrs. and one representative of each platoon will be at Battalion Trench Hd.Qrs. at 9-30 a.m. except "B" Coy. and the representatives of the other 3 platoons of "C" Coy. who will be at the N. end of SHAFTESBURY AVENUE at the same hour.
     These parties will arrange to take over all trench stores etc.

5...   The Machine Gun Officer will visit the trenches and arrange to take over all Machine Gun Emplacements at the same hour.
     The 4 Machine Guns belonging to the battalion will be in the front line, and in addition he will arrange to "man" 2 machine guns belonging to the 8th Yorks Regt. in the BOIS GRENIER LINE.

6...   The Signalling Sergt. will report to Trench Hd.Qrs. and take over all lines at 10 a.m.

7...   The battalion Sergt.Major will proceed to Trench Hd.Qrs. and take over all stores at 2 p.m.

8...   One officer and 20 men of each Coy. in support will be told off to act as Grenadiers and will be grouped together.

9...   Transport will be arranged as follows :-
         1 G.S. Limber   "A" and "C" Coys.   4 p.m.
         1 G.S. Limber.   "B" and "D" Coys.   4 p.m.
         1 G.S. Limber.   Hd.Qrs. and Sigs.   4 p.m.
         Maltese cart.   Medical Officer.   4 p.m.
         Mess Cart.   Hd.Qrs.   3 p.m.

Coy. Messes will be carried on Coy. Limbers and will be in charge of Officers' servants.
All Coy. Cookers will be ready to move to transport lines by 3 p.m.
Water cart arrangements as heretofore.

10..   The battalion will move as follows :-
         Hd.Qr. Party ...... 4-15 p.m.
An interval of 100 yards between platoons and 5 minutes between Coys. will be observed. The Head of the column will pass the starting point H.24.a.8.7. at 4-45 p.m.
Order of march :-
         Hd.Qrs.
         "D" Coy.
         One platoon "C" Coy.
         "A" Coy.
         3 platoons "C" Coy.
         "B" Coy.
Coys. and M.Gun Section will telegraph Battn. Trench Hd.Qrs. when relieve is complete.

xxxx~~MINIMUM~~.

11... RATIONS. Rations for "D" Coy. will be dumped at TRAMWAY FARM and for the remainder of the battalion at the Farm I.19.c.5.1½.
They will be left in charge of Coy.Qr.Mr.Sergts. who will be held responsible that they are handed over complete to their Coys.

12... Officers spare kits will be left in charge of a ~~service~~ servant who will remain with them until collected by the transport. He will then rejoin his Company.

13... Representatives of the 8th Yorks will ~~takexsxerx~~ come to take over billets in the course of the day.

14. Coy.Commdrs. will be held responsible that all xxxxx the men in their Coy. rub their feet with anti frostbite grease before starting.

                         sd. H.L. Waite. Lieut. & A/Adjt.

13.12.15.   sdxxWxLxxWaitx.

         Copy No. 1 Major L.E. Buchanan.
                   2 Lieut. H.L. Waite.
                   3.O.C. A. Coy.
                   4.   B. Coy.
                   5.   C. Coy.
                   6.   D. Coy.
                   8.Lt.R.S.S. Ingram.
                   9.Quartermaster.
                   17.M.Gun Officer.
                   10.Transport Officer.
                   11.Regtl.Sergt.Major.
                   12.Signalling Sergt.
                   13.War Diary.

10TH (S) BN. DUKE OF WELLINGTON'S (WEST RIDING) REGIMENT.

Operation Order No. 6.   Copy No. 14

1... The battalion will be relieved in the trenches by the 8th Yorks Regt. tomorrow evening.

2... Guides (1 per platoon) to be at COX'S CORNER at 4-30 p.m.

3... Return of trench stores to be handed over to relieving unit to be handed into Orderly Room by 2 p.m. tomorrow.

4... O.C. Coys. will ensure that all empty cases and damaged ammunition are collected, placed in sandbags and dumped at the authorized place at the entrance to SHAFTESBURY AVENUE.
All other articles for salvage to be dumped at the same time.

5... Transport is allotted as follows :-
   1 G.S. Limber per Company.
   2 "   "   for Hd.Qrs.
   2 "   "   for Machine Guns.
Officers Messes may be sent ahead after dinners tomorrow to "B" Coy. Hd.Qrs. where they will be collected by the Officers Mess Cart.

6... Coys. on relief will take over their former billets.

7... 2 men per Coy. will meet their Coy.Q.M.S. at Farm at 4 p.m., to take over and load Company Blankets.

8... All Companies in the front line will send a runner and report verbally at Trench Headquarters on completion of relief.

9... Before leaving trenches Coys. will hand over to the 8th Yorks trench boots as follows :-
   "A" Coy.   100
   "B" "   48
   "C" "   75
   "D" "   100
Receipts to be obtained and handed in to Orderly Room.

10... The Signalling Officer will arrange to take over signal communications at LA ROLANDERIE by 12 noon.

sd. H.L. Waite. Lieut. & A/Adjt.

17.12.15.

Copy No. 1 C.O.
        2. Major L.E. Buchanan.
        3. Lieut. H.L. Waite.
        4. O.C. A. Coy.
        5. O.C. B. Coy.
        6. O.C. C. Coy.
        7. O.C. D. Coy.
        8. Capt. A.P. Harrison.
        9. Lieut. R.S.S. Ingram.
       10. 2/Lt. R.C. Perks.
       11. Transport Officer.
       12. Quartermaster.
       13. Battn. Sergt. Major.
       14. War Diary.

10TH (S) BATTN. DUKE OF WELLINGTON'S (WEST RIDING) REGIMENT.

Operation Order No. 7.   Copy No.

1... The Battalion will move into Divisional Reserve tomorrow and will take over billets from the 10th North. Fusiliers at RUE DORMOIRE.

Companies will march as follows :-

	Hour.	Route.	Starting Point.
Hd.Qrs. & "D" Coy.	3-45 p.m.	Road Junction H.4.d.7.7.	Billets.
"A" & "C" Coys.	4 p.m.	Road Junction. H.5.d.	Billets.
"B" Coy.	4 p.m.	Cross Roads H.22.6. Road Junction H.16.c. RUE DES MOULINS.	Billets.

2... One Officer per Company and Coy.Q.M.Sgts. will proceed in advance at 10 a.m. tomorrow to take over billets.

3... All Coys. will detail a Corporal to report at Transport Lines at 12 noon tomorrow for the purpose of drawing rations and conducting same to billets.

4... All Blankets and Officers' kits will be ready for loading by 3 p.m. Cookers and watercarts to be ready for "hitching in" at the same time.
All baggage and transport will follow the Company to which it belongs.

5... Coy. reserve ammunition will be packed at the bottom of blanket wagons.

6... Should only two blanket wagons be available, it will be necessary for them to make two journeys as follows :-
    1st journey   "A" & "C" Coys. & Hd.Qrs.
    2nd   "   "D" & "B" Coys.
"D" and "B" Coys. will each detail 1 N.C.O. and 6 men to act as loading and conducting parties.

7... The Signalling Officer will arrange to take over communications by noon tomorrow;; there are three stations.

        sd. H.L. Waite. Lieut. & A/Adjt.

21.12.15.

Copy No. 1. C.O.
2. Major L.E. Buchanan.
3. Lieut. H.L. Waite.
4. O.C. A. Coy.
5. O.C. B. Coy.
6. O.C. C. Coy.
7. O.C. D. Coy.
8. Capt. A.P. Harrison.
9. Lieut. R.S.S. Ingram.
10. 2/Lt. R.C. Perks.
11. Transport Officer.
13. Quartermaster.
14. War Diary.
13. Sergt Major

PROGRAMME

OF BATTALION CONCERT, 25TH DECEMBER 1915.

To be held in RECREATION ROOM, HEADQUARTERS.

$$$$$$$$$$$$$$$$$$$$$$$$$$$$$$$$

1.	Humourous Song. (Johnson when I met you.)	L/Cpl. Nunn. "D" Coy.
2.	Song.	L/Cpl. McAndrew. "B" Coy.
3.	Recitation. (Kissing Cup's Race.)	Pte. Clarkson. Hd.Qrs.
4.	Song. (The Gallery Boy.)	Pte. Conley. "C" Coy.
5.	Song. (Down in Lousiana)	Pte. Brennan. "C" Coy.
6.	Song.	Pte. Wood. "B" Coy.
7.	Song.	Sergt. Oldfield. "A" Coy.
8.	Selected.	Pte. Needham. "C" Coy.
9.	Recitation. (The Delirium).	Pte. Bolton. "C" Coy.
10.	Bones & Whistle.	L/Cpl. Randle.

Interval of 10 minutes. Gramaphone Selections.

11.	Song. (Little Grey Home in the West).	Pte. Duggan. "A" Coy.
12.	Duet.	(L/Cpl. Dury. "A" Coy. (Pte. Dudley. "C" Coy.
13.	Recitation. (The Tramp Musician.)	Pte. Binns. Hd.Qrs.
14.	Song.	Pte. McMath. "A" Coy.
15.	Parody.	Pte. Stockell. "D" Coy.
16.	Song.	Pte. Needham. "C" Coy.
17.	Song.	L/Cpl. Greenard. "A" Coy.
18.	Song. (I put on my Coat and went Home.)	Pte. Beaver. "D" Coy.
19.	Song.	L/Cpl. Nunn. "D" Coy.
20.	Song. (Old King Cole.)	Pte. Richardson. "D" Coy.

GOD SAVE THE KING.

!!!!!!!!!!!!!!

Commence 5p.m.

COPY NO. 12

10th. BATTALION. WEST RIDING REGT.

Ref. Map Sheet 36.   Operation Order No. 8.
1/40000.

Reference Preliminary Move Orders issued last night.

1. Billetting Parties of 1 Officer per Coy, Coy Qr Mstr Sgt &
   1 representative per platoon.
   1 representative for Machine Gun.
   1 representative for Signallers.
   will parade under Lieut. Laverack at Battn Hdqrtrs. at
   1'30 p.m. on 29th. inst. and will proceed to RUE MARLE.
   to take over Billets and Stores from 2nd. East Lancs.
   Coys will send a Ration Corporal to transport lines by 12' noon
   to draw and escort rations.

2. The Signalling Officer will arrange to take over all Lines from
   East Lancs at 2'30 p.m. 29th. inst.
   He will leave sufficient signallers behind to keep touch with
   the Brigade until they are relieved by the incoming unit.

3. Companies will be billetted as follows:-
   "C" Company - I.8.a. 55.
   "A","B",&"D" Coys - East side of RUE MARLE.

4. Companies will march out as follows:-

   Starting Point — Road Junction in H.9. b.
   Route.   — Road Junction in B.30. C.31.
       3'25 p.m. = C. Coy & Headquarters.
       3'35 p.m. = A. Coy & 2 Sections of Machine Gun.
       3'45 p.m. = B. Coy.
       3'55 p.m. = D. Coy.
   The 2 Sections of Machine Gun who are handing over guns to "A"
   Battalion will move under arrangements to be made by M.G.O.

TRANSPORT. The transport is allotted as follows:-

   1 Blanket Wagon for each Coy to be on the road outside
   Company Lines at 2. p.m.
   The Headquarter party blankets will be put on "D" Coys Wagon.
   Machine Gun Blankets will be carried on the Machine Gun Limbers.

   1 Baggage Wagon for Officers Kits, Company Stores and reserve
   ammunition at "A" Companies lines at 2. p.m.
   1 Baggage Wagon for Headquarters and Officers kits at 2 p.m.
   1 Limber for tools and signalling stores to be at Hdqrtrs at 2 p.m.
   1 Limber for Soyers Stoves to be at Hdqrtrs at 2 p.m.
   1 Mess Cart for Coy Messes = "A" Coy billetts 1'30 p.m. thence
   to other Companies.
   1 Maltese Cart for M.O's use. to be at Headquarters at 1'30 p.m.

2.

TRANSPORT.
Cont.

Four men per Company to proceed with Blanket Wagons to unload same.

Two men and two Officers Servants per Company to march behind the Baggage Wagons.

Cookers and Watercarts will be ready to be horsed in by 2'30 p.m.

All Transport will move in rear of the Battalion under the orders of the Transport Officer.

(SD)   C. BATHURST.

Capt & Adjt.
10th. Btn. Duke of Wellington'
(West Riding Regt.).

28.12.15.

AFTER OPERATION ORDER NO. 8.

Companies will take over Billets as follows from the 2nd. East Lancs :-

"A" Coy. 10th. West Ridg. take over from "B" Coy E. Lancs in H.12.b.

"B" Coy.   "   "   "   "   " "C" "   "   " H.12.C.9.7½.

"C" Coy   "   "   "   "   " "A" "   "   " I.8. a.central.

"D" Coy.   "   "   "   "   " "D" "   "   " H.b.d.7.8.

(sd) C. Bathurst. Capt & Adjt.

Copy No. 1. C. O.
2. Major L. E. Buchanan.
3. O.C. "A" Coy. No.12 War Diary.
4. O.C. "B" Coy.
5. O.C. "C" Coy.
6. O.C. "D" Coy.
7. Capt A.P. Harrison.
8. Lieut A. K. Laverack.
9. 2nd. Lieut R.C. Perks.
10. Transport Officer.
11. Quar...

DEFENCE ORDERS.

1. While in RUE MARLE the Battalion will be known as "C" battalion.

2. In case of alarm the Battalion will move up to Bois Grenier line in battle order; waterproof sheets will be carried.

3. DISTRIBUTION.

   HEADQUARTERS at entrance to PARK ROW AVENUE.

   C. Company will hold the line from LILLE RD to BREASTWORK AV. (exclusive)

   D. Coy   "   "   "   " BREASTWORK AV TO HAYSTACK AV.
                                (inclusive)   (exclusive)

   A. Coy   "   "   "   FARM DESPLANQUES to DOGS LEG RD.
                                                     inclusive.

   B. Coy.   "   "   "   DOGS LEG RD to LA GUERNERIE.

   The section HAYSTACK AV. (inclusive) to FARM DESPLANQUES (exclusive) is held by 1 Coy. South Staffords Regt.

   The Machine Gun Section (less 2 guns attached to "A" Btn.) will rendezvous at the N. end of Dogs Leg Rd. where they will await orders.

4. The 1½ Section M.M.G. Battery will retain its present position in Bois Grenier line.

5. BLOCKING PARTIES.
   Companies will arrange to block avenues as follows :-
   COWGATE AVENUE   )   WINE AVENUE.   )
   BREASTWORK AVENUE.) C. COY.   HAYSTACK AV.   ) D. COY.
                                      SALOD AVENUE.   )

   RAILWAY AVENUE.   )
   WELLINGTON AVENUE.) A. Coy.   PARK ROW AVENUE. B. COY.
                                       N.C.O.
   Each Blocking Party will consist of 1 N.C.O. and 6 men of which 2 must be trained bombers.
   On reaching their posts Company Commanders will at once assure themselves that tools, sandbags and knife rests are assembled at the selected spot for blocking.

6. On the alarm being given "C" Coy will detail a subaltern to report at Battalion Headquarters.
   Companies will move off to their respective posts on receiving the order to do so from Battalion Headquarters.

7. All Officers will make themselves acquainted with the various emergency roads and communication trenches up which they may have to move. Especial attention should be paid to possible lines of advance to Wine Avenue or Park Row Avenue having due regard to Artillery positions.

                              (SD)   C. BATHURST.
                              Capt & Adjt. 10th. Duke of
   28.12.15.   Wellington's, West Riding Regt.

EM 5.4.
36 sheets

108 West Ridge
vol. 6
Jan 16

23

Army Form C. 2118

WAR DIARY
or
INTELLIGENCE SUMMARY
(Erase heading not required.) 10th (Ser.) BATT. DUKE OF WELLINGTON'S
(WEST. RIDING REGIMENT)

Place	Date	Hour	Summary of Events and Information	Remarks and references to Appendices
R.U.E. MARLE. (Bde Reserve)	1/1/16.	1-25 a.m.	Received orders that the Battalion would "Stand to arms". The reason being issued orders for a Raid upon the German Trenches to take place at the time named above. Penetrated to time the artillery as arranged commenced to send a fairly good quantity of shells towards the enemy line. The Bombardment lasted 50 minutes. It was difficult to ascertain the number of batteries engaged. The 9th Yorkshire Regt. raided the enemy lines 5 Officers 100 other ranks, and it is believed that the desired results were obtained. It is thought that they accounted for 20 Germans (killed). The enemy returned with strong artillery fire upon our front line, reserve and support trenches. The Casualties of the 9th Corps are particularly slight. 7 O.R. wounded, 6 being very slight. We received word to Stand down about 4 a.m. during the remainder of the night great vigilance. We also received orders during the evening to relieve the 9th Yorks in the left section Operation orders marked "A" attached	

WAR DIARY
or
INTELLIGENCE SUMMARY

(Erase heading not required.)

Army Form C. 2118

Place	Date	Hour	Summary of Events and Information	Remarks and references to Appendices
RUE MARLE	2/1/16	morning afternoon Twelve evening	The weather is much better, some light rain; our Artillery has shown marked activity all along the line. Repairs were duly carried out without casualties and completed about 7pm. The Germans appear to be more active here than when we were here previously. We had one man wounded.	
	3/1/16		Weather Good. our Artillery is persistent another sent a good number of shells into the Enemy lines. Observers report the Germans have increased sending a number of heavy shells into (Chapelle de Armentieres) they also spotted one of our working parties, which was erecting a dummy station immediately behind the Headquarters. They sent about 6 Whizz bangs, no harm was done, for the time being during the same evening our officers were instructed to keep a good look out for Enemy machine guns, it is thought that one or two were located; the information was sent to the Brigade office. The night passed quietly	

WAR DIARY
or
INTELLIGENCE SUMMARY
(Erase heading not required.)

Army Form C. 2118

Place	Date	Hour	Summary of Events and Information	Remarks and references to Appendices
	4/1/16.		Weather less bright, more light rain. The artillery is again fairly busy. The Germans sent a number of heavy shells into CHAPELLE d'(ARMENTIERES, also into the very much battered village BOIS GRENIER. The night passed off quietly.	
	5/1/16		Received orders to move into Brigade reserve billets. The 9th Yorks are to relieve the bombardment the 6th Inst. Copies of orders issued to all concerned, copy marked "B" attached. There is pronounced aerial activity, particularly between 9 am and 12 noon. Our Artillery is still busy, the Germans are paying special attention to CHAPELLE d'ARMENTIERES. During the night rifle and machine gun fire was very busy on both sides. Our Artillery sent the enemy a few salvoes which had the effect of quieting the enemy. Our Artillery also sent a few shells into LILLE	
	6/1/16.		Weather dull, but no rain, the enemy shelled the s/of terrain on our left very heavily between 9 am and 11 am. Nothing of importance transpired on our front. The enemy sent the usual shells into CHAPELLE d'ARMENTIERES, also a few a few into the town of ARMENTIERES. The BOIS GRENIER line also had a good number of shells from the enemy. JOCKSTOY and the Battn HEAD Qrs had also certainly been air covered. As the enemy really allow a day	

Army Form C. 2118

WAR DIARY
or
INTELLIGENCE SUMMARY
(Erase heading not required.)

Instructions regarding War Diaries and Intelligence Summaries are contained in F.S. Regs., Part II. and the Staff Manual respectively. Title Pages will be prepared in manuscript.

Place	Date	Hour	Summary of Events and Information	Remarks and references to Appendices
Corps	6/1/16		To pass without paying it every attention. The relief was carried out satisfactorily. Casualties nil. All Companies reported relief complete by 7 pm	
	7/1/16		Weather again improved, found working parties, everything very quiet.	
	8/1/16		As for the 7th inst. Nothing further to report.	
	9/1/16		Weather still good. Things generally quiet. Issued orders to all concerned regarding relief which takes place tomorrow the 10th inst. Copy marked "C" attached. Found working parties.	
	10/1/16		Weather good. 3 of our men (Officers Servants) of B Company arrested a subject this morning, according to his report the men was asking for information regarding the residence of the General and commanding Officers. Relieved where we are. About 7 pm. We relieved the 9th Hants. Relief complete about 7 pm. Casualties nil. Enemy quiet during the night.	
	11/1/16		Weather dull, inclined for rain. The enemy about 9 am began to send very heavy shells into or near RUE MARIE CHAPPELLE &c. ARMENTIERES and the town of ARMENTIERES, in the latter place according to report a number of Civilians were killed and wounded. Our Artillery retaliated. Quiet. Regiment worked	

WAR DIARY
or
INTELLIGENCE SUMMARY

Army Form C. 2118

Place	Date	Hour	Summary of Events and Information	Remarks and references to Appendices
Contd	11/1/16		About 11.30pm when no artillery opened on Trenches bombardment on the German Trenches opposing the 2nd Division. The men had evidently been raiding the enemy who seemed very excited and threw a large number of varied coloured lights. He retaliated feebly with his artillery. The remainder of the night passed quietly.	
	17/1/16		Fairly good weather. Aeroplanes active. I regret a that one of our aeroplanes was shot down by the enemy. He passed over our line in the night and had travelled about 2 miles beyond our line when a shot from one of our Anti Air Craft guns hit the machine. He fell quickly for about 100', then the machine caught fire. According to further reports both pilot and observer were seen to jump from the machine. The end of them is not known. About 5pm my artillery on my right opened a heavy bombardment accompanied by rifle & machine gun fire on the enemy trenches. The Germans were seen sending up coloured lights. This lasted for about 40 minutes I further regret to record the loss of an Officer which is the first since the Batth arrived in the Country viz 2nd Lieut SAMUEL LAWRENCE GLOVER. He and one N.C.O. and two men went on patrol duty at 12.30 am. The OFFICER and Cpl Waddington	

WAR DIARY or INTELLIGENCE SUMMARY

Army Form C. 2118

Place	Date	Hour	Summary of Events and Information	Remarks and references to Appendices
Contd	12/1/16		got through the enemy wire when they were observed by the enemy and heavily fired upon, also one of the men returned and he reports that the officer boy quite still, the Cpl rolled over and said "I am done for." of the other man Pte A/S Horton nothing is known except that he was near the other two when the firing took place. The man who returned (Pte Reed) thinks that the 3 of them were killed.	
	13/1/16		The weather has broken, some heavy rain. Artillery on both sides has been fairly quiet. The enemy has sent just a throw trench and Shrapnel shells over. About 5.30 pm the Germans were busy with their machine Guns. The night passed quietly.	
	14/1/16		Weather good, a fairly good wind. Nothing happened until about 11.30 am when our artillery opened a keen bombardment on the enemy trenches. The infantry assisted with rifle, machine guns and Trench Mortar Battery. The Germans retaliated principally with whizz bangs but we had no casualties, neither have we had other damage done. His shells fell in his desired position. If there were any of the enemy on or about there they must have suffered severely. At 3.20 pm an enemy Aeroplane came	

Army Form C. 2118.

WAR DIARY
or
INTELLIGENCE SUMMARY
(Erase heading not required.)

Place	Date	Hour	Summary of Events and Information	Remarks and references to Appendices
Cuffs	14/1/16	cont.	Fine and was constantly bent on spotting our batteries. Our Air Craft gun opened fire and succeeded in driving the machine back. The day has been full of excitement, we received orders in the early afternoon that the Artillery covering us would bombard the enemy lines at 4.10pm for 5 minutes, after which we the 10th (WEST RIDINGS) would send smoke bombs all along our front. The wind was favourable for us. The machine guns and Trench mortars to be fired also. The Artillery opened fire a own. As the smoke got under weigh and after a few minutes interval they sent out a few shells but the enemy reserve and support lines. As soon as the enemy spotted the smoke there was great excitement. They were heard shouting, blowing whistles & ringing bells. The enemy artillery though slow to retaliate opened vigorously, both things hang and a few howitzer shells. N Cm-walker were 7 or 8 wounded some slightly damaged. One done to parapets which was speedily repaired also reported that the 6th Inf Bde would be relieved by the 6th Inf Bde. The 13th D.L.I. are taking over our trenches. We are to proceed to Divisional Reserve at Wallaston. Copies of orders issued to all concerned. Copy marked "D" attached.	

WAR DIARY
or
INTELLIGENCE SUMMARY
(Erase heading not required.)

Army Form C. 2118

Instructions regarding War Diaries and Intelligence Summaries are contained in F. S. Regs., Part II. and the Staff Manual respectively. Title Pages will be prepared in manuscript.

Place	Date	Hour	Summary of Events and Information	Remarks and references to Appendices
Trenches running out between Armand Redoubt at Nullebien evening	15/1/16		The weather fairly good, nothing of importance transpired # reliefs carried out, our Emplacer without casualties about 7pm	
	16/1/16		Bright morning, nothing to report.	
	17/1/16		Weather still good, about 1.30 pm one of our aeroplanes flew very low out our lines and descended to earth a few hundred yards away, he had alighted on account of engine trouble.	
	18/1/16		Some rain. A few guns are heard in the distance. nothing further to report.	
	19/1/16		A bright day, all quiet along the line, aeroplanes about our guns are continually heard bombarding near # LAVENTIE a good many colored flares were noticed in the enemy lines B Company found a working party of 100 N.C.O's and men for work in ERQUINGHEM. nothing further to report.	

1875 Wt. W593/826 1,000,000 4/15 J.B.C. & A. A.D.S.S./Forms/C. 2118

WAR DIARY
or
INTELLIGENCE SUMMARY

(Erase heading not required.)

Army Form C. 2118

Instructions regarding War Diaries and Intelligence Summaries are contained in F.S. Regs., Part II. and the Staff Manual respectively. Title Pages will be prepared in manuscript.

Place	Date	Hour	Summary of Events and Information	Remarks and references to Appendices
	20/1/16		Not so fine as yesterday. The Coys carried out training in accordance with programme issued.	
	21/1/16		Weather again bitter, things generally quiet with the exception of aeroplane activity.	
	22/1/16		As far as the 21st nothing exciting happened. Received orders that the 69th Inf. Bde. would relieve the 21st Inf Bde. in the night section on the evening of the 23rd inst. The 8th and 9th Yorkshire Regts taking over the fire trenches and the 10th West Riding and 11th West Yorks being allotted brigade reserve. Copies of orders issued to all concerned. Copy marked E attached.	
Duroval Werne & morning & Afternoon then Relief towing	23/1/16		A German morning. The Aeroplane which came to search on the 17th inst got away during the early afternoon. The Battalion marched to ROLANDERIE FARM in accordance with orders issued on the 22nd inst. The relief was carried out without incident and Completed about 7-30 p.m. nothing further to report.	

WAR DIARY
or
INTELLIGENCE SUMMARY

Army Form C. 2118

Place	Date	Hour	Summary of Events and Information	Remarks and references to Appendices
	24/1/16		Some rain during the day. Weather dull. Artillery active on both sides. The enemy sent a number of large shells into RUE MARLE during the morning, otherwise all quiet.	
	25/1/16		The weather good. Observation good. Aeroplanes active. Artillery also fairly busy. A German aeroplane passed over our lines during the afternoon, in each case he passed over our billets. He was flying fairly high, on two occasions the first pass over ARMENTIERES. On our way to see one of our batteries was very busy during the day. Between 11 pm and 12 mn. this battery fired about 300 rounds. Answered by rifles, machine guns &c.	
	26/1/16		Weather dull, everything quiet. We received a wire and issued orders to all concerned that the Batth. would relieve the 9th Yorkshire Regt. in the trenches tomorrow the 27th. Copy marked F attached. We also received advice that a Battn. of the 16th Royal Scots (3rd Division) would be attached to us during our tour in the trenches. Copy marked attached. Again between 11 pm and 12 mn. heavy musketry rifle machine gun fire from both sides, also artillery was very busy. Our guns carried on an irregular bombardment throughout the night	

1875 W. W 593/826 1,000,000 4/15 J.B.C. & A. A.D.S.S./Forms/C. 2118.

WAR DIARY
or
INTELLIGENCE SUMMARY

(Erase heading not required.)

Army Form C. 2118

Place	Date	Hour	Summary of Events and Information	Remarks and references to Appendices
	27/4/16		weather not good, a quiet time during the day, reliefs carried out without casualties and completed about 8 p.m. a few of our guns were fired during the latter part of the night, the German Howitzers fairly strongly. At about 4.15 a.m. the Germans opened a rather heavy bombardment on our trenches, principally support and reserve, with whizz bangs and a few Howitzers. No casualties caused, neither was there much damage done, our artillery replied effectively.	
	28/4/16		Still morning, the Germans about 9 am began to make numerous trips and are carrying out a bombardment on our reserve and support trenches, altho the bombardment is not over intense, it is regular and is somewhat apparent to understand as they do not appear to have a definite object in view. The 16th Royal Scots are having a rather rough time of it as this is their first experience under fire, the The bombardment has became more intense, the Germans must have been registering during the morning. They gradually brought more guns to bear until eventually it became a perfect hurricane. Our Guns retaliated effectively the trumes making particularly good practice.	

Army Form C. 2118

WAR DIARY
or
INTELLIGENCE SUMMARY
(Erase heading not required.)

Place	Date	Hour	Summary of Events and Information	Remarks and references to Appendices
(cont'd)	29/1/16		During the afternoon the R.F.A. cut enemy wire opposite I.26.2. and machine guns were training on the gaps during the night. Our Cavalry are. One man killed. One man wounded. The 16th Royal Scots having one man killed and one man slightly wounded who has since returned to duty. The remainder of the night passed quietly.	
	29/1/16		Dull morning, rather misty. The Germans have put out but a few whizz bangs and are carrying on an irregular and erratic bombardment on our nearer support trenches. Our guns have replied to them effectively and succeeded in quietening them. Things have quietened and considerably. The machine guns on both sides are somewhat active. Our's have instruction to give attention to the enemy wire opposite I.26.2. The remainder of the night passed quietly.	
	30/1/16		Very dull morning, also misty. One light rain, everything quiet except for an occasional gun or rifle shot. Receiving report from the 69th Bde. under cover of 29 & B.M.s got yesterday to make a raid upon the enemy trenches opposite I.26.2. And the report of the attempt is as follows.	

WAR DIARY
or
INTELLIGENCE SUMMARY
(Erase heading not required.)

Army Form C. 2118

Place	Date	Hour	Summary of Events and Information	Remarks and references to Appendices
Continued	30/1/16		The raiding party of the 10th West Riding Regt. assembled in readiness in rear of trench I.26.2. at 9-30 pm yesterday evening. The wire cutting party and two scouts left our line at 9.15 pm and proceeded towards point I.26.c.9½.2½. They returned at 11pm and stated that a strong hostile patrol, strength about 20 men, moving S.W. and running N.E. along the enemy's wire had prevented them from approaching the wire and completing the gap for the raiding party. After reporting progress to the 69th Infy Brigade I ordered a strong patrol of 12 men to go out to the selected point and to lie up about 60 yards from the enemy wire, in the hope of encountering and dealing with the enemy patrol. At 12.35 am the above patrol returned, stating that they had met no enemy. As all the party were by this time very cold and wet, I suggested to the 69th Infy Bde that operations be discontinued, and received orders to do so. The night was starlit but fairly clear, with very little mist.	

WAR DIARY
or
INTELLIGENCE SUMMARY

Army Form C. 2118

Place	Date	Hour	Summary of Events and Information	Remarks and references to Appendices
(contd)	30/1/16		A copy of orders issued by me are attached. G attached. I am of opinion that the failure to carry through scheme No 1 was due to excessive caution on the part of our wire cutters, who should have tackled the hostile patrol. As no enemy working party was met with Scheme No 2 did not come into operation. We also received advice that the 8th Yorks Regt would relieve us from the front line tomorrow the 31st inst. Copies regarding relief were issued to all concerned. Copy marked H attached	
	31/1/16		Dull morning, some mist. Nothing to report, everything particularly quiet. Reliefs carried out without incident. Casualties nil.	

31-1-1916.

J.A. Ballandine
Lieut Colonel
Commanding 10th (Ser) Battalion
Duke of Wellingtons Regt

A

OPERATION ORDERS.

1. The Battalion will releive the 9th Yorks in the left Section Trenches to-morrow evening.

2. Distribution.

   ### In fire trenches.

   "A" Coy on right.
   "B" Coy in centre.
   "C" Coy on left.

   ### IN BOIS GRENIER.

   "D" Coy (Less 1 Platoon at Fme Du Biez.).

3. Hours of starting. Companies will march off as follows:-

Coy.	Starting Pnt.	Route.	Hour.
C.	Billets.	COWGATE AV.	4'15 p.m.
A.	Billets.	WINE AV.	4. p.m.
B.	BOIS GRENIER LINE.	WINE AV.	To arrive at N. end of Wine Av. at 5'15 p.m.
D.	Billets.	Arret.	4'30 p.m.
Hd. Qrtrs.	Billets.	WINE AV.	4.5 p.m.

   The Signal Officer will arrange to take over Signal Stations at 12' noon to-morrow.
   Machine Gun Emplacements to be taken over in daylight.
   The 9th. Yorks will hand over 2 Machine Guns one in Fire Trenches and one in Bois Grenier Line which will be manned by part of the Btn. Machine Gun Section.
   The 9th. Yorks will take over the billets occupied by the Battalion on relief.

4. A. B. & C. Companies will each detail 4 first class bombers for Headquarters Grenadier Party under Lt Laverack, they will be rationed by the Headquarter Party.
   They will report to Lieut Laverack to-morrow at 4' at Btn. Headquarters.

5. One representative from each Platoon will reach the portion of the Trench allotted to it at 2'30 p.m. for the purpose of taking over TREnch Stores.

   (SDX C. BATHURST. Capt & Adjt.
   1.1.16. 10(S) Btn. Duke of Wellington's.W.R. Re

Reference.
No. 5.   Please add. The Sergeant Major will take over Battalion Stores at Headquarters at 2. p.m.
The Grenadier officer will arrange to take over all bombs in the Trenches.

MOVE ORDERS.

1. The following Transport will be required for the move to the Trenches to-morrow:-
        Heeadquarters. = 2 Limbers.
        A.C. &D.Coys. = 1 Limber each.
        Machine Gun. = 1 Limber.

2. Blankets will be rolled and stacked in Company Headquarters by 3. p.m. to-,orrow where they will be taken over by Coy Qr Mstr Sgts.
"D" Coy will furnish a loading party of 1. N.C.O. and 10 men to report to the Quartermaster at Battalion Headquarters to ~~assis~~ assist in storing blankets at 4.p.m.

~~2~~. This party will rejoin its Company at 4ation Farm on compleetion.

3. Company reserve ammunition will be returned to the Transport Lines by Ration Carts to-morrow. It will be stacked at Headquarters by 2 a.m. to-morrow.

4. Companies will arrange to return all Bombs to the Brigade Bomb Store by 12' noon to-morrow.

                              (SD) C. BATHURST. Capt & Adjt.
1.1.16.   10th. Btn. Duke of Wellington's. W.R. Regt.

OPERATION ORDERS.   NO. 10.

1. The Battalion will be relieved to-morrow by the 9th. Yorks Regt.

2. Coys, on relief, will take over billets from 11th. West Yorks as under:-

      B & A Coys.   H.5.b.7.7. on ERQUINGHEM - ARMENTIERES RD.
      C. Coy.   RUE MARLE.(West side)
      D. Coy.   RUE MARLE.(W.side opposite H.Qrtrs.).
      HEADQUARTERS. Just S. of Bgde Office.

3. The Quartermaster and Coy Q.M.Sgts will take over all billets at noon to-morrow.
All Coys and Hdqrtrs will send one N.C.O. to assist and act as Guide.

4. Officers baggage and Stores will be stacked as follows by 4-45 pm. to-morrow. Not more than 10 men in each Coy to be employed as carrying party.
      H.Q., A, B, & D. Coys.   Entrance to WINE AV.
      C. Coy.   Entrance to Cowgate Av.

5. The TRANSPORT OFFICER will allot the following TRANSPORT to be at Dumps at 5. p.m.:-
      1. G. S. Limber for A & B Coys.
      1. "   "   "   " C & D Coys.
      2. "   "   "   " HEADQUARTERS.
      1. "   "   "   " MACHINE GUN.
Officers Mess Carts, and Medical Cart.

Water Carts will be removed to billets at the same hour.

6. 2 Cooks per Coy & 1 for Hd Qrtrs may precede the Battalion for the purpose of preparing teas.

7. The Machine Gun Officer will arrange to hand over 2 M/c Guns to O/c. 9th. Yorks in BOIS GRENIER LINE.

8. Trench Stores etc will be assembled in readiness for handing over by 12 noon to-morrow and log books will be completed up to date

9. On arrival at the New Billets the Battalion will be known as "D" Btn. In case of alarm Companies will assemble by the shortest route in the Field N. of D. Coy billets on W. side of RUE MARLE.

10. O.C. Signals will arrange to take over all Communications in the New Billets at 2 p.m. to-morrow.

                                      (SD) C. BATHURST. Capt & Adjt
5.1.12.   10th. Duke of Wellington's W.R. Regt.

OPERATION ORDERS.   No. 11.

1. Commencing from to-morrow the 6th inst. the Garrison of the Trenches held by the Battalion will be reduced from 3 Coys to 2 Coys made up to 180 strong.

2. The dividing line between Companies is the bridge crossing the stream in the middle of I.51.1.

3. At intervals in the front line trenches there will be small groups of not less than a section, a proportion of whom should be bombers. There will be a bomb store near them and they will be prepared to counter attack, right or left in case the enemy should break through. They must be prepared to work up or defend the traffic trench as well as the fire trench. One of these posts will be established as near as possible to the night position of each Machine Gun.

4. These dispositions will come into force at 12' noon to-morrow by which time A. & C. Coy Commanders will have completed their dispositions. Arrangements
The right and left Platoons of "B" Coy will be attached to and come under the orders of O.C. "A" & "C" Coys respectively "B" Coy less two platoons, will after the above named hour be withdrawn into any convenient dug outs. At 4'15 p.m. they will move down to that part of the Bois Grenier line at present occupied by 1. Coy 9th. Yorks Regt. and remain there until the relief is complete or orders are received to march to billets.

5. The signal station now used by B. Coy will remain as an extra line and the dug out occupied by O.C. "B" Coy will be taken over by the 2nd in command of A.

6. All Trench Stores will be distributed redistributed with A & C. Coys and a careful list made. Orders are being awaited as to the disposal of the gum boots taken over from 24th. Brigade. Special attention should be paid to the placing of all rifle-racks and sniperscopes in the bays occupied under the new distribution scheme.

(SD)   C. BATHURST. Capt & Adjt
10(S) Btn. Duke of Wellington's.
West Riding Regt.

5.1.16.

10TH (S) BATTN. DUKE OF WELLINGTON'S (WEST RIDING) REGIMENT.

Operation Order No. 12.   Copy No. 15

1...   The battalion will relieve the 9th Yorks Regt. in the Left Section Trenches tomorrow evening, 10th Inst.

2... DISTRIBUTION :-   In Fire Trench.

"D" Coy. on right.
"B" " in centre.
"C" " on left.

In BOIS GRENIER Line.

"A" Coy. (less 1 platoon at Fme. du BIEZ.)
The latter to report to O.C. LILLE POST on taking over.

3... HOURS OF STARTING. Companies will march off as follows :-

Coy.	Starting Point.	ROUTE.	Hour.
"D"	WINE AVENUE.(N.end)	WINE AVENUE.	4-30 p.m.
"B"	Billets.	WINE AVENUE.	4-30 p.m.
"C"	Billets.	COWGATE AVENUE.	4-45 p.m.
"A"	Billets.	WINE AVENUE	4-30 p.m.
Hd.Qrs.	Billets.	WINE AVENUE.	4-15 p.m.

4...   The Signalling Sergeant will arrange to take over Signal Stations at 12 noon tomorrow.

Machine Gun Emplacements to be taken over in daylight.
The 9th Yorks will hand over 2 M.Guns, one in Fire Trenches and one in BOIS GRENIER Line, which will be manned by part of the battalion Reserve M.Gun Section.

The 9th Yorks. will take over the billets occupied by the battalion on relief.

5...   "A" Coy. will detail 12 first class bombers for Hd.Qr.Grenadier Party under Lt. Lavarack; they will be rationed by the Hd.Qr. Party. They will report to Lieut.Lavarack at Battn. Trench Hd.Qrs. at 4-30 pm.

6...   One representative from each platoon and one officer per Coy. will reach the portion of the trench allotted to it at 2-30 p.m. for the purpose of taking over trench stores.
         More care must be taken in taking over trench stores. The latest list of articles to be classed as trench stores is to be strictly complied with and all articles mentioned on the list which are in the trenches are to be taken over.
         The Sergeant Major will take over all Headquarter Trench Stores at 2 p.m.
         The Grenadier Officer will arrange to take over all Bomb Stores during the course of the afternoon.

7... TRANSPORT is allotted as follows and will be at Hd.Qrs. at 4 p.m. unless otherwise stated :-
         1 limber Machine Gun.
         2 limbers Hd.Qrs.
3 pack animals per "A","B", & "C" Coys. for officers' kits.

— 2 —

1 Mess Cart will collect Coy. Messes of "A","B", & "C" Coys., commencing with "A" Coy. at 4 p.m.

Blankets will be rolled and stacked at Coy.Hd.Qrs. A guard will be left in charge at each Coy. until the blankets are removed when the guard will rejoin their companies in the trenches.

8... Each man proceeding to the trenches is to take with him two sandbags which will afterwards be collected at Coy.Hd.Qrs.
They will be drawn from Battn.Hd.Qrs. at 10 a.m. tomorrow.

9... Special attention of all platoon commanders is to be drawn to the pamphlet issued to all platoon commanders ~~yesterday~~ yesterday.

10.. RATIONS. Ration parties are not to be at the dumps until 6-30 p.m. tomorrow. Rations will arrive at the dumps at that hour.
~~After that,~~ rations will be at the dumps at 5 p.m. daily.

From 11th inst. onwards

9.1.16.   sd.   C. Bathurst. Capt. & Adjt.

             Copy No. 1 Lt.Col. H.J. Bartholomew, D.S.O.
                      2 Major L.E. Buchanan.
                      3 Capt. C. Bathurst.
                      4 O.C. "A" Coy.
                      5 O.C. "B" Coy.
                      6 O.C. "C" Coy.
                      7 O.C. "D" Coy.
                      8 Capt. A.P. Harrison.
                      9 Lieut. A.K. Lavarack.
                     10 Transport Officer.
                     11 Quartermaster.
                     12 Battn. Sergt. Major.
                     13 Signalling Sergt.
                     14 O.C. 9th Yorks Regt.
                     15 War Diary.

10TH (S) BATTN. DUKE OF WELLINGTON'S (WEST RIDING) REGIMENT.

Operation Order No. 13.   Copy No. 14

1... The battalion will move into Divisional Reserve tomorrow, and will take over billets from the 13th D.L.I. at HALLOBEAU.
The 12th D.L.I. will relieve the battalion in the trenches.

2... Companies will march to the new billets as soon as relieved, and will report to Battn.Hd.Qrs. at HALLOBEAU when they are all in their billets.

3... One Officer per Company. and one for Hd.Qrs. will proceed in advance at 10 a.m. tomorrow to take over billets.
The Quartermaster will send all men who returned from the Bomb School yesterday to HALLOBEAU to act as unloading parties, guides, etc. by 1 p.m. at which hour they will report to their respective Company Officers.

4... All baggage and kits of "B","D", & Hd.Qrs., are to be at N. end of WINE AVENUE at 5-15 p.m. All baggage and kits of "C" & "A" Coys. will be at N. end of COWGATE AVENUE by the same hour.
Not more than 10 men per Coy. are to be away from their Coy. at the same time to carry out the above order.
Cooks will proceed to billets with the baggage. They will not leave their Coy. Lines before 4-15 p.m.

5... The ration warmers at present in the trenches are to be included in the baggage to be taken away by companies.

6... The Signalling Sergeant will arrange to take over all lines of communication at HALLOBEAU tomorrow morning.

7... The M.Guns of relieving unit will be taken to their emplacements during daylight tomorrow.

8... Trench Stores will be handed over in the usual manner. Lists of Stores to be handed over will reach Orderly Room by 12-30 p.m. tomorrow. These lists must be very carefully compiled and everything that is trench stores in accordance with the last list issued are to be included if in the trench.

9... The Transport Officer will make arrangements for the removal of baggage from the ends of WINE and COWGATE AVENUES to HALLOBEAU.

14.1.16.   sd. C. Bathurst. Capt. & Adjt.

Copy No. 1 Lt.Col. H.J. Bartholomew, D.S.O.
        2 Major L.E. Buchanan.
        3 Capt.C.Bathurst.
        4 O.C."A"Coy.
        5 O.C."B"Coy.
        6 O.C."C"Coy.
        7 O.C."D"Coy.
        8 Capt.A.P.Harrison.
        9 Lt.A.K.Lavarack.
       10 Transport Officer.
       11 Quartermaster.
       12 Battn.Sergt.Major.
       13 Signalling Sergt.
       14 War Diary.

10TH (S) BATTN. DUKE OF WELLINGTON'S (WEST RIDING) REGIMENT.

Operation Order No. 14.   Copy No. 14

Ref. Map - Sheet 36. 1/40,000.

1... The 69th Infantry Brigade will relieve the 24th Infantry Brigade in the right section on the evening of January 23rd. 1916.

2... The battalion will take over billets from 1/Sherwood Foresters as follows :-

   Battn. Hd. Qrs.   LA ROLANDERIE.
   "A" Coy.   H.18.c.3.6.
   "B" "   H.17.c.9.1.
   "C" "   H.11.d.0.4.
   "D" *less 1 platoon*   H.24.c.4.5. ~~and CEMETRY POST~~
   1 Platoon D Coy.   CEMETERY POST

   2 M.Guns and   )
   their teams.   )   LA ROLANDERIE.

   2 M.Guns and   )
   their teams.   )   CEMETRY POST.

3... The battalion whilst in the above billets will be known as "D" Battn.

4... The 1/Sherwood Foresters will take over billets at present occupied by the battalion.

5... Billeting parties, as under, will reach the billets they are taking over by 2 p.m. tomorrow :-
   1 representative for Headquarters.
   1 Officer per Coy. & 1 representative per platoon.
   2 representatives for Machine Gun.
   1 representative for Signallers.
In addition to taking over billets, the officer from each company will also take over Company Bomb Stores.

6... The Signalling Sergt. will arrange to take over all lines from the 1/Sherwood Foresters at 2 p.m. tomorrow.
   He will leave sufficient Signallers behind to keep touch with the Brigade until they are relieved by the incoming Unit.

7... The battalion will march out as follows :-
Starting point - Road Bend H.1.b.9.5.
Route - ERQUINGHEM - RUE DU BIEZ.

   4-35 p.m.   "D" Coy. & Battn.Hd.Qrs.
   4-45 p.m.   "A" Coy.
   4-55 p.m.   "C" Coy. and details of "B" Coy.

The 2 sections of M.Gun who are proceeding to CEMETRY POST will proceed with "D" Coy. The remaining 2 sections will proceed with H.Q.

8... Blankets will be tied in bundles ready for loading by 12 noon tomorrow.

9... All Straw in billets will be collected after breakfast tomorrow and burnt, together with all refuse, in the incinerator.

10.. Receipts will be obtained from relieving unit for all pallaises, basins, etc., handed over.

11.. The Company taking over RUE CHARLES billets ("D" Coy.) will be responsible for the maintenance of the defences of, and posting the necessary sentries in, CEMETRY POST. One platoon will occupy the post at night.

— 2 —

11. **TRANSPORT.** Transport ~~Oxffxxxx~~ is allotted as follows :—

    1 baggage wagon ..... Hd.Qr.Stores & Hd.Qrs. Officers Kits.
    1   "   "   ..... Companies Officers' Kits.
    The Mess Cart will collect the Company Messes.
    The Maltese Cart will collect the Medical Stores.

22.1.16.   sd. C. Bathurst. Capt. & Adjt.

            Copy No. 1   Lt.Col. H.J. Bartholomew, D.S.O.
                   2   Major L.E. Buchanan.
                   3   Capt.C.Bathurst.
                   4   O.C. "A" Coy.
                   5   O.C. "B" Coy.
                   6   O.C. "C" Coy.
                   7   O.C. "D" Coy.
                   8   Machine Gun Officer.
                   9   Lt.A.K.Lavarack.
                 10   Transport Officer.
                 11   Quartermaster.
                 12   Battn.Sergt.Major.
                 13   Signalling Sergt.
                 14   ~~Sigxxkkxxxxxxxx~~ War Diary.

AFTER OPERATION ORDER NO. 14.

10TH (S) BATTN. DUKE OF WELLINGTON'S (WEST RIDING) REGIMENT.

Reference Operation Order No. 14, para 7 is cancelled.
INSERT - The battalion will march out in column of route in the following order :—

        Hd. Qrs. and Signallers.
        "D" Coy.
        "A" "
        "B" "
        "C" "

The 2 sections of Machine Gun who are proceeding to CEMETERY POST will proceeding with "D" Coy, the remaining 2 sections will march in rear of battalion.
Starting point - Road bend H.1.b.9.5.
Route - ERQUINGHEM - RUE DU BIEZ.
The Head of the column will pass the starting point at 4-25 p.m.

23.1.16.   sd.   C. Bathurst. Capt. & Adjt.

10TH (S) BATTN. DUKE OF WELLINGTON'S (WEST RIDING) REGIMENT.

Operation Order No. 16.   Copy No. 15

1... The 10th Duke of Wellington's Regt. will relieve the 8th Yorks Regt. in the Left sub-sector of the Right Section on the afternoon of the 27th January.

2... The battalion will be termed "B" Unit whilst in this sub-sector.

3... Companies will take over trenches I.32.1. to L.26.4. as follows :—

    "A" Coy. on the right.
    "B" "   in the centre.
    "D" "   on the left.
    "C" "   in BOIS GRENIER.

4... Company Commanders and one representative of each platoon will be at Company Trench Headquarters at 10 a.m. tomorrow, except those of "C" Coy. who will be at the N. end of SHAFTESBURY AVENUE at the same hour.
    These parties will arrange to take over all trench stores. Special note should be taken of all available dug-outs in view of the attachment of 2 companies Royal Scots.

5... The Machine Guns at present at Battn.Hd.Qrs. will be left in the BOIS GRENIER Line near SHAFTESBURY AVENUE tonight under arrangements to be made by the M.Gun Officer.
    All M.Gun emplacements in front line will be taken over in daylight tomorrow.
    The 2 guns in CEMETERY POST and the 2 guns left overnight in BOIS GRENIER Line will be man handled to the front line under arrangements and at a time to be decided by the M.Gun Officer.

6... The Signalling Sergt. will arrange to take over all lines of communication in the Left sub-sector by 12 noon tomorrow. He will leave sufficient operators at present Battn.Hd.Qrs. to keep in touch with the Brigade. These operators will not proceed to the trenches until relieved by 8th Yorks Regt.

7... The Battalion Sergt.Major will proceed to Battn.Trench Hd.Qrs. to take over trench stores at 2 p.m. tomorrow.

8... Ration parties will not leave the trenches for the dumps until SHAFTESBURY AVENUE is reported clear from Battn.Hd.Qrs.
    No baggage or kit will be taken up to the trenches until the relief is complete and the 8th Yorks are clear of the trenches.

9... Transport will be allotted as follows :—
    1 G.S. Limber for "A" & "B" Coys.   5 p.m.
    1 G.S. Limber for "C" Coy.   5 p.m.
    1 G.S. Limber for "D" Coy.   5 p.m.
    1 Baggage wagon for Hd.Qrs. and Signallers. 5 p.m.
    1 Maltese cart for Medical Officer.   5 p.m.
    1 Mess Cart for Hd.Qrs., "A"& "B" Coys.Messes. 5 p.m.
"C" & "D" Coy. Messes will be carried on Coy. Limbers and will be in charge of Officers' Servants.
All Cookers will be ready to be moved to the Transport Lines by 3 p.m.

10.. All blankets will be rolled in bundles ready for loading at Coy.Hd.Qrs. at 2 p.m. tomorrow.

11... The battalion will move off as follows :-

	Starting Point.	Time.
Hd.Qr.Party.	Billets.	5-15 p.m.
"A" Coy.	"	5-15 p.m.
"B" "	"	5-45 p.m.
"D" Coy.(via REGENT CIRCUS)	"	5 p.m.
"C" Coy.	"	5-50 p.m.

An interval of 100 yards between platoons will be observed. When proceeding up the road from GRIS POT to BOIS GRENIER, platoons will proceed by sections, and will march in single file on either side of the road.

12.. Companies and M.Gun Section will report by wire to Battn.Hd.Qrs. when relief is completed.

13.. Trench Stores will be taken over as usual. Attention is called to Battn. Routine Order No. 1 of date.

14.. Rations for "D" Coy. will be dumped at TRAMWAY FARM, and for the remainder of the battalion at the Farm I.19.c.5.1½.
They will be left in charge of C.Q.M.S's. who will be held responsible that they are handed over complete to their Companies.
Tomorrow's rations will not be at the dumps until 7 p.m.

15.. Officers' spare kits will be left in charge of Officers' Servants who will load them and accompany them throughout.

16.. O.C. "C" Coy. will detail 1 N.C.O. and 3 men to report at Hd.Qrs. 8th Yorks (JOCK'S JOY) to take over Battn.Hd.Qrs. Guard at 2 p.m. tomorrow.

26.1.16.   sd. C.Bathurst. Capt. & Adjt.

Copy No. 1 Lt.Col. H.J. Bartholomew, D.S.O.
2 Major L.E. Buchanan.
3 Capt. C. Bathurst.
4 O.C. 8th Yorks. Regt.
5 O.C. "A" Coy.
6 O.C. "B" Coy.
7 O.C. "C" Coy.
8 O.C. "D" Coy.
9 Machine Gun Officer.
10 Lt.A.K.Lavarack.
11 Transport Officer.
12 Quartermaster.
13 Battn.Sergt.Major.
14 Signalling Sergt.
15 War Diary.

10TH (S). BATTN. DUKE OF WELLINGTON'S (WEST RIDING) REGIMENT.

ATTACHMENTS.

1.. Two Companies of the 16th Royal Scots. (34th Division) will be attached to the battalion for instructional purposes from 27th January to 31st January inclusive.

2.. These Companies will join the battalion tomorrow, 27th Inst., and will proceed to the trenches with the Companies to which they are attached.

3.. Attached Companies will indent for rations through their own battalions.

4.. Casualty returns will be rendered to the Orderly Room with the Company Returns.

5.. The instruction will commence with a course of 2 days individual instruction, i.e., Officers being linked with officers; N.C.O's. with N.C.O's.; and Privates with Privates.
For instance – "A" platoon sergeant will have a platoon sergeant of the attached company told off to work with him and receive instruction in all his duties.
This will be followed by a period of 2 days during which the platoons of attached companies will work together as platoons.

6.. The two Companies of the 16th Royal Scots will be attached as follows :-
    (Right). "A" Coy. 10th W.Rid.R. to have 3 platoons.
    (Left). "D" " " " " " " " 3 platoons.
    (Centre)."B" " " " " " " " 2 platoons.

7.. Two Machine Guns of the 16th Royal Scots will be attached to this Battn. They will be employed in the front line.
The Machine Guns of the 16th Royal Scots, will be taken up in their limbers to arrive at BOIS GRENIER at 3-30 p.m. tomorrow. Thence they will be man handled to SHAFTESBURY AVENUE (W.end) where the M.Gun Officer 10th West Riding Regt. will meet them and direct them to their positions in the front line.

8.. Platoon guides from "A", "B", & "D" Coys. and a guide from M.Gun Section 10th West Ridings will report to Battn.Hd.Qrs. LA ROLANDERIE FM. at 10-45 a.m. tomorrow. Instructions will be issued to them at that hour. These guides will direct the incoming platoons to the Company to which they are attached.
Here the platoons will be divided as directed in para 5 of these orders.

9.. The Transport Officer will send a guide to the Transport Lines, 16th Royal Scots Regt. H.S.G.d.6. in sufficient time to guide ration carts to the ration dumps daily.

26.1.16.   sd. C.Bathurst, Capt. & Adjt.

Copy No. 1 Lt.Col. H.J. Bartholomew, D.S.O.
        2 Capt. C. Bathurst.
        3 O.C. 16th Royal Scots Regt.
        4 O.C. "A" Coy.
        5 O.C. "B" Coy.
        6 O.C. "D" Coy.
        7 Transport Officer.
        8 Machine Gun Officer.
        9 Quartermaster.
       10 War Diary.

10TH (S) BATTN. DUKE OF WELLINGTON'S (WEST RIDING) REGIMENT.

Operation Order No. 17.   Copy No. 16.

1... The battalion will be relieved by the 8th Yorks. Regt. tomorrow evening, 31st Inst..

2... The Detachment of the 16th Royal Scots will march out with the companies to which they are attached when the latter are relieved.
   They will not proceed to Coys. billets but companies will detail guides to conduct them to LA ROLANDERIE FME. where both companies will assemble prior to marching back to the Hd.Qrs. 16th Royal Scots.

3... Unless prevented by hostile shell fire, all baggage and company stores will be sent out of the trenches and dumped at N. end of SHAFTESBURY AVENUE by 5-15 p.m.
   The ROYAL SCOTS will dump at MOAT FARM, the 10th WEST RIDINGS opposite Brigade Tool Stores.
   By 5-15 p.m. SHAFTESBURY AVENUE will be clear of all baggage or troops other than the incoming Unit.

4... Two cooks per Company may leave the trenches at 4-45 p.m. and proceed to billets.
   No other person is permitted to leave the trenches until relief is complete, except those ordered to do so from Battn.Hd.Qrs.

5... Companies when relieved will not enter SHAFTESBURY AVENUE until all the relieving Unit are up.
   When they may proceed, word will be sent to companies by telephone, and they will go out in the following order :-
      "D" Coy. (via REGENT STREET)
      "A" Coy.
      "B" Coy.
"C" Coy. may proceed to their billets as soon as relieved.
The remaining companies will inform the company which follows them, when they are clear of the trenches.
2 Machine Gun Sections will proceed in rear.

6... Companies will proceed to billets as follows :-
      "A" Coy.   H.18.c.2½.6.
      "D" Coy.   H.17.c.9.1.
      "C" Coy.   H.11.d.0.4.
   "B" Coy.(less 1 platoon).   H.24.c.4.5.
   1 platoon "B" Coy.   CEMETERY POST.
      Battn.Hd.Qrs.   LA ROLANDERIE FME. (H.11.c.6.5.)

      2 M.Guns   ) LA ROLANDERIE FME.
      and their teams.)

      2 M.Guns and   ) CEMETERY POST.
      their teams.   )

7... Lists of trench stores to be handed over will be rendered to Orderly Room by 12 noon tomorrow.
   Company Log Books will be sent to the Orderly Room at the same hour for inspection.

8... Transport will be allotted as follows :-
      1 Baggage wagon.   Hd.Qrs. stores and officers' kits.
      1 Limber for "B" Coy.
      1 Limber for "C" Coy.
      1 Limber for "A" and "D" Coys.
      Maltese cart for Medical Stores.
      Mess cart for Hd.Qr. "A" & "D" Coy's. Messes.
The Company Messes of "B" & "C" Coys. will be carried on their limber.

   1.Limber for the 2 M.Guns at Battn. Hd.Qrs.
   Transport will be at Brigade Tool Shed at 5-30 p.m.

— 2 —

9... Officers' Servants will be in charge of Officers' Kits and will load the same.
Each Company will detail 1 L/Cpl. and 4 men to load baggage and proceed with transport to unload same in billets.

10.. Companies will notify Battn.Hd.Qrs. by wire when they are in their billets.

11.. The Signalling Sergt. will arrange to proceed to billets and take over all Company and Brigade Lines as soon as relieved in the trenches.

30.1.16.   sd. C.Bathurst. Capt. & Adjt.

         Copy No. 1 Lt.Col. H.J. Bartholomew, D.S.O.
                  2 Major L.E. Buchanan.
                  3 Capt.C.Bathurst.
                  4 O.C. 8th Yorks. Regt.
                  5 O.C. 16th Royal Scots Regt.
                  6 O.C. "A" Coy.
                  7 O.C. "B" Coy.
                  8 O.C. "C" Coy.
                  9 O.C. "D" Coy.
                 10 Machine Gun Officer.
                 11 Lt. A.K. Lavarack.
                 12 Transport Officer.
                 13 Quartermaster.
                 14 Battn.Sergt.Major.
                 15 Signalling Sergt.
                 16 War Diary.

SECRET.

10TH (S) BATTN. DUKE OF WELLINGTON'S (WEST RIDING) REGIMENT.

Operation Order No. 18.   Copy No.

Reference Map 1/10,000 Edition 6.

1... A selected party of "C" Company, 10th (S) Bn. Duke of Wellington's Regt., strength 3 Officers and 60 O.R. under MAJOR L.E. BUCHANAN, will raid the enemy's trenches at I.26.c.9½.2½. tonight,

2... The objects of the raid are :—

    (1). To kill or capture as many of the enemy as possible.

    (2). To collect papers, equipment, etc., which may furnish information.

3... Formation of Raiding Party :—

    (1). 2 Wire Cutting parties, each of 1 bomber & 3 men.

    (2).

LEFT PARTY.	RIGHT PARTY.
Lieut. A.K. LAVARACK.	Lieut. G.R.C. HEALE.
3 groups, each of - 1 N.C.O.	3 groups, each of -
2 Bombers	1 N.C.O.
2 Bayonet men.	2 Bombers.
1 Carrier.	2 Bayonet men.
	1 Carrier.

SUPPORT.

2/Lieut. C. SNELL.
10 Bayonet men.
5 Bombers.
4 Stretcher Bearers.
2 Telephonists.

4... The O.C. Raid Party will remain behind our trenches at I.26.c.5½.6.

5... Wire cutters will leave our line at point I.26.c.5½.6. at zero time. They will proceed to cut 2 lanes, 5 yards wide and at 20 yards interval, through the enemy wire at I.26.c.7½.2½.
    They will lay a fine line from the point of exit to the points in the enemy wire which they have cut.
    On completion of their task, two men will be left in observation of the gaps they have cut, the remainder returning to our trenches to report to O.C. Raid.
    If hindered by the enemy, or if a hostile working party is discovered at the point selected, they will immediately send back word to O.C. Raid.

6... The Raiding Party will assemble in the traffic trench in rear of I.26.2. ~~█████████~~ half an hour after zero time.
    O.C. "B" Coy. will arrange that this trench is kept clear from zero time ~~████~~. onwards except for despatch riders and runners.
    On receiving orders to form for the attack, the Raiding Party will pass through our parapet at I.26.c.5.5. and form up just beyond our wire thus :—

```
                              ↑
                    ▮<..20 yds....>▮
LEFT PARTY.    <5 yds>            <5 yds>         RIGHT PARTY.
             ▮                          ▮
       <5 yds>                              <5 yds>
     ▮                                            ▮
     <.................40 yds.................>
                              ↑
                              ·
                           20 yds.
                              ·
                              ▮  SUPPORT.
```

7... Orders for the advance will be given by the O.C. Raid.

8... Should the Raiding Party succeed in entering the enemy's trenches, their subsequent action is left to the discretion of the Officers in command of parties. They must not, however, remain in the enemy's trench for a longer period than 5 minutes, and must not proceed more than 50 yards to the right or left.

   The signal for the return will be a succession of notes on the horn carried by the Officers.

9... Unless the lanes through the enemy wire have been successfully cut, or if the enemy opens fire from his parapet before the wire is reached by the Raiding Party, the latter will not attempt to enter the enemy trench.

   Should a hostile working party be found in front of enemy wire it will be attacked with vigour and driven in, every effort being made to secure at least one prisoner.

   Should a hostile listening post be encountered, it will be bombed and rushed with the bayonet.

   FLANK PATROLS. O.C. "B" Coy. will furnish two flanking patrols each of 1 N.C.O. and 6 men including 2 bombers.

   Instructions have been given to O.C. "B" Coy. as to the action of these flanking patrols.

10.. DISTINGUISHING MARKS. The face of every officer or man who proceeds beyond our own parapet after dusk this evening will be blacked.

11.. The Pass Word will be communicated in sealed message to all concerned at a later hour.
   Zero time will be communicated in the same manner.

12.. An Advanced First Aid Station will be formed at the old gun emplacement at I.26.c.5.4½.

   The Stretcher Bearers of "B" Coy. and those of "D" Coy. 16th Royal Scots will report to the Medical Officer there at 9 p.m.

   The M.O. 8th Yorks. Regt. and 4 stretcher bearers will remain at the Battalion 1st Aid Post near JOCK'S JOY.

13.. The O.C. Battalion will remain at the Advance Signal Station at I.26.c.7.7.
    The O.C. Raid will keep him constantly informed of the progress of operations.

14.. If and when Artillery support is required, it will be asked for by the O.C. Battalion.
    The F.O.O. will remain with him throughout.

15.. The 10th West Riding Companies and the attached platoons of 16th Royal Scots, both in the fire trenches and the BOIS GRENIER Line will "stand to arms" at 10 p.m.

16.. Special orders have been communicated to the M. Gun Officer.

17.. Please acknowledge these orders.

                                               sd. C. Bathurst. Capt. & Adjt.

30th January 1916.

Copy No.	
1	Lt.Col. H.J. Bartholomew, D.S.O.
2	Major L.E. Buchanan.
3	Capt. C. Bathurst.
4	O.C. "A" Coy.
5	O.C. "B" Coy.
6	O.C. "C" Coy.
7	O.C. "D" Coy.
8	O.C. "D" Coy. 16th Royal Scots.
9	Lt. G.R.C. Heale.
10	Lt. A.K. Lavarack.
11	2/Lt. C. Snell.
12	Medical Officer.
13	War Diary.

Action in case of attack

D Coy will support B battalion, acting under the orders of the OC that unit

A~~B~~ will at once reinforce BOIS GRENIER POST

B~~B~~ will occupy BOIS GRENIER LINE S. of SHAFTESBURY AVENUE

C will ....
N. f

~~Those~~ B + C will arrange to have Grenadier & blocking parties in Readiness to block SHAFTESBURY AVENUE.

The Machine Gun Sect less 2 guns will

move to a position in BOIS GRENIER LINE in close proximity to SHAFTESBURY AVENUE.

All Officers will make themselves with the various emergency roads and communication trenches up which they may have to proceed.

Army Form C. 2118

WAR DIARY
or
INTELLIGENCE SUMMARY

(Erase heading not required.) 10th (Ser) Batt'n DUKE of WELLINGTON'S REGIMENT

Place	Date	Hour	Summary of Events and Information	Remarks and references to Appendices
LA ROLANDERIE FARM (Brigade) Resr.	1/7/16		An ideal summers morning a little frost we are in Brigade reserve. Our Guns are bombarding to our right wing. Our trenches generally quiet on our front line. Nothing unusual happened during the night.	
	2/7/16		A fine morning, very cold, some Artillery activity during the day, during the day evening and early morning bursts of rifle and machine gun fire and occasional exchanges of Artillery shots otherwise nothing to report.	
	3/7/16		A fine morning a strong breeze is blowing which is having a good drying effect upon the ground. The enemy has sent a number of heavy shells to our right. Our Artillery has replied effectively. Received orders to relieve the 8th Yorks Regt. in the trenches tomorrow evening. Move orders issued to all concerned. Copy marked "A" attached.	

Army Form C. 2118

WAR DIARY
or
INTELLIGENCE SUMMARY

(Erase heading not required.)

Instructions regarding War Diaries and Intelligence Summaries are contained in F.S. Regs., Part II. and the Staff Manual respectively. Title Pages will be prepared in manuscript.

Place	Date	Hour	Summary of Events and Information	Remarks and references to Appendices
Rue Recipe Trenches morning & afternoon & evening	4/2/16		A stiff breeze blowing, weather still cold. Everything very quiet. We relieved the 8th Yorks Regt in the evening. Reliefs carried out without casualties. All along our front for the past few days has been most unusually quiet. During the eve evening the enemy machine guns were somewhat active. The night passed quietly.	
	5/2/16		A beautiful morning. Our artillery opened fire on the enemy, sending them a few salvoes. The enemy replied feebly and without doing any damage, his artillery is not very effective, he appears to be searching for a mark. Our artillery sent over a number 9 or 10 of shells and it is thought he enemy line and it is thought there were a raiding party. As far as the eye could follow they were all flying in perfect order hundreds of shots were fired upon them. In the late afternoon	

1875 Wt. W593/826 1,000,000 4/15 J.B.C. & A/ A.D.S.S./Forms/C. 2118.

WAR DIARY
or
INTELLIGENCE SUMMARY
(Erase heading not required.)

Place	Date	Hour	Summary of Events and Information	Remarks and references to Appendices
	5/7/16 (m.2)		Afternoon One of our planes also worried the enemy very much, he was constantly over their lines and shots were never upon him. He escaped without injury. The day was very clear which made observation good.	
	6/7/16		The day passed off extremely quiet - nothing to report.	
	7/7/16		Received orders to move into Divisional reserve at FORT ROMPU tomorrow the 8th inst. The 68th Infantry Brigade relieving the 69th Bgde. in the night. Action operation orders issued to all concerned Copy marked "B" attached. The day passed off quietly the only a desultory kind of bombardment taking place. We had one man wounded at night in the front of our wire.	

Army Form C. 2118

WAR DIARY
or
INTELLIGENCE SUMMARY
(Erase heading not required.)

Instructions regarding War Diaries and Intelligence Summaries are contained in F. S. Regs., Part II. and the Staff Manual respectively. Title Pages will be prepared in manuscript.

Place	Date	Hour	Summary of Events and Information	Remarks and references to Appendices
Trenches running southward from Mineral Point Trench	8/9/16		Day very quiet. relief carried out in a downpour of rain and it was nearly midnight before the Battalion reported present at Billets at FORT ROMPU	
	9/9/16		Weather fine, received orders from 69th Inf Bde that the Brigade would move into Corps reserve on the 14th inst. nothing of importance transpired	
	10/9/16		Weather fine. nothing to report	
	11/9/16		Weather broke much rain. we form a working party for the BOIS GRENIER line = 1 officer 80 other ranks. nothing further to report.	
	12/9/16		Weather improved, found a working party of one officer and 50 other ranks nothing further to report	

WAR DIARY
or
INTELLIGENCE SUMMARY

(Erase heading not required.)

Army Form C. 2118

Place	Date	Hour	Summary of Events and Information	Remarks and references to Appendices
	13/9/16		Fine day. Much Aeroplane Activity, two enemy machines dropped bombs in the vicinity, good kills in the late afternoon. No damage caused. Issued orders to all concerned with regard to the move into Corps Rest Camp tomorrow.	
	14/9/16		"C" attacked. Nothing further to report. A strong wind blowing. the Battn was employed in making preparation for the march to STEENBECQUE. We formed up at 9.45 p.m. and marched away with a good step via STEENWERCK and CROIX du BAC, VIEUX BERQUIN. Arriving at the latter place about 3 a.m. where we rested until 9.30 a.m.	
	15/9/16		fine morning. Continued our march to STEENBECQUE via LA MOTTE and arrived at our destination about 2.30 p.m. The troops marched	

WAR DIARY
or
INTELLIGENCE SUMMARY

(Erase heading not required.)

Army Form C. 2118

Place	Date	Hour	Summary of Events and Information	Remarks and references to Appendices
Camp	13/7/16		Week only a few cases of men falling out were reported.	
	14/7/16		A strong wind got up during the night accompanied by heavy rain. A number of Tents were blown down during the day. The air is very pure. The Camp is situated about one mile north of STEENBECQUE. Owing to recent heavy rain there is much mud about. The water is reported not good, and the farmers milk is also considered of questionable quality. Orders have been issued that water and milk must be too boiled before drinking. Training is being carried out in accordance with programme issued by 69th Inf BDE.	

Army Form C. 2118

WAR DIARY
or
INTELLIGENCE SUMMARY

(Erase heading not required.)

Place	Date	Hour	Summary of Events and Information	Remarks and references to Appendices
	17/9/16		Continued the training as mentioned on the 16th	
	18/9/16		As above — weather good	
	19/9/16		as above "	
	20/9/16		as above "	
	21/9/16		as above "	
	27/9/16		Received orders late at night that all training be suspended and that the Battn must be held in readiness to move off at a moments notice. All concerned were duly advised of this	
	28/9/16		The Battalion marched off at 11 am at the head of the 69th Infantry Bde. the weather was fine	

WAR DIARY
or
INTELLIGENCE SUMMARY
(Erase heading not required.)

Army Form C. 2118

Place	Date	Hour	Summary of Events and Information	Remarks and references to Appendices
Camp	23/9/16		Much snow and sleet, also very cold. Arrived at our destination at 6 pm.	
	24/9/16		Nothing further has transpired. We were however intimated to "Stand to". The weather is bad.	
	25/9/16		As for the 24th.	
	26/9/16		As above. During the evening received advice that the Battn. would return to STEENBECQUE. This information was later to all Concerned copy marked D attached.	
	27/9/16		The morning broke dull. Some snow & rain. The Battn. was formed up at 9-30 am and marched in rear of the 69th Inf Bde and arrived at Camp at 3-30 pm. Instructions were received and issued	

WAR DIARY
or
INTELLIGENCE SUMMARY

Army Form C. 2118

Place	Date	Hour	Summary of Events and Information	Remarks and references to Appendices
En S	25/4/16		To all concerned to resume training.	
	26/4/16		Weather fine. Received information to the effect that the Battn is to be held in readiness to move at short notice. This information was passed to all concerned. Copy marked E attached.	
	27/4/16		Weather Good. The Battn formed up at 7 am and marched to STEENBECQUE STATION and there entrained for a station named CALONNÉ RICOUART. We were making for a station named CALONNÉ RICOUART. Arriving there about 11 am. The Battn was again formed up and marched to HESDIGNEUL via BRUAY.	

H.A.S. Borders? Lt Colonel
Commanding 10th (S.) Battn
Duke of WELLINGTON'S Regt

10TH (S) BATTN. DUKE OF WELLINGTON'S (WEST RIDING) REGIMENT.

OPERATION ORDER. NO. 19.

1... The 10th Duke of Wellington's Regt. will relieve the 8th Yorks Regt. in the Left sub-sector of the Right Section tomorrow, 4th Inst..

2... The battalion will be termed "B" Unit whilst in this sub-sector.

3... Companies will take over trenches I.32.1. to I.26.4. as follows :-
   "A" Coy. on the right.
   "C" " in the centre.
   "D" " on the left.
   "B" " in BOIS GRENIER Line.

4... Coy. Commdrs. and one representative of each platoon will be at Coy. Trench Hd.Qrs. at 10 a.m. tomorrow, except those of "B" Coy., who will be at the N. end of SHAFTESBURY AVENUE at the same hour. These parties will arrange to take over all trench stores.

5... All M.Gun emplacements in front line will be taken over in daylight tomorrow, under arrangements to be made by the M.Gun Officer. No M.Gun limbers are required.

6... The Signalling Officer will arrange to take over all lines of communication in the Left sub-sector by 12 noon tomorrow. He will leave sufficient operators at present Battn.Hd.Qrs. to keep in touch with the Brigade. These operators will not proceed to the trenches until relieved by 8th Yorks. Regt.

7... The Battn. Sergt. Major will proceed to Battn. Trench Hd.Qrs. to take over trench stores at 2 p.m. tomorrow.

8... Ration parties will not leave the trenches for the dumps until SHAFTESBURY AVENUE is reported clear from Battn.Hd.Qrs. No baggage or kit will be taken up to the trenches until the relief is complete and the 8th Yorks are clear of the trenches.

9... Transport will be allotted as follows :-
   1 C.S. Limber for "A" & "D" Coys.   5 p.m.
   1 C.S. Limber for "C" Coy.   5 p.m.
   1 C.S. Limber for "B" Coy.   5 p.m.
   1 baggage wagon for Hd.Qrs. & Signallers. 5 p.m.
   1 Maltese cart for Medical Officer.   5 p.m.
   1 Mess cart for Hd.Qrs., "A" & "D" Coys. Messes 5 p.m.

"C" & "B" Coy. Messes will be carried on Coy. Limbers and will be in charge of Officers' Servants.
1 baggage will collect officers' spare kits, etc., commencing at "B" Coy. at 5 p.m. Coy.Commdrs. will leave sufficient men behind to load this wagon and other baggage. The men so left behind will be marched to rejoin their Coys. by an N.C.O.
All Cookers will be ready to be moved to the Transport Lines by 4.30 p.m.

10.. All blankets will be rolled in bundles ready for loading at Coy. Hd.Qrs. at 2 p.m. tomorrow.

11.. The battalion will move off as follows :- Hd.Qrs. party...... 5 p.m.
   "D" Coy.(via REGENT
                Circus)..... 5-15 p.m.
   "C" Coy................. 5 p.m.
   "A" Coy................. 5-15 p.m.
   "B" Coy................. 6-15 p.m.

An interval of 100 yards between platoons will be observed. When proceeding up the road from GRIS POT to BOIS GRENIER, platoons will proceed by sections, and will march in single file on either side of the road.

— 2 —

12... Coys. and M.Gun Section will report by wire to Battn.Hd.Qrs. when relief is completed.

13.. Rations for "D" Coy. will be dumped at TRAMWAY FARM, and for the remainder of Battalion at Farm I.19.c.5.1½.
They will be left in charge of C.Q.M.S. who will be held responsible that they are handed over complete to their Companies.
Tomorrow's rations will not be at the dumps until 7 p.m.

14.. Officers' Kits will be left in charge of Officers's Servants who will load them & accompany them throughout.

15.. O.C. "B" Coy. will detail 1 N.C.O. & 3 men to report at Hd.Qrs. 8th Yorks (JOCK'S JOY) to take over Battn.Hd.Qr. guard at 2 p.m. tomorrow. They will find this guard daily during this tour in the trenches.

3.2.16.   sd. C.Bathurst. Capt. & Adjt.

ATTACHMENT.

1... "C" & "D" Coys. and 2 M.Guns with detachments of 11th SUFFOLK REGT. will be attached to the battalion in the trenches from tomorrow evening.

2... They will be taken over from the 8th Yorks on relieving the latter in the trenches.

3... The instruction will consist of (1). one period of two days during which the platoons of the attached Coys. will work together as platoons. (2). For the remaining 2 days, the attached Companies will work as Companies, one Coy. being in the front line and the other in the BOIS GRENIER Line, for one period of 24.hours each.

4... Attached Coys. will indent for rations through their own battalions.

5... Casualty returns will be rendered to Orderly Room with Coy.Cas. returns. Ammunition required to replace that expended by attached Coys. will be indented for by O.C. Coys. to which attached.

5... The Transport Officer will arrange to send a guide to the transport lines 11th SUFFOLK Regt. (H.9.c.4.6.) in sufficient time to guide ration transport to ration dumps daily. He will inform the SUFFOLKS that for tomorrow, rations are not to be at dumps till 7 p.m.

3.2.16.   sd. C.Bathurst. Capt. & Adjt.

Copy No.	
1	Major L.E. Buchanan.
2	Capt. C. Bathurst.
3	O.C. 8th Yorks. Regt.
4	O.C. "A" Coy.
5	O.C. "B" Coy.
6	O.C. "C" Coy.
7	O.C. "D" Coy.
8	Machine Gun Officer.
9	Lt. A.K.Lavarack.
10	Transport Officer.
11	Quartermaster.
12	2/Lt. R.C. Parks.
13	Battn.Sergt.Major.
14	War Diary.

10TH (S) BATTN. DUKE OF WELLINGTON'S (West Riding) Regiment.

OPERATION ORDER. NO. 29.   Copy No. 14

Ref. Map: Sheet 36. 1/40,000.

1... The battalion will move into Divisional Reserve tomorrow, 8th Inst., and will take over billets from the 13th D.L.I. at FORT ROMPU.
   The 11th Northumberland Fusiliers will relieve the battalion in the trenches.

2... Companies will march to the new billets as soon as relieved, and will report to Battalion Hd.Qrs. when they are all in their billets, but no one is to move into SHAFTESBURY AVENUE until all relieving battalion is in the trenches. This information will be sent to Coys. from Bn.Hd.Qrs.

3... The Quartermaster will arrange to take over billets.

4... One Officer per Company will proceed to the billets at 10 a.m. tomorrow, and will inspect and take over their respective Coy.Billets.
   The Quartermaster will arrange about Headquarters, M.Gun, and Signallers billets.

5... Each Company will send one N.C.O. & 3 men to H.10.d.3.2. by 2 p.m. tomorrow, 8th Inst., to load blankets. They will escort the wagons to billets where they will unload the blankets.
   Later these men will act as platoon guides when their company marches in.

6... Transport is allotted as follows :-
   1 G.S. Limber for "A" & "D" Coys.
   1 G.S. Limber for "C" Coy.
   1 G.S. Limber for "B" Coy.
   1 baggage wagon for Hd.Qrs. & Signallers.
   1 Maltese Cart for Medical Officer.
   1 Mess cart for Hd.Qrs., "A" & "D" Coys. Messes.
"C" & "B" Coy. Messes will be carried on Coy.Limbers and will be in charge of Officers' Servants.

7... All baggage and kits are to be at Coy.Ration Dumps by 5-15 p.m. Coys. will leave an N.C.O. & 3 men with baggage to load and escort wagons to new billets. Officers' Servants will take charge of Officers' kits. Transport will be at these points at 5-30 p.m.

8... The Signalling Officer will arrange to take over all lines of communication at FORT ROMPU tomorrow morning.
He will hand over three D.3. telephones to relieving battalion.

9... Trench Stores will be handed over in the usual manner. Lists are to be carefully compiled and checked and copy to be sent to Orderly Room by 12 noon, tomorrow, 8th Inst.

10.. Machine Gun Detachments will be relieved during daylight. They will not move out before 5-30 p.m.

11.. All Coys., M.Gun, & Hd.Qrs. will march via RUE DU BIEZ.

7.2.16.   sd. C.Bathurst. Capt. & Adjt.

Copy No.		Copy No.	
1	Major L.E. BUCHANAN.	8	Machine Gun Officer.
2	Capt. C. Bathurst.	9	Lt. A.K. Lavarack.
3	O.C. 11th. North. Fus.	10	Transport Officer.
4	O.C. "A" Coy.	11	Quartermaster.
5	O.C. "B" Coy.	12	2/Lt. R.C. Perks.
6	O.C. "C" Coy.	13	Battn. Sergt. Major.
7	O.C. "D" Coy.	14	War Diary.

10TH (S) BATTN. DUKE OF WELLINGTON'S (WEST RIDING) REGIMENT.

OPERATION ORDER No. ...   COPY No. 13

1... The battalion will assemble in column of route (fours) at 9-15 p.m. tomorrow evening and march to VIEUX BERQUIN, via [illegible] – [illegible] – [illegible] – LE VERRIER.
Starting point:- Entrance to 69th Field Ambulance; the battalion will march in the following order:-
  H.Q'RS. & Signallers.
  "A" Coy.
  "B" "
  "C" "
  "D" "
  M.Guns.
  1st. Line Transport Echelon "A".
  1st. Line Transport Echelon "B".
Intervals & distances as laid down in F.S. Regulations.
DRESS:- "Marching order". Great coats will be worn.

2... The 1st Line Transport will move at 1-15 p.m. A baggage guard of 1 N.C.O. per Coy. under an N.C.O. to be detailed by "A" Coy. will accompany 1st Line Transport. This party will assemble outside the Orderly Room at 1-30 p.m. and they will carry the remainder of the day's rations on their person.

3... All Coy. and Officers' kits will be ready for loading, and loading parties detailed to deal with the same, by 11 a.m.
No unauthorised article will on any account be carried on the 1st Line Transport.

4... The Ammunition and M. Gun Limbers and toolcarts will park in the road between the Orderly Room and H.Q. Tpt. Park at 12 noon tomorrow; the horses and pulls will be led back to the Transport Lines until evening.

5... O.C. "B" Coy. will detail a party of one Officer and 10 men for loading Marker's Baggage tool wagons at 2 p.m.
O.C. "D" Coy. will detail a party of 1 N.C.O. and 10 men to load [illegible] at 11 a.m.; this party will parade outside the Orderly Room.

6... All watercarts and field cookers will draw out on to the Main Road at 5-30 p.m.

7... O.C. Coys. will ensure that every man's water bottle is full before starting.

8... Lieut. Laverack and the 4 Coy. Or.MR.Sergts. will parade outside the Orderly Room at 5 a.m. tomorrow and march to VIEUX BERQUIN. They will report to Town Captain at M.24.c.7.2. at 9 a.m.

9... All Officers' Mess kits to be at Orderly Room by 5-30 p.m. for loading on Mess Cart.

10... Mackintoshes and range finders on Coy. charge may be packed in the camp wagons.

11... Unless orders are received to the contrary, the wagons containing Officers' and Mens' kits and blankets will not be sent out on the morning of the 13th to VIEUX BERQUIN.

                        (Sd) C.L. White, Lieut. & A/Adjt.

12.Q.M.

10TH (S) BATTN. DUKE OF WELLINGTON'S (WEST RIDING) REGIMENT.

OPERATION ORDER. NO. 23.   Copy No.

1... The battalion will march to STEENBECQUE tomorrow and will occupy the Camp vacated on the 23rd Inst.

2... Starting point, - road junction L.17.d.3.5.

3... Order of march :-
    Signallers & Hd.Qrs. pass starting point at 10 a.m.
    "B" Coy.
    "C" "
    "D" "
    2 platoons "A" Coy.
    "A" Coy. (less 2 platoons) will march in rear of 2nd Line Transport.
    2nd Line Transport passes Road Junction L.13.b.2.6.
    at 11-35 a.m.

    DRESS - Full marching order. Great coats will be worn unless orders are received to the contrary.

4... Transport is allotted as under :-
    1 G.S. wagon (Reserve Park) per Coy. for blankets.
    ½ Motor Lorry per Coy. for kits.
    1 "   "   for Officers' Kits.
    2 baggage wagons (train) for Qr.Mr's. Stores.
    Transport, M.Gun., Hd.Qrs. blankets will be packed on Qr.Mr's. Stores wagons and will be loaded by 8-30 a.m.

5... 1st Line Transport will be ready to move by 9 a.m.
O.C. "D" Coy. will detail a fatigue party of 1 Officer and 30 O.R. to load C.S. limbers and baggage wagons at 7-15 a.m.

6... Coys. will each detail 1 N.C.O. and 2 men to parade at Road Junction L.24.c.7.3. at 8-45 a.m. tomorrow to act as guides to lorries and wagons. These N.C.O's. and men will act as baggage guards until arrival at STEENBECQUE.

7... All blankets and sandbags are to be rolled and packed by 7 a.m. tomorrow, and stacked by Coys. outside Coy. Hd.Qrs. Parties will be held in readiness to load them.
Coy.Commdrs. are held responsible that no unauthorized articles are carried in either blankets or sandbags.

8... The Motor Lorry for Officers' kits will start at "D" Coy. Hd.Qrs, at 9 a.m.
The Officers' Mess Cart will start at Battn.Hd.Qrs. at the same hour. All kits must be outside Coy.Hd.Qrs billets in readiness for loading at 9 a.m.

9... All tools and stretchers are to be returned to the tool carts and Maltese cart tonight.

10.. L/Cpl. DENHAM and L/Cpl. HEBBLETHWAITE will report to Q.M.S.Patrick at 69th Bde. Hd.Qrs. at 8-15 a.m. tomorrow to take over lorries and G.S. wagons.

11.. O.C. "A" Coy. will detail 1 Officer and 20 O.R. who will march from their billets at 9 a.m. and will proceed to camp at STEENBECQUE. This party will make every endeavour to unload the lorries before the arrival of the battalion.

— 2 —

12.. Strict attention is to be paid to march discipline, especially the Transport.
The following points require particular attention:-
One brake man only to march in rear of each wagon, or two if ther are two brakes.
Cooks (other than brakesmen) to march in a formed body in rear of their cookers.
No rifles or equipment are to be placed on the wagon.
Troops and Transport when halted will keep the centre of the road clear
The instructions contained in this order are to be read and explained to all men accompanying the transport before marching off.

13.. All men of the East Lancs. Regt. attached to the battalion will march in rear of "D" Coy.

26.2.16.   sd. C. Bathurst. Capt. & Adjt.

69/23.

10 County
Richny

Vol 8

23

Franchise

T.Y.
7 sheets

10TH (S) BATTN. DUKE OF WELLINGTON'S (WEST RIDING) REGIMENT.

OPERATION ORDER. No. 25.   Copy No.

Reveille for today 4 a.m.
Breakfast   5 a.m.

2... The battalion will pass the starting point in the following order:-
  Hd.Qrs. & Signallers.
  "C" Coy.
  "D" "
  "B" "
  "A" "
  Lewis Gun Section.

3... Starting Point C.30.b.7.0.

4... The Head of the Column will pass the starting point at 7 a.m.

5... DRESS - Full marching order. Great coats to be worn.
  One blanket per man will be carried on top of the pack.
  Waterproof cape & sheet to be carried in pack

6... All other blankets will be rolled in bundles of "10" and stocked in the barn of the Estaminet in Camp by 6 a.m.
  Fur coats and surplus kits will be packed in sandbags and stacked in the same place as the blankets by 6 a.m.

7... Lieut. LAVARACK and 1 N.C.O. to be detailed by O.C. "D" Coy. will report to Hd.Qrs. 69th Inf.Brigade at 6-50 a.m.

8... O.C. "C" Coy. will detail 1 N.C.O. and 5 men to report to N.C.O. in charge of guard over baggage in the barn of the Estaminet in the Camp by 6-30 a.m. They will received further instructions from the Adjutant.

9... No horse or vehicle will accompany the battalion.

10... Orders will be issued to the Transport for moving as soon as received. They will be moving at or about 8-30 a.m.

11... Officers' valises will be at the Guard Room ready for loading at 6 am.
  A fatigue party of 1 N.C.O. and 12 men from fatigue company will report to Battn.Hd.Qr Farm C.30.b.6.2. at 6 a.m. today.
  A fatigue party of 1 N.C.O. and 20 men from fatigue company will report to Qr.Mr. Stores at 6 a.m. today.

sd. C.Bathurst. Capt. & Adjt.

29.2.16.

WAR DIARY
or
INTELLIGENCE SUMMARY

(7th (Se) Batn Rifle of Wellington Regt)

Place	Date	Hour	Summary of Events and Information	Remarks and references to Appendices
HESDIGNEUL	1/3/16 to 5/3/16		From 1st to 5th inst. we were encamped at the place named in the margin, which time the weather was indifferent. As our movements are uncertain, we are simply instructed to "stand to". For this date in question training was carried out as far as circumstances permitted. On the 1st inst. we received information from the 69th Inf Bde. that the 69th Inf Bde would be inspected by the 4th Corps Commander (Sir Jas Wilson) K.C.B. The Battn was duly formed up at 8.45 A.m on the 2nd inst. and marched to the inspection ground which was at HALLICOURT. Late in the evening of the 5th inst. we received orders from the 69th Inf Bde to relieve a portion of the 17th French Division in the trenches concerned. Copies of orders were issued to all Concerned Copy marked "A" attached	

WAR DIARY
or
INTELLIGENCE SUMMARY
(Erase heading not required.)

Army Form C. 2118

Place	Date	Hour	Summary of Events and Information	Remarks and references to Appendices
	6/2/16		The Battalion paraded at 3-45 pm and marched to the forest BOIS. de BOUVIGNY arriving here about 8 pm. The roads were in a very bad state and there was a large hill to climb which for a great deal of the men who were thoroughly tired out on arrival. About midnight a draft of 100 C.O's men reported their arrival. Orders were issued that the Battn moved the following day.	
	7/2/16		Weather very bad, some snow. The Battn formed up at 3pm and marched to VILLERS-au-BOIS. whilst on the march snow fell fast and a very cold wind was blowing. The hills are of a very important quality, the room being cramped. The Battalion marched to the trenches under the most trying conditions. The village of ABLAIN is a very	

Place	Date	Hour	Summary of Events and Information	Remarks and references to Appendices
	8/3/16		2nd sight being absolutely in ruins; the third of the Battn was left at the village in support of those in the front line trenches. We relieved the 9th York's Regt. All reliefs completed at 7-15 pm. Casualties nil. Snow on the ground. Cruel cold day. Enemy shelled our front line continuously throughout the day with heavy minenwerfer and aerial torpedoes. The trenches are in a very bad condition in fact the front line can scarcely be called trenches since they consist of shell craters joined by shallow ditches.	
	9/3/16		More snow. During the day enemy continually bombarded us with trench mortars, aerial torpedoes, and shells of every calibre. The Centre station officer was named the officer of "C" Company suffered concussion, one killed and 18 wounded	

WAR DIARY
or
INTELLIGENCE SUMMARY

Army Form C. 2118.

Place	Date	Hour	Summary of Events and Information	Remarks and references to Appendices
	10/3/16		early in the day. The medical Officer (Lt. John Inlan) was killed whilst in performance of his duty (dressing the wounded. The undermentioned Officers N.C.O. men were awarded the Military Cross & Distinguished Conduct medal respectively for their gallantry upon several occasions whilst in action under severe conditions. Lt. G.R.C. Henle 11988 Sergt R Earnshaw 15537 Pte J Hawkridge was attached to the 2nd Northants Regiment. The Battn. to the 24th Infantry Brigade returning the 6.9.5 Inf Bde. 8.30 pm The Embussment under which the Battn. Landed would not permit the issue of the usual orders. The Battalion arrived at Bellets in the BOIS DE BOUVIGNY arriving here about 3 a.m.	

Army Form C. 2118.

WAR DIARY
or
INTELLIGENCE SUMMARY.
(Erase heading not required.)

Instructions regarding War Diaries and Intelligence Summaries are contained in F. S. Regs., Part II. and the Staff Manual respectively. Title pages will be prepared in manuscript.

Place	Date	Hour	Summary of Events and Information	Remarks and references to Appendices
	11/3/16		The men were very dirty as a consequence of wading through mud and also lived out and were exceedingly dirty. Some artillery activity. There was nothing to report	
	12/3/16		Nothing to Report	
	13/3/16		Received orders that the Battn would proceed to BRUAY. There was a great change in the weather. The sun shone out and it became very hot. The Battn left the reserve Billets at 10-20 am arriving in BRUAY about 4 p.m. Some difficulty was experienced in procuring the billets, no however was surmounted, accomplished and all ranks made comfortable	
	14/3/16		The Battn was employed in cleaning clothing and general interior economy. Equipment a bath and the french people in the town of BRUAY appears	

Army Form C. 2118.

WAR DIARY
or
INTELLIGENCE SUMMARY.

(Erase heading not required.)

Instructions regarding War Diaries and Intelligence Summaries are contained in F.S. Regs., Part II. and the Staff Manual respectively. Title pages will be prepared in manuscript.

Place	Date	Hour	Summary of Events and Information	Remarks and references to Appendices
	15/3/16		to be pleased with the troops and great friendliness prevails. Weather fine nothing to report. An enemy plane dropped 4 bombs about 10 p.m. this is no information to hand that damage was done or otherwise.	
	16/3/16		Weather fine nothing to Report.	
	17/3/16		Received orders to relieve the 2nd Oxford & Bucks Light Infantry in the trenches Angres Section. This information was duly passed to all Concerned. Copy marked @ attached	
	18/3/16		The Battn was formed up at 11.30am today and marched to CORON-FOSSE arriving there at 3-45pm The weather was very good. The distance between BRUAY & CORON is about 10½ Kilometres. we marched via HALLICOURT + BARLIN + HERSIN. On our way we passed the 6th Inf Bde (2nd Divs)	

WAR DIARY
or
INTELLIGENCE SUMMARY.

Army Form C. 2118.

Place	Date	Hour	Summary of Events and Information	Remarks and references to Appendices
	19/3/16		They employed the King. Scissors Scope & Telescope Rgt's. They each had a half a dozen which was much appreciated by no men. They appear a fine body of men. Things are generally quiet here just as aeroround gun being fired. Aircraft have been over all day however nothing to report. The weather was very fine while carried out Coueches and CORON. Stores are in CORON. The transport lines and ammunition cooking purposes to be carried up in tin from BULLY GRENAY — during darkness a distance of two miles.	
	20/3/16		The day very dull much aeroplane activity especially by our own Airmen. Artillery during the day quiet but before dark the enemy Artillery opened fire and continued to do so for about 11 minutes then into our support trenches. Our artillery retaliated and succeeded in quietening the enemy	

WAR DIARY
or
INTELLIGENCE SUMMARY

Army Form C. 2118.

(Erase heading not required.)

Place	Date	Hour	Summary of Events and Information	Remarks and references to Appendices
	21/3/16		During the afternoon an enemy rifle grenade was fired and burst in the open trap window killing one man and wounding 3 other men. A sentries ring observed during the night. We had 1 other man wounded.	
	22/3/16		The day was very dull otherwise was uneventfully not great. Artillery was quiet. The enemy was moving and very many flying rifle grenades amongst our dead. He went very many flying rifle grenades about me on to a two or three foot trap. Enemy succeeded in placing one 8 other rounds being wounded when walked in. I opened sweeping on him who uneventfully. Day dull. No casualties to report. Hoping to report.	
	23/3/16		Some men, rifle grenades and trench mortars active on both sides were very active. We had the following casualties as a result of enemy rifle grenades. One Officer wounded. 5 other ranks killed. 10 O.R. wounded. There were very little artillery in action during the dull weather. During the night there was a big fall of snow.	
	24/3/16		There was practically nothing doing. No had no Casualties.	

WAR DIARY
INTELLIGENCE SUMMARY

Army Form C. 2118.

Place	Date	Hour	Summary of Events and Information	Remarks and references to Appendices
	25/3/16		Beautifully clear day, but very cold. Much aeroplane activity. The 9th Yorks Regt relieved in commencing at 7 pm. Carried out without casualties all reliefs completed by about midnight.	
	26/3/16		Weather fine. Nothing of importance happened. Received orders that the S.O.S. 23rd Divn would replace the Battn on the 27th inst. Enemy working parties heard on the 28th inst. Inspection reports to the 75th inst. weather dull. Fired off well, Enemy working parties was made and passed off well.	
	27/3/16		Weather fine. Enemy working parties reported from 75 – 28. inst. Received orders to relieve the 9th Yorks Regt in the trenches & copy marked "E" attached.	
	29/3/16		Fine morning much aeroplane activity. The	
	30/3/16		Battn marched to the trenches nothing of importance happened reliefs carried out and completed by 11 pm Casualties nil	

Army Form C. 2118

WAR DIARY
or
INTELLIGENCE SUMMARY.
(Erase heading not required.)

Place	Date	Hour	Summary of Events and Information	Remarks and references to Appendices
	31/3/16		Beautiful morning. Aeroplanes again active the enemy more than usual. Some little artillery activity. The enemy has sent some heavy shell into a place known as FOSSE 10. (Pit head) about 12 shells before noon + two about 3.30 pm. Nothing further to report.	

H.J. Bath Agnes
Lieut-Colonel
Commdg 10th (Batta) Duke of Wellington Regiment

ORDERLY ROOM.
No. ......
31 MAR 1916
10th (SER) Bn. DUKE of WELLINGTON'
W. RIDING REGT.

10th (Ser) Battn. Duke of Wellington's (West Riding) Regiment.
OPERATION ORDERS, NO. 27.

1... The Brigade will relieve a portion of the 17th (French) Division in the trenches.
The line to be taken up extends from SOUCHEZ RIVER to and including the "ERSATZ" communication trench about point S.15.a.3.2.

2... The 9th Yorks Regt. will be the left battalion on night of 7/8th.
    8th Yorks Regt. will be the centre battalion -do-
    11th West Yorks Regt. will be the right battn. -do-
    10th West Ridings. will be in close support -do-

3... "A" Coy. 10th West Ridings will be in close support in or about the CABARET ROUGE.
This Company will march with the 11th West York on evening of 7th Inst., and will join that battalion at GRANDE SERVINS at 5 p.m. that day.
"B" Coy. 10th West Ridings will be in CARENCY.
Battn.Hd.Qrs., "C" & "D" Coys. 10th West Ridings will be in VILLERS.

4... 1,000 detonated grenades will be taken by "B" Coy. to CARENCY.
1,000 detonated grenades will be taken by "A" Coy. to CABARET ROUGE.
These grenades will be picked up at CARENCY.

5... Before leaving billets tomorrow evening, each man will carry 220 rounds S.A.A.
As soon as the ammunition to complete this number has been drawn from the limbers, the latter will proceed to the Brigade S.A.A. Dump in the Square GRANDE SERVINS and refill.
A limber containing 16 boxes S.A.A. will follow "A" Coy. This ammunition is to be taken into the CABARET ROUGE Trenches.
This limber will then proceed to S.A.A. Dump to refill.

6... All ranks will carry rations for the 8th Inst. when moving from the huts on the evening of the 7th Inst.

7... When relieving in the trenches absolute silence must be maintained owing to the close proximity of the enemy's trenches.

8... The transport of the battalion will move to GOUY SERVINS not later than 4-45 p.m. 7th Inst. Lines will be allotted by the Staff Captain.

9... The battalions in the trenches will be designated as follows :-
    RIGHT Battalion .... "A" Battalion.
    CENTRE   "   .... "B"   "
    LEFT   "   .... "C"   "
    SUPPORT "   .... "D"   "

6.3.16.   sd. C.Bathurst. Capt. & Adjt.

10TH (S) BATTN. DUKE OF WELLINGTON'S (WEST RIDING) REGIMENT.

OPERATION ORDERS. NO. 28.

1... The battalion will march to BRUAY tomorrow about 12 noon.

2... Reveille tomorrow, 13th Inst., will be at 6 a.m.
Breakfast 7 a.m.
Orderly Room 9-30 a.m.

3... All kits, blankets, and fur coats, are to be ready for loading by 8-30 a.m. tomorrow.

4... Transport is allotted as follows :-
- 1 Lorry .... "A" & "B" Coys. blankets.
- 1 Lorry .... "C" & "D" Coys. blankets.
- 1 Lorry .... (Hd.Qrs. & M.Gun Blankets.
  (Qr.Mr's. Stores & Hd.Qrs. Officers' Kits.
  (Hd.Qr. Officers' Mess.
- 1 G.S. wagon ...... Company Officers' Kits & Coy.Officers' Mess
- 1 G.S. wagon ...... Qr.Mr.Stores.

5... All fur coats will be packed in sandbags, carefully labelled, and stacked in the empty hut on the West side of camp.
Nothing but fur coats are to be placed in the sandbags. <u>If any unauthorized articles are found in the bags they will be left behind.</u>
One lorry will return to pick up the above sandbags.
An Officer, to be detailed by O.C. "C" Coy., with 4 men per Coy., will remain behind to load the above lorry.
This party, after the departure of the battalion, will search all huts in camp to ensure that nothing is left behind.
They will afterwards hand over the camp to the relieving Unit.

6... All 1st Line Transport will be ready to load by 11 a.m. tomorrow.
Teams for Cookers, Watercarts, M.Gun Limbers, will be at Battn.Hd.Qrs. by 11 a.m.
G.S. Baggage wagons will be at Battn.Hd.Qrs. ready for loading at 8-30 a.m.
Orders as to where the remainder of 1st Line Transport will join the battalion will be issued later.

7... Great care must be taken to ensure that the camp is handed over in a clean condition. Company etc. Commanders are responsible for the cleanliness of the ground in the vicinity of their Company etc. Lines.

8... Further orders will be issued later.

12.3.16.   sd. C.Bathurst. Capt. & Adjt.

10TH (S) BATTN. DUKE OF WELLINGTON'S (WEST RIDING) REGIMENT.

OPERATION ORDER. NO. 29.

Reference Map, Sheet 36b.

1... The battalion will relieve the Oxford & Bucks L.I. in the ANGRAS Sector tomorrow, and will march to billets at CORON, FOSSE 10 (R.8.Central) tomorrow.

2... Starting Point - Road Junction J.16.a.5.7.

3... The battalion will march in the following order :-
    Hd.Qrs. & Signallers.
    "C" Coy.
    "D" "
    "A" "
    "B" "
    Lewis Gun Detachment.
    Transport.
DRESS - Full marching order. Great coats will be carried in or on the pack.

4... The Head of the Column will pass the starting point at 11-45 a.m.

5... Transport is alloted as under :-
    1 Lorry........ "A" & "B" Coys. blankets.
    1   "   .... "C" & "D" "   "
    1   "   .... Qr.Mr's. Stores.
    1 G.S.Wagon... Officers' kits.
    1   "   "   ... Hd.Qrs. Stores.
The lorries will return, and on the second journey will be loaded :-
    1 Lorry........ Fur coats "A" & "B" Coys.
    1   "   ....   "   "   "C" & "D" "
    1   "   .... Blankets of Hd.Qrs.Party & Signallers.

6... Company Commdrs. will detail an N.C.O. & 3 men each to accompany the lorries containing their blankets. These men will act as unloading parties.
In addition, the fatigue Company will detail 4 men to accompany the lorry containing Qr.Mr's. Stores.
Each Company will detail 1 N.C.O. & 4 men to remain behind at Qr.Mr's. Stores and wait for the return of the lorries. This party will then load and accompany the lorries to the billets.
The Regtl.Qr.Mr.Sergt. will superintend the latter party.

7... All blankets, rolled in bundles of 10, and accompanied by a loading party of 10 men per Company, will be at the Qr.Mr's. Stores at 8-15 am. tomorrow.
    Officers' kits and Messes will be brought to the Qr.Mr's.Stores for loading by 9.30 a.m.
    O.C. "A" Coy. will detail a fatigue party of 1 Officer and 20 men to load the 2 G.S. wagons.

8... On arrival at billets, no man is to quit his billet without permission. As the vicinity is liable to shell fire, no unnecessary movement will take place.

9... On the morning of the 19th Inst :-
    Company Commdrs. & 1 runner each.
    Lewis Gun Officer.
    Grenadier Officer.
    Medical Officer.
    Signalling Officer.
will visit the trenches to be taken over. One guide will meet this party at the road junction R.11.c.3.9., at 9 a.m. and will direct the party to Battn.H.Q. where guides will be met to direct the above officers to their respective positions.

sd. C. Bathurst. Capt & Adjt.

10TH (S) BATTN. DUKE OF WELLINGTON'S (WEST RIDING) REGIMENT.

OPERATION ORDERS.   NO. 30.

1... The battalion will relieve the 2nd Oxford & Bucks L.I. in the Centre Section tomorrow, 19th Inst.
Companies will take over as follows :-   "A" Coy.   Right.
               "B" " Centre.
               "D" " Left.
               "C" " Support.

2... The battalion will march to the trenches by Companies as follows, via CROSS ROADS R.3.d. and CROSS ROADS R.11.c.3.9.:-   "B" Coy.   5-30 pm.
                        "D" " 6-30 pm.
                        "A" " 7-30 pm.
                        "C" " 8 pm.
Guides will be met at CORONS D'AIX (R.11.c.3.9.).

3... Advance parties as detailed in Operation Order No. 29 para 9, will proceed to the trenches tomorrow morning, 19th Inst., to take over. In addition, the Sergeant Major will proceed at the same time to take over stores for Battn.Hd.Qrs.

4... Whilst in the trenches the battalion will be known as "B" Battalion.

5... Companies, etc. will notify the Adjutant by wire or runner on completion on relief.

6... All rations for the 20th will be carried up on the men.

7... "C" Company will detail sufficient men daily to carry rations and water etc. from the dump to Battn.Hd.Qrs.
Hour of arrival of rations at the Dump will be notified later.

8... The S.O.S. Signal will consist of 5 white rockets, to be sent up as fast as possible, one after the other.
The signal will be repeated at two minute intervals until required Artillery fire has been opened.
The Brigade on the Right use Red rockets.
 " " " " left " Green "

9... Hd.Qr.Signallers will take over at 3 p.m. tomorrow. Company Signallers will march with their Companies.

10.. All water bottles are to be filled before starting to the trenches.

11.. "Stand to Arms" in the trenches will be:- 4-30 a.m. & 6-15 p.m.

12...Officers' valises will not be taken to the trenches and Officers are recommended only to take what they can carry.

13...Lewis Guns will take over emplacements at hours to be arranged by the Lewis Gun Officer.

14...Lists of all stores taken over in the trenches will be rendered to Battn.Hd.Qrs. tomorrow night as soon as possible after the trench relief has taken place.

15...One G.S. wagon will be sent to the Gum Boot Stores (R.11.a.7.4.) BULLY GRENAY to draw 350 pairs of Gum Boots. These will be conveyed to CORONS D'AIX (R.11.c.3.9.) by 5-45 p.m. where they will be handed out to Companies etc. by Regtl.Q.M.S. on their way to the trenches.

10TH (S) BATTN. DUKE OF WELLINGTON'S (WEST RIDING) REGIMENT.
OPERATION ORDERS NO. 32.

1... The 10th West Ridings will relieve the 9th Yorks Regt. in the Centre Sector tomorrow, 30th Inst..

2... Dispositions :—   "C" Coy. on the right.
   "B" " in the Centre.
   "D" " on the left.
   "A" " in Support.

3... One Officer and one N.C.O. per Coy. will proceed to the trenches on the morning of 30th Inst. to take over trench stores.
The Sergt. Major and Pioneers will proceed to trenches at 6 p.m., and the former will take over all Hd.Qr. Stores and all water carrying vessels.

4... The Lewis Gun Officer will receive his orders separately.

5... Gum boots will be picked up at the W. end of CORON D'AIX Communication Trench as follows :—
   Each Company in front line.... 90 pairs.
   Support Company .... 50 "
   Lewis Gun Detachment .... 20 "
   Hd.Qr. Party .... 10 "

6... Guides will be met as follows :—

Coy.	Place.	Time.
"B" Coy. W. end of CORONS D'AIX Trench.		7 p.m.
"D" "	—ditto—	7-30 p.m.
"C" "	—ditto—	8 p.m.
"A" "	—ditto—	8-30 p.m.

7... Company Signallers will follow their own Coys. Hd.Qr. Signallers will take over in trenches at 3 p.m.

8... All rations for the 31st. Inst. will be carried on the man.

29.3.16.   sd.   C. Bathurst. Capt. & Adjt.
_____
AFTER ORDERS.

1.....Reference above order No. 6. Coys. will parade as follows :—
   "B" Coy.   6-15 p.m.
   "D" "   6-45 p.m.
   "C" "   7-15 p.m.
   "A" "   7-45 p.m.
Dress – Marching Order. Great coats will be worn. Fur coats will be carried in the straps of the pack.
Coys. will march by the following route – Railway Crossing R.9.a.6.9. Track N. of railway to R.3.d.8.5, thence by main road to CORON D'AIX & CORON D'AIX ALLEY.
Platoons will vacate their billets 1 hour before the hour of parade & the former will be thoroughly cleaned. Each platoon is to be inspected before moving off by an officer.

2.WATER. Officers will ensure that all water bottles are full. No water will be available in the trenches till 6 a.m. on the morning of 31st.

3.OFFICERS' KITS. 2 c.s. limbers will be at Qr.Mr's. Stores at 6 p.m. to collect same.

29.3.16.   sd. C.Bathurst. Capt. & Adjt.

16... MOVEMENT BY ROAD.
Between FOSSE 10 and BULLY GRENAY via Road R.3.d.1.8. to R.10.b.6.2., Infantry Only by day with intervals of 200 yards between sections and in single file alongside of road.

Limbers by day will move by PETIT SAINS - MAZINGARBE - L.5.3. - BREVIS.

No movement is permitted from FOSSE 10 to AIX NOULETTE until 6 p.m. and then by platoons with 100 yards intervals.

17... Transport Lines and Quartermaster's Stores will be at FOSSE 10, R.8.Central).

The Transport Officer and Quartermaster will detail a party to take over the above tomorrow morning, 19th Inst.

18.3.16.   sd. C.Bathurst. Capt. & Adjt.

WAR DIARY or INTELLIGENCE SUMMARY

10 W Riding
Vol 9
10th (Sv) Bn. Duke of Wellington's Regt.

Place	Date	Hour	Summary of Events and Information	Remarks and references to Appendices
TRENCHES	1/4/16		Weather fine. Good visibility. Aeroplanes on both sides active. About 9.30 am our Anti Aircraft guns appeared to hit an enemy machine which descended some distance in rear of the enemy lines. The enemy were also active with rifle grenades and trench mortars. We retaliated similarly vigorously. It is noticed that guard & aircraft retaliation keeps the enemy well in hand. The bugler guns on both sides showed some activity. No Man's Land is pitted with shell holes, in the bottom of which, in several cases, there is barbed wire. These form particularly nasty traps. At 3.15 pm a French aeroplane was brought down by the enemy Anti Aircraft gun. It fell immediately behind the Battalion French Headquarters. The pilot was picked up "dead", the observer and a few minutes later	

S.Y.
11 sheets

WAR DIARY
or
INTELLIGENCE SUMMARY.
(Erase heading not required.)

Army Form C. 2118.

Place	Date	Hour	Summary of Events and Information	Remarks and references to Appendices
TRENCHES	1/4/16		Fine warm day, the weather is much appreciated by all ranks as trench life is considerably improved. Artillery on both sides very active. The enemy fired a number of rifle grenades & trench mortar shells into, and behind our front line without doing any damage. We retaliated with similar missiles a little more vigorously than the enemy. The night passed quietly.	
"	2/4/16		Hazy but fine morning, as the day advanced the sun shone out & it was very pleasant. The large cloud away and aeroplane made their appearance, no being the 1st on the scene. During the day we had 3 casualties caused by rifle grenades. The night passed quietly.	
"	4/3/16		Quiet change in the weather, much colder and dull. Nothing of importance transpired. Received and carried out to all concerned a relief which took place at night. The 9th Yorkshire Regt taking our place. Relief completed about midnight. Casualties nil. We moved into Billets at FOSSE 10 Copy marked "A" attached	

Army Form C. 2118.

WAR DIARY
or
INTELLIGENCE SUMMARY.
(Erase heading not required.)

Instructions regarding War Diaries and Intelligence Summaries are contained in F. S. Regs., Part II. and the Staff Manual respectively. Title pages will be prepared in manuscript.

Place	Date	Hour	Summary of Events and Information	Remarks and references to Appendices
RESERVE BILLETS	5/4/16		Fine day a good amount of artillery activity, also much aeroplane activity. The enemy sent several shells into FOSSE 10. No damage reported. Our guns were particularly active in the late evening, nothing further to report.	
FOSSE 10	6/4/16		Weather continues fine a devil of a lot of shelling is taking place, activity in the Air continues. FOSSE 10 has been in receipt of a few more shells of small calibre nothing further of importance transpired.	
"	7/4/16		Still fine. Everything very quiet, the enemy tried hard to locate one of our batteries without success nothing further to report.	
	8/4/16		Fine morning. Things everywhere within sight generally quiet.	
	9/4/16		Same as for the previous day. Received orders to relieve the 9th Yorks in the trenches. Orders issued to all	

WAR DIARY
or
INTELLIGENCE SUMMARY.

Army Form C. 2118.

Place	Date	Hour	Summary of Events and Information	Remarks and references to Appendices
Contd	9/4/16		concerns accordingly. Copy marked "B" attached.	
Billets morning afternoon trenches evening	10/4/16		Beautifully fine. All very quiet, which were completed about 10pm Casualties nil. Enemy quiet during the night. Afternoon an intense bombardment took place by the brigade on our left. No particulars as to results to hand	
T.R.E.N.C.H.E.S	11/4/16		Weather broke, some rain, not any real activity shewn by either side the enemy has sent a number of rifle grenades and trench mortor shells into the left company lines without making any answer. In the afternoon we had 11 men wounded by the premature bursting of one of our rifle grenades. The remainder of the day passes off quietly	
"	12/4/16		Small rain, everything quiet, during the morning. The enemy artillery very quiet also. In the afternoon the enemy used rifle	

WAR DIARY
or
INTELLIGENCE SUMMARY.

Army Form C. 2118.

Place	Date	Hour	Summary of Events and Information	Remarks and references to Appendices
[Crud]	17/4/16		in fairly large numbers. We had no casualties. The night passed quietly.	
TRENCHES	13/4/16		Some rain. The enemy is sending over rifle heavy shells into BULLY GRENAY. Our artillery is replying. the weather is bad for observation and aeroplanes. Nothing further to report.	
"	14/4/16		Still raining. Things generally quiet, enemy aircra[ft] enemy sent a shell into FOSSE 10. We receive advice that the 5th Inf[antr]y Bde (2nd Division) would relieve the 69th Inf[antr]y Bde. Prior to the relief the time was redistributed. Copy marked 6 attached. It will be noticed that B Company will be relieved tomorrow the 15th but the 4B Company remaining in support until the 16th.	
"	15/4/16		Beautiful morning. The enemy shelled the BULLY 4 Communications	

WAR DIARY
or
INTELLIGENCE SUMMARY.

Army Form C. 2118.

Place	Date	Hour	Summary of Events and Information	Remarks and references to Appendices
Carty	13/4/16		Trenches. The whole were well dressed. The Bangours were relieved by noon. Casualties nil. We moved into Billets in CORON D'AIX for the night. Found orders to relief to the 2nd Oxford Bucks which would take place on the 16th inst. Copy marked "D" attached. During the late evening our artillery was very active, particularly on the left. About 11 pm an enemy aeroplane flew over the viciniy of our billets and dropped a number of bombs.	
	14/4/16		The Companies which were ordered to march out commencing at 10.30 am an interval of 200 yards being observed between half platoons. About 11-20 am the enemy big air to shell the various billets at CORON D'AIX. He sent some very heavy shells but beyond demolishing a few already badly damaged houses there was no damage or casualties reported. The Battn marched to HERSIN by Companies starting a few	

Army Form C. 2118.

WAR DIARY
or
INTELLIGENCE SUMMARY.
(Erase heading not required.)

Place	Date	Hour	Summary of Events and Information	Remarks and references to Appendices
(contd)	16/4/16		distance between Head quarter Coy leading. Arrived HERSIN about 3pm all ranks were made comfortable for the night. Received orders to move to OURTON Copy of march table marked "E" attached.	
	17/4/16		The Battalion formed up at 12 noon and marched to OURTON via HOUDAIN arriving at OURTON at 5 pm. Reached orders to proceed to the Marquise area and take over billets on the 19th inst at BEAUMETZ &c. This information was passed on to all concerned on the 18th inst. Copy marked "F" Attached	
	18/4/16		One van the Companies are placed at the disposal of Coy Commanders. General cleaning up and interior economy	
	19/4/16		The Battn formed up at 7.45 am the condition being miserable here being a drizzly rain. We marched via PERNES – SAINS – FIEFS arriving at BEAUMETZ at	

Army Form C. 2118.

WAR DIARY
or
INTELLIGENCE SUMMARY.
(Erase heading not required.)

Instructions regarding War Diaries and Intelligence Summaries are contained in F. S. Regs., Part II. and the Staff Manual respectively. Title pages will be prepared in manuscript.

Place	Date	Hour	Summary of Events and Information	Remarks and references to Appendices
Contd	19/4/16	2.30 p.m	The march was 16 miles distance and the Men marched well. There were 12 cases of men who were unable to keep pace with the Battn and were consequently allowed to place their packs on the 1st line transport. These cases were investigated by the Medical Officer in charge and were found to be genuine. The rain was constant throughout the day.	
	20/4/16		Fine day. The Companies were placed at the disposal of Coy Commanders during the morning. In the afternoon the Battn was supervised by the Commanding Officer in Company & Battalion drill	
	21/4/16 to 25/4/16.		During this period the Battn has been employed in general training being taken for good route marches having	

T./134. Wt. W708—776. 500000. 4/15. Sir J. C. & S.

WAR DIARY
or
INTELLIGENCE SUMMARY.
(Erase heading not required.)

Army Form C. 2118.

Place	Date	Hour	Summary of Events and Information	Remarks and references to Appendices
			Physical exercises, Platoon, Company, & Battalion drill, also receiving instruction on the value of care of arms, handling of arms and general interior economy. The weather for the most part has been favourable and good results have been obtained. Received instructions above on the 28th that the Battn would proceed to HERSIN on the 26th inst. The order of the move being that the Transport should move by road the whole of the distance. The Battn to march to PERNES station entraining here and conveyed to BARLIN station, march from BARLIN to HERSIN. Copy marked "G" attached	
	26/4/16		The Battn formed up at 7 a.m. Head 2nd Coy leading and marched via LAIRES - SAINS. marqz the town of PERNES to the station arriving here about 11 am. The distance is 19 kilometres to PERNES station The day was very hot and consequently very trying. 4 N.C.Os	

WAR DIARY
or
INTELLIGENCE SUMMARY.
(Erase heading not required.)

Army Form C. 2118.

Place	Date	Hour	Summary of Events and Information	Remarks and references to Appendices
CALM	28/4/16		and men fell out before reaching PERNES. Those however picked up before the train started away at 11-50 pm. The Route taken by rail was somewhat roundabout we travelled via BOURS, BRYAS, HOUDAIN, HALLICOURT, RRUAY, arriving at BARLIN 1-55 pm. The train was very long and carried 2.5 Battns and the Brigade Headquarters. Formed up outside BARLIN station immediately on arrival and marched to HERSIN. Here we were met by the billeting parties and made comfortable.	
HERSIN	29/4/16		Fine day. We found strong working parties and Received orders about 7-30 pm that the Germans were using Gas at HULLOCH. The necessary precautions were at once observed. The enemy Artillery has been active they have sent a large number of heavy shells into the Mines in HERSIN. Between 9 pm & 10 pm there was a heavy Artillery	

WAR DIARY
or
INTELLIGENCE SUMMARY.

Army Form C. 2118.

Place	Date	Hour	Summary of Events and Information	Remarks and references to Appendices
	27/4/16		engagements. The night passed fairly quiet	
	28/4/16		Aeroplanes very active. Heavy shelling by both sides from about 8 p.m. to midnight.	
	29/4/16		As for preceding day except that reports to hand shew the enemy to be using gas. There is no information to hand that they have met with any success. night passed quietly.	
	30/4/16		Fine day. Morning quiet. Remainder of the day also passed quietly.	

E.P. Hargrett(?)
Comdg 1st N. North'n Rhy Regt

Operations Orders.

1. The Battⁿ will be relieved by 9 Yorks tonight and will proceed to same billets as they occupied on the previous occasion at FOSSE 10.

2. C.Q.M.S's will take over billets from their boys & the R.Q.M.S for Hd Qrs & Lewis Guns during the morning.

3. Guides will only be required from "C" & "A" Coys. These Coys will each send 4 guides to report at Battⁿ Hd Qrs by 7 pm.
Each guide will have a slip of paper on which will be written

"C" Coy No. 1 guide — Right front platoon
  " 2 " — Left front platoon
  " 3 " — Right Support platoon
  " 4 " — Left Support platoon

"A" Coy No. 5 guide — Boracco South Right platoon
  " 6 " —   "   "   Left   "
  " 7 " — Mackaine Right "
  " 8 " —   "   Left   "

4. All baggage will be in the Provost Sgt's house by 6-30pm. Sgt Cole will take charge of this baggage until it is removed

- 2 -

by the Transport Officer.
The latter will arrange to remove
the baggage after dark.

5. Extra bandoliers at present on the
men will be handed over to
relieving Unit.

6. Lewis Detachment will be relieved
during daylight

7. All gum boots will be carried out
round the man's neck & will be
handed in to the Brigade Gum Boot
Store on the way to billets. Receipts
are to be obtained for all boots
handed in & the total numbers
handed in will be notified to the
Orderly Room by 10 am tomorrow

8. List of Trench Stores to be handed
over are to reach Orderly Room
by 1 pm today

sd C Bathurst
Capt & Adjt.

4/11/16.

10TH (S) BATTN. DUKE OF WELLINGTON'S (WEST RIDING) REGIMENT.

OPERATION ORDERS. No. 34.

1.... The 10th Duke of Wellington's will relieve the 9th Yorks in the Centre Sector tomorrow, 10th Inst.

2... Dispositions :-   "C" Coy. on the Right.
                        "B" " in the Centre.
                        "A" " on the Left.
                        "D" " in Support.

3... One Officer and one N.C.O. per Company will proceed to the trenches on the morning of the 10th Inst. to take over trench stores.
The Sergt. Major and Pioneers will proceed to trenches at 4 p.m. and the former will take over all Hd.Qr. Stores and all water carrying vessels.

4... The Lewis Gun Officer will receive his orders separately.

5... Gum Boots will be picked up at the W. end of CORON D'AIX Communication Trench as follows :-
   Each Company in front line.... 90 pairs.
   Support Company .... 50 pairs.
   Lewis Gun Detachment .... 20 pairs.
   Hd.Qr. Party .... 10 pairs.

6... Guides will be met at Battn. Trench Hd.Qrs. xxxxxxxxx for the Left and Support Companies only.

7... Company Signallers will follow their own Companies. Hd.Qrs. Signallers will take over in trenches at 3 p.m.

8... All rations for the 11th Inst. will be carried on the man.

9... Companies will march off as follows :-
   "B" Coy. 6-45 p.m.
   "A" "   7-15 p.m.
   "C" "   7-45 p.m.
   "D" "   8-15 p.m.
Dress - Marching order, great coats will be worn.
Plattons will vacate their billets 1 hour before the hour of parade & the former will be thoroughly cleaned. Each platoon is to be inspected before moving off by an officer.

10.. WATER. Officers will ensure that all water bottles are full. No water will be available in the trenches till 6 a.m. on the morning of 11th.

11.. OFFICERS' KITS. 2 G.S. limbers will be at Qr.Mr's. Stroes at 7 p.m. to collect same.

9.4.16.   sd. C. Bathurst. Capt. & Adjt.

To. O.C. Coys. etc.

Reference Operation Order No. 34 issued yesterday, please note the following amendments :—

Para 5. Cancel. No gum boots will be taken to the trenches.

Para 6. Guides for all Coys. will be met at Battn. Trench Hd.Qrs.

Para 9. Should read :- Coys. will march off as follows :
          "C" Coy. 6-45 p.m.
          "B" " 7-5 p.m.
          "A" " 7-25 p.m.
          "D" " 7-45 p.m.

ADDITIONS.

12... 20 Bombers of "D" Coy. will be in FOREST ALLEY under the orders of Lt. Lavarack.
    They will have with them 20 boxes of bombs and 20 sandbags.

13... Immediately on arrival in trenches, all steel helmets are to have the outside dipped in mud, which will be allowed to dry on.
This will be repeated when necessary.

14... All vessels for drinking-water will be distributed evenly between Coys They will be marked will the letter of the Coy. & numbered consecutively.
No. Coy. will draw another Coys. vessel and no company will draw more full vessels than it has returned empty ones.

15... One cook per Company will be left behind to clean and paint the cookers.

                              sd. C. Bathurst. Capt. & Adjt.

10.4.16.

10TH (S) BATTN. DUKE OF WELLINGTON'S (WEST RIDING) REGIMENT.

OPERATION ORDER. NO. 35.

1... The 5th I.Bde. will take over the ANGRES Sector on Sunday next with two battalions holding the front line.
To enable this to be done easily, the front now held by the 69th I.B. will be redistributed on Saturday as follows :-
- (a). The Companies of the 11th West Yorks and 8th Yorks Regts. now at CORON D'AIX will relieve the 3 Companies of the 10th West Ridings now in the front line.
- (b). 8th Yorks will take over all "A" Coys trench, and "B" Coys. as far as VASSEAU TRENCH (M.25.d.8½.5½.) inclusive. 11th West Yorks will take over all "C" Coys. trench and "B" Coys. as far as VASSEAU TRENCH (exclusive).

2... Hd.Qrs. and "A","B","C" Coys. 10th West Ridings will move on relief to CORON D'AIX billets.
"D" Coy. will remain at MECHANICS.
Lt. Lavarack and the 20 bombers at present under his command will remain at MECHANICS.
The use of MOROCCO SOUTH will be lent by O.C. 8th Yorks for accommodating portion of "D" Coy.

3... "D" Coy. and the bombers under Lt. Lavarack and the Reserve Lewis Gun at MECHANICS will be in immediate support at the call of O.C. "A" Unit. The remainder of the battalion will form Brigade reserve, except as mentioned in para 4.

4... Two Lewis Guns, 10th West Ridings, in front line will exchange places with 2 Lewis Guns 8th Yorks now between BULLEY ALLEY and ALGIERS Trench They will be under the orders of O.C. 8th Yorks Regt. (O.C."B" Unit).
Two Lewis Guns, 10th West Ridings, will remain in position in front line and be under the orders of O.C. Unit in whose front they are.
One Lewis Gun, 10th West Ridings, will be held in reserve in MECHANICS (see para 3) at the call of O.C. "A" Unit (11th West Yorks.)

5... Companies when relieved will report to Battalion Hd.Qrs. by wire, and will then proceed to billets in CORON D'AIX by small parties of not more than half platoons with 10 minutes intervals.

6... O.C. "A" Coy. will hand over trench stores from Sap 11 (exclusive) to VASSEAU Trench (inclusive) to 8th Yorks.
O.C. "C" Coy. will hand over trench stores thence to the right of his company to 11th West Yorks.
Lists of stores handed over to reach Battn. Hd. Qrs. by 12 noon tomorrow.

7... The Quartermaster will make arrangements to deliver rations on Saturday for "D" Coy., Lt. Lavarack, & 3 Lewis Gun Teams, on the present battalion dump.
He will arrange to dump rations for 2 Lewis Guns Teams on the dump at present used by 8th Yorks Regt.
The time at which the rations will be dumped will be notified to all concerned by wire.

8... O.C. "B" Coy. and O.C. "C" Coy. will send respectively 8 and 2 guides to be at Battn.Hd.Qrs. at 9-30 a.m. tomorrow to guide in the 11th West Yorks.

14.4.16.   sd.   C. Bathurst. Capt. & Adjt.

1/6TH (S) BATTN. DUKE OF WELLINGTON'S (WEST RIDING) REGIMENT.

OPERATION ORDER. NO. 36.

1... The battalion will be relieved by the 2nd Oxford & Bucks L.I. tomorrow, 16th Inst.

2... The battalion will proceed to HERSIN where they will take over billets from the 17th Royal Fusiliers.

3... The battalion will spend the night at HERSIN.

4... A billeting party consisting of :-
    Lieut. A.K. Haversack.
    1 representative per platoon.
    1   "   for Hi.Qrs.
    1   "   for Lewis Gun.
will parade at Battn. Hi.Qrs. at 7-30 a.m. tomorrow. They will proceed to FOSSE 10 where they will pick up at Gr.Mr. Stores:-
    C.Q.M. Sgts.
    1 representative for transport.
The party will then march to HERSIN where they will take over the billets from 17th ROYAL FUSILIERS.

6... Coys. will move by sections at intervals of 200 yards as far as FOSSE 10 by a route to be notified later. Here they will form up outside the Gr.Mr. Stores into half companies. As each half-Coy. is formed, it will march off to HERSIN.
Lt. Haversack will ensure that platoon guides are well this side of HERSIN to meet each party.
When sections are waiting at FOSSE 10 to form up, men are on no account to be allowed to wander about the road, but must be kept well to the side under the FOSSE 10 walls. All ranks will be informed that the whole Brigade is carrying out a daylight relief and as little movement as possible is to be shown.

7... O.C. "D" Coy. will receive special instructions.

8... The Lewis Gun Officer has received special instructions.

9... The Transport Officer will send (with MALINGA'SE and LES BREBIS) the Officers' Kit S.A. wagon to be at COHON D'AIX by 10 a.m. to collect Officers' trench kits and messes.

10.. All rations for the day will be carried on the man.

11.. All men must be shaved, and as clean as possible, before marching off from COHON D'AIX.

12.. The battalion moves about 12 noon on the 17th, by which time all ranks must be clean.

13.. All this afternoon and tomorrow will, subject to marching out parade, be devoted to cleaning. All dry mud to be rubbed off and all boots well dubbed.
All mud will be washed from actual billets.

15.4.16.   sd. C. Bathurst. Capt. a/Adjt.

(Omission from above.)

5... Coys. will march out from COHON D'AIX as follows :-
        "C" Coy, "B" Coy., "A" Coy.
    commencing at 10-30 a.m.

ORDERS BY LIEUT. COLONEL S.S. HAYNES, COMMDG.
10TH (S) BATTN. DUKE OF WELLINGTON'S (WEST RIDING) REGIMENT.

Reference 1/40,000 Sheet B.

1. The battalion will march to OURTON Area on Monday, 17th Inst. The Order of march will be -
    Signallers,
    Headquarters,
    "A" Coy.
    "B" "
    "C" "
    "D" "
    Lewis Gun Detachment.
    1st Line Transport.
Starting point - Road junction K.34.d.7.1.
The battalion will be formed up ready to march off at 12 noon in above order.
ROUTE — BARLIN — MAISNIL — HOUDAIN — DIVION — OURTON

2. Billeting parties - strength (Lieut. Lavarack, C.Q.M.S.) and 82 men per Company and Headquarters will leave HERSIN for OURTON at 8-45 a.m. tomorrow. Party to parade outside Battalion Orderly Room. Cyclists will leave for OURTON at 10 a.m. and will report to R.Q.M.S. on arrival. They will meet the battalion on road near Fme. D'ESTRAYETT I.29.c.2.8. and act as guides.

3. O.C. Coys. will satisfy themselves that their respective billets are thoroughly clean before marching off.

4. TRANSPORT. Lorries will leave for OURTON at 8 a.m.
    3 men per Coy. to accompany lorries. These men will report to R.Q.M.S. at 7-45 a.m.
    Blankets to be immediately unloaded on arrival at OURTON and lorries sent back for Quartermaster's Stores.
    O.C. "B" Coy. will detail 1 N.C.O. & 6 men to remain at Quartermaster's Stores and on the return of the lorries, to load same with Qr.Mr's. Stores and accompany them to OURTON.
    Headquarters, all Officers and Company Kits to be ready for loading by 10-30 a.m.
    No. 1 baggage wagon :— "A" & "B" Coys and Officers
    C.O. & Adjutant.

    No. 2 baggage wagon :— "C" & "D" Coys and Officers.
    Senior Major and M.O.

    No. 1 limber :— C.O. & Adjutant.
    Horse blankets.

    No. 2 limbers :— Senior Major & M.O.
    Horse blankets.

Cookers will start under Sgt. Smithers at 10 a.m. and dinners will be on the arrival.

sd. C. Bathurst.
Capt. & Adjt.

16.4.16.

OPERATIONS ORDERS NO. 2 BY LIEUT. COLONEL S.S. HAYNES, COMMDG.
10TH (S) BATTN. DUKE OF WELLINGTON'S (WEST RIDING) REGIMENT.

Reference 1/40,000 Sheet 36B.   OURTON. 18.4.16.

1. The battalion will march to BEAVMETZ les-AIRE tomorrow morning.
Order of march :-
          Headquarters & Snipers.
          "C" Coy.
          "A" "
          "B" "
          "D" "
          Lewis Gun Detachment.
          1st Line Transport, Cookers in front.

Coys. will be formed up, Headquarters and Coys. in above order at Cross Roads xxxxxxxxxx I.34.a.6.3. ready to march off at 7-35 a.m.
ROUTE - : PERNES - SAINS - FIEFS - BEAVMETZ.

2. Breakfast will be at 6 a.m. O.C. Coys. will see men carry bread and bully beef rations in havarsacks.
Dinners will be on the march about 12 noon.

3. TRANSPORT.
1 Sergeant & 5 men per Company will be at Qr.Mr's. Stores to load up Company blankets at 6-45 a.m.
     No. 1 Lorry.   "A" & "B" Coys. blankets & waterproof sheets.

     No. 2 Lorry.   "C" & "D" Coys. blankets & waterproof sheets.

1 Sergeant "A" Coy. & 3 men to proceed with No. 1 Lorry.
1 Sergeant "C" Coy. & 3 men to proceed with No. 2 lorry.

Lorries will be despatched as soon as loaded.

2/Lieut. W.D. Taylor will proceed with lorries and see that kit is unloaded without delay.

No. 1 lorry on being unloaded will immediately return for Quarter Master's Stores.

     No. 1 G.S. wagon will call for Officers' Mess Kit and valises "A" and "C" Coys. at 7 a.m.

     No. 2 G.S. wagon Valises Headquarters & Officers "B" & "D" Coys. and Mess Kit "B" & "D" Coys. at 7 a.m.

Headquarters Mess Kit will be loaded on Mess Cart and ready to march off by 7-30 a.m.

18.4.16.   sd. C. Bathurst. Capt. & Adjt.

OPERATION ORDERS. NO. 3, BY LIEUT.COLONEL S.S. HAYNE,
COMMANDING,
10TH (S) BATTN. DUKE OF WELLINGTON'S (WEST RIDING) REGIMENT.

Reference 1/40,000 Sheet 36 B.   BEAUMETZ LES AIRES.
                                   25.4.16.

1. The battalion will march to PERNES Station tomorrow and will entrain from there to HERSIN Area.
    Route : LAIRES - SAINS - PERNES.
    Order of march : Headquarters, Signallers & Snipers, made up to 2 parties of 40 under Lieut. Heale.
                    "B" Coy.
                    "C" "
                    "D" "
                    "A" "
                    Lewis Gun Detachment, to parade 40 strong.
    6 bombers per Coy. and Signallers (less H.Q. Signallers) to parade with their Companies.
    O.C. Coys. will "tell off" their companies into parties of 40 ready to entrain.
    Coy. Commdrs. in succession from the leading company are to inform the O.C. Coys marching in their immediate rear, of the number of surplus men of their Companies. These will be made up to 40 from the Company marching in their immediate rear. This must be done before leaving BEAUMETZ.

    Companies will be formed up <u>ready</u> to march off at 7 a.m.

    Starting point : LAIRES-RECLINGHEM and BOMY-LUGY Cross Roads.

2. Breakfast 5-15 a.m. The unconsumed portion of the day's ration to be carried in haversack.

3. <u>TRANSPORT</u>. "A" & "D" Coys. 1 lorry. (No. 1).
                     "B" & "C"   "   1 lorry. (No. 2).
    Lorries to be loaded up and despatched at 6-30 a.m., returning as soon as possible for surplus baggage.
    Officer in charge of lorries : Capt. J. Atkinson, who will see lorries unloaded without delay.
        1 Sergt. & 3 men "D" Coy. to proceed with No. 1 lorry.
        1 Sergt & 3 men "B" Coy. to proceed with No. 2 lorry.
    Officers' Mess Kit and valises to be stacked at Quartermaster's Stores ready for loading by 5-45 a.m.
    1st Line Transport to move off at 6 a.m. Lieut. Hammond will report to O.C. 192nd Coy. A.S.C. at Road Junction G.6.c.1.4. at 8-18 a.m.
    Transport of the Brigade will march under orders of O.C. 192 Coy. A.S.C. in the following order :
                    192nd Coy. A.S.C.
                    Brigade Headquarters.
                    11th West Yorkshire Regt.
                    Machine Gun Company.
                    9th Yorkshire Regt.
                    8th Yorkshire Regt.
                    10th West Riding Regt.
    Officers' Chargers will proceed by road from PERNES to HERSIN with their respective grooms in one party under L/Cpl. Thornton.

4. O.C. Coys. will see their respective billets are thoroughly clean before marching off.

5. ENTRAINING & DETRAINING ORDERS.
O.C. Coys. will halt their respective Coys. by whistle opposite the trucks alloted to their Companies.

On 1st Whistle sounding : Coys. will turn facing the train in fours.

2nd Whistle : Sections of fours to enter the train commencing from the left section.

Each party of 40 will be kept closed up towards their respective trucks as much as possible.

There is to be no talking or noise of any description during entrainment. Arms to be slung.
No man is to leave his truck once he has entrained.

On arrival at HERSIN. On whistle sounding Coys. will fall in outside their carriages and await orders.

25.4.16. sd. C. Bathurst. Capt. & Adjt.

10 West Riding
Vol 16

Army Form C. 2118.

WAR DIARY or INTELLIGENCE SUMMARY.

(Erase heading not required.)

10th (Svc) Battn Duke of Wellington's Regt

Place	Date	Hour	Summary of Events and Information	Remarks and references to Appendices
HERSIN	1/5/16		During the period the weather has been very fine, hot during the day, pleasant during the evening. Artillery on both sides active each evening & lasting from 2 to 3 hours. The Battn has been kept well employed having found large working parties, and all available spare time has been utilised in training. Received orders on the evening of the 4th inst that the Battn would proceed to PERNES on the 5th inst. This information was duly passed on to all concerned. Copy marked "A" attached.	
PERNES	5/5/16		Battn formed up as shown on copy "A" and marched to HERSIN station, there entrained & travelled via BRUAY-BRYAS and arrived PERNES at 7pm were marched to billets which were not in a good condition. A Confland has been lodged at Bde HQrs	C.S.D
	6/5/16		Battn was inspected by G.O.C. 23rd Division. Found working parties for the IV Corps school that not so employed have been employed in training.	
	7/5/16		Nothing to report weather good	
	8/5/16		Weather broke, much rain	
	9/5/16		Weather improved, continued to find working parties for the IV Corps school nothing of importance transpired	9.4. 17 sheets
	11/5/16		On the evening of 10th inst received orders to proceed to HERSIN. The Battn was formed up at 10.45 Am moved off to PERNES station there we entrained. The train	

WAR DIARY or INTELLIGENCE SUMMARY

Army Form C. 2118.

Place	Date	Hour	Summary of Events and Information	Remarks and references to Appendices
			left PERNES at 11-37 and arrived at HERSIN about 2-30pm. Just before the arrival of the train it was noticed that the enemy was shelling the station. In spite of this however the train was stopped at the usual detraining place and all units were instructed to retrain their units. The train was standing in the shelled area 10 minutes during which time about 70 shells were discharged. It was decided to run the train back towards BARLIN, & the troops detrained in an obscure place just before entering at the stop named station. Some of the shells were very near to doing damage members of his of shells penetrating portion of the carriages. Casualties nil. He marched from BARLIN and arrived at HERSIN 5-30pm. Operation order number "B"+"C" attached	
	12/5/16		The Batt'n relieved the 17th Royal Fusiliers in Trench Dumpshift, leaving HERSIN at 7-30pm. marching small parties via FOSSE.10 and BULLY GRENAY. The relief was extrapolation accomplished, we had no casualties. Companies reported relay complete at 8 p.m. all quiet along our front.	
TREN CH F5	13/4/16		Rain fell during the morning near much extent. The enemy put a number of	

Army Form C. 2118.

WAR DIARY
or
INTELLIGENCE SUMMARY.
(Erase heading not required.)

Instructions regarding War Diaries and Intelligence Summaries are contained in F.S. Regs., Part II. and the Staff Manual respectively. Title pages will be prepared in manuscript.

Place	Date	Hour	Summary of Events and Information	Remarks and references to Appendices
	14/5/16		"C" Shells into the SET OF 5 behind the BULLY CRATERS. No aeroplanes are to be seen still quiet along our Battn. front day and night.	
	15/5/16		Cold dull day. The enemy have fired a number of rifle grenades into our night tray and occasioned in slightly wounding one man. There is still an absence of artillery activity, a number of our aeroplanes made their appearance during the late evening, nothing further to report. Weather continues cold and dull, very little activity with hostile or airplanes ibut a considerable amount in the use of Rifle Grenades is noticed to be used by the enemy. # No hostile aircraft to be seen.	
	16/5/16		Weather improved. Observation good. The enemys artillery very active at long range. Our aeroplanes active during the afternoon. The night passed quietly.	
	17/5/16		Beautiful day. All quiet during the morning. Issued orders re. relief copies marked attached. The 11th West Yorks Regt. marching from FOSSE 10 to relieve us at 4.30 p.m. relief completed at 9 p.m. A battery of our heavy guns has sent a few shells over to the enemy, no retaliation. Our aeroplanes active.	

WAR DIARY or INTELLIGENCE SUMMARY

Army Form C. 2118.

Place	Date	Hour	Summary of Events and Information	Remarks and references to Appendices
Rouen Billets	18/5/16		There was nothing of importance transpired on our front, though both to our right and left there have been heavy artillery duels. Weather good. Things generally quiet, aircraft also a reduced kind of bombardment the night passed quietly.	
	19/5/16		Weather fine, visibility good. The enemy sent a number of shells which resulted in killing a Frenchman and a boy & wounding a young woman. The rest of the day passed quietly until 9 pm when our artillery commenced a bombardment upon the enemy lines. It commenced just to the left of the ARRAS road and was confined to a small portion of the front and continued for 1/2 hour the portion bombarded was ablaze with very lights. The bombardment was then extended to the left considerably and became most intense, the enemy replied with some violence. About 10pm it decreased in violence and developed into a big gun duel. Our machine gun casting a forward, probably with the intention of harassing work the smaller guns sending salvoes at irregular intervals as far as can be judged	

T/134. Wt. W708-776. 500000. 4/15. Sir J.C. & S.

WAR DIARY or INTELLIGENCE SUMMARY

Army Form C. 2118.

Place	Date	Hour	Summary of Events and Information	Remarks and references to Appendices
	25/5/16		the duel to over a 2½ to 3 mile front, the operation continued until midnight though occasional shots were exchanged throughout the night.	
			The enemy Artillery is shewing a marked activity and is ranging upon various places with a high velocity gun of small calibre. This gun can easily be distinguished from others. During the morning the enemy fired a very heavy shell into a trench of 4/ he pit railway (FOSSE 10) which resulted in wounding one of our men severely and killing a French Civilian. He was belonging to an aide he following day. They also succeeded in demolishing the house he was also continued to send shells within the vicinity of our billets, he had no casualties.	
	27/5/16		Beautiful day. about 11 am the enemy commenced a heavy bombardment on our front line trenches which extended to the whole of the front visible to the eye. This continued until the early afternoon after which he lengthened his range and rained shells of heavy calibre on the supports, and roads leading to the trenches, and	

WAR DIARY
or
INTELLIGENCE SUMMARY.
(Erase heading not required.)

Army Form C. 2118.

Place	Date	Hour	Summary of Events and Information	Remarks and references to Appendices
			also within the rang of our batteries. At 4.50pm we received advice from the 68th Brigade that the enemy was sending gas over to our lines, this was accompanied by a torrent of shells from the enemy which were principally composed of what is known as tear shells. The enemy got very near to a number of our batteries but the damage done generally is not obtainable. A battery of R.G.A. which was in action played a very important part in the days proceedings. This battery was supposed to work a hail of shells for 5 or 6 hours what can only be explained by the word tempo, needless to say the men of this battery stuck to their guns in the good old fashioned way, and when the enemy thought he had succeeded in silencing them they roared forth again and again. This battery continued the fight throughout the night and the enemy gave it up as a hopeless case about 11pm.	
27/5/16			At 12.15 am we received the following message from the 69th Trench Mortar Office	

WAR DIARY
or
INTELLIGENCE SUMMARY.
(Erase heading not required.)

Army Form C. 2118.

Place	Date	Hour	Summary of Events and Information	Remarks and references to Appendices
Cont⁴	25/5/16		Situation an Enemy attacked VIMY RIDGE today, British Counter attacked situation still undecided and Heavy shelling but no attack CALONNE and SOUCHEZ sectors. All ranks in trenches to be warned to keep good lookout ends. Found orders in the morning regarding relief we are to relieve the 11⁵ West Yorks Regt commencing at 5.30 p.m. from Battn H.Q⁵ at FOSSE 10. This relief was completed at 8 p.m. The enemy shelled Brigade Headquarters and roads in rear. We had no Casualties, he being slightly wounded by shrapnel. Our aeroplanes were very active during the relief period & being warned was a short front. Our artillery fired at irregular intervals during the most of the night.	
	26/5/16		Beautiful weather. The enemy's artillery opened fire very early and kept it up until late in the afternoon. At times a fusilade of shells passed over us which at it is thought were intended for batteries. Our artillery was also heavily engaged in the enemy works. About 7 p.m. our Artillery opened a very heavy bombardment on the enemys	

WAR DIARY
or
INTELLIGENCE SUMMARY.
(Erase heading not required.)

Army Form C. 2118.

Instructions regarding War Diaries and Intelligence Summaries are contained in F.S. Regs., Part II. and the Staff Manual respectively. Title pages will be prepared in manuscript.

Place	Date	Hour	Summary of Events and Information	Remarks and references to Appendices
	24/5/16		fairies, some very heavy shells being amongst them. The enemy released smoke on our front line. The bombardment was also carried on to the right and left of us. The enemy was very liberal in the use of colored lights. We had 4 casualties (wounded) This morning but during during the rest of the day. A good deal of rifle grenade trench mortars were exchanged by both sides. At 1.30pm the enemy shelled our communication trenches, he also sent a large number of shells in rear. We had one man (killed) one man wounded	
	25/5/16		All morning everything very quiet. About 4pm the enemy started firing shells over us in rapid succession. Night proved quietly.	
	26/5/16		This morning. All quiet. Issued orders regarding relief Capt. Mar(?)J.E. attacked Relief commenced about 2.30pm. Completed about 11pm. (No casualties) weather continued fine. Much Artillery activity on both sides, this	
	27/5/16		continued throughout the day. About 11pm we received S.O.S from the right Batt. 1st Brigade 1st Division. It appears that a number of the enemy were caught in an attempt to reach our trenches. There were	

WAR DIARY
or
INTELLIGENCE SUMMARY.

(Erase heading not required.)

Army Form C. 2118.

Place	Date	Hour	Summary of Events and Information	Remarks and references to Appendices
			smartly dealt with. The number of casualties inflicted upon the enemy is not known. Our artillery kept up a well regulated bombardment. S.O.S. was withdrawn at 1 AM 28th inst.	
	28/8/16		Good weather. Artillery and Aeroplanes active. The enemy was not doing very heavy shells into the rest area. We received orders to move the transport lines. Mine had been nearly completed when the enemy started to put a shell into the old standings. The enemy had fresh howitzers in the vicinity of FOSSE 10 and SAINS en GOHELLE.	
	29/8/16		The guns were firing at it from morning. Aided by aircraft the enemy began to reply at 8 am and kept up a constant bombardment of positions on the rest, which we were not able to see from here. We had two men wounded at the transport lines this morning. This bombardment continued until late evening. Received and issued orders relieving the 9th Inf. Bde relieving the 69th Inf. Bde. Copies marked F attached. At 4 PM we received orders to be on the alert for gas. All the necessary precautions were taken.	

Army Form C. 2118.

WAR DIARY
or
INTELLIGENCE SUMMARY.
(Erase heading not required.)

Place	Date	Hour	Summary of Events and Information	Remarks and references to Appendices
BOUVIGNY Huts	20/5/16		Our Artillery commenced a desultory kind of bombardment on the enemy lines at 7 a.m. The enemy replied to portions in rear of their lines. The enemy replied in a similar fashion. The Battn. marched to BOUVIGNY HUTS arriving here at 8:30 pm	
	21/5/16		Nothing further to report. The day was utilized for a general cleaning up. Nothing further to report.	

21/5/16.

OBathurst Capt
for Major
Comdg 10th (Ser) Batt. Duke of Wellington's Regt

OPERATION ORDERS, NO. 4, BY LIEUT.COLONEL S.S. HAYNE, COMMANDING,
10TH (S) BATTALION, DUKE OF WELLINGTON'S (WEST RIDING) REGIMENT.

Reference 1/40,000. Sheets B. & C.   HERSIN. 4.5.16.

1. The battalion will proceed by train to ~~XXXXX~~ PRESSY-LES-PERNES tomorrow afternoon, marching for entrainment to HERSIN or BARLIN Station according to whether the former is being shelled or otherwise. The battalion will be formed up ready to march to HERSIN Station on the road outside billets in the following order :-

    Hd.Qrs., Sigs., Bombers, & Snipers, under Lt. Heale.
    "A" Coy.
    "B" "
    "C" "
    "D" "
    Lewis Gun Det.
  Time ~~3-15~~ 3·50 p.m.
  Starting Point :- *Gate of boy Billets*

2. O.C. Coys. will satisfy themselves their respective billets are thoroughly clean before 2-15 p.m. All billets to be evacuated ready for relieving Unit by 2-15 p.m. Coys., Parties, etc. will pile arms outside their respective billets.

3. Blankets to be rolled in bundles of 10, labelled and securely tied under the supervision of an Officer per Company and to be ready for loading by 6-15 a.m. outside billets.

4. ~~Blankets to be rolled in~~ Officers' valises and mess kit and Coys. spare kits to be ready for loading by 10-30 a.m.

5. TRANSPORT. No. 1 lorry.   "A" & "B" Coys. blankets and small portion of Hd.Qrs. Kits.
   No. 2 lorry.   "C" & "D" Coys. blankets.
   No. 1 G.S. wagon.   Allotted to Hd.Qrs. "A" & "B" Coys.
   No. 2 G.S. wagon.   Allotted to Qr.Mr., Transport Officer, "C" & "D" Coys.

6. Guides will be sent to meet lorries at Brigade Hd.Qrs. at 6 a.m. tomorrow.

   All transport under Lt. Hammond to proceed via BARLIN-HOUDAIN-DIVION to PRESSY-LES-PERNES to pass Cross Roads Q.5.a.7.3. at 12-30 p.m. Lt. Hammond will meet the G.S. wagons at Battalion Hd.Qrs. at 10 a.m. and despatch same for their respective loads.

7. *Lt. R Bolton* will be in charge of lorries, see them loaded and despatched as soon as possible. They will be unloaded at PRESSY-LES-PERNES as soon as possible and return to pick up spare kit at HERSIN without delay.

   Officers' Chargers under Corpl. Thornton will leave for PRESSY-LES-PERNES at 10 a.m.

   Coys. to have a party of 1 N.C.O. & 5 men to assist in loading up lorries at 6-15 a.m.
   1 Sergt & 3 men "A" Coy. to proceed with haversack rations with No. 1 lorry.
   1 Sergt & 3 men "C" Coy. to proceed with haversack rations with No. 2 lorry.

8. 2/Lt. Lester will be at HERSIN Station to take over train at 3-30 p.m. on the 5th Inst.

   4.5.16.   sd. C. Bathurst. Capt. & Adjt.

OPERATION ORDERS NO. 5, BY LIEUT.COLONEL S.S. HAYNE, COMMDG.,
10TH (S) BATTALION, DUKE OF WELLINGTON'S (WEST RIDING) REGIMENT.

Reference 1/40,000.   Sheets B. & C.   PERNES.   10.5.16.

1. The battalion will march to PERNES Station and entrain from there to HERSIN tomorrow.
   The battalion will be formed up ready to march off at 10-45 a.m.
   Starting Point : H.11.c.6.7. (PERNES Square).
   Order of march :- Hd.Qrs, Sigs., Bombers, Snipers, under R.S.M.
               "A" Coy.
               "B" "
               "C" "
               "D" "
               Lewis Gun Det.
   Train leaves PERNES at 11-37 a.m.

2. Blankets to be rolled in bundles of ten, labelled & securely tied, and stacked ready for loading outside Coy. Billets. by 7-15 a.m.
   1 Officer per Coy. to supervise.

3. Officers' valises and spare kit to be ready for loading by 8 a.m.

4. Coy. and other Commdrs. will satisfy themselves their respective billets are thoroughly clean before marching off.

5. TRANSPORT. Lorries are allotted as under :-

        No. 1 lorry "A" & "B" Coys.)
) Blankets.
        No. 2   "   "C" & "D" Coys.)

   O.C. Coys. will detail an officer to supervise loading. They will be loaded without delay and will report to Quartermaster who will see them despatched as soon as possible. They will return for second load without delay.
   O.C. "C" Coy. will detail a full Sergeant to meet lorry at PERNES Market Square (H.11.b.7.8.) at 7 a.m.
   O.C. "A" Coy. to comply with above for the lorry of "A" & "B" Coys.
        1 Sergt. & 3 men "B" Coy. to proceed with haversack rations with No. 1 lorry.
        1 Sergt. & 3 men "D" Coy. to proceed with haversack rations with No. 2 lorry.

        No. 1 G.S. wagon. allotted to "A" & "B" Coys., Quartermaster, and Transport Officer.

        No. 2 G.S. wagon. allotted to "C" & "D" Coys., and Headquarters.

   Lieut. Wolfe will assemble transport at Market Square (H.11.b.7.8.) at 9 a.m. and march to HERSIN.
   Route :- CAMBLAIN-CHATELAIN-DIVION-BRUAY-BARLIN-HERSIN.
   Officers' Chargers to follow in rear of transport.

   10.5.16.   sd.   C. Bathurst. Capt. & Adjt.

OPERATION ORDERS, NO. 7, BY LIEUT.COLONEL S.S. HAYNE, COMMDG.
10TH (S) BATTALION, DUKE OF WELLINGTON'S (WEST RIDING) REGIMENT.

Reference: 1/40,000 Sheets B & "C". No 36   HERSIN. 11.5.16.

1. The situation on our front is reported normal.

2. The battalion will relieve the 13th Royal Fusiliers on the evening of the 12th Inst. and will hold the ANGRES right sub sections as under :-
   "D" - "B" - "A"
   "C" Support.
   The battalion will march to the trenches in the following order :-
   Headquarters.
   "A" Coy.
   "C" "
   "B" "
   "D" "

   Starting point : Q.6.c.2.8½.
   Headquarters will pass the starting point at 2-45 p.m.
   Route: HERSIN-FOSSE 10-BULLY GRENAY-CORONS D'AIX.
   Companies will march to FOSSE 10 at 100 yards distance, after which they will proceed by sections at 100 yards distance. Leading sections of each platoon to halt when 250 yards up CORONS D'AIX COMMUNICATION TRENCH until the whole platoon has closed up on leading section.
   O.C. platoons will then march their platoons to MECHANICS where guides will be met

GUIDE NO:	TO GUIDE.
H.Q.	H.Q.Party.
"A" Coy.	
No. 1.	Right front platoon.
No. 2.	Centre "
No. 3.	Left "
No. 4.	Support.
"C" Coy.	
No. 5.	
No. 6.	MOREAU Trench.
No. 7.	
No. 8.	F.C. 4.
"B" Coy.	
No. 9.	Right centre platoon.
No. 10.	Centre "
No. 11.	Left "
No. 12.	Support.
"D" Coy.	
No. 13.	Right platoon.
No. 14.	Centre "
No. 15.	Left "
No. 16.	Support.

3. O.C. Platoons must ensure their platoons being kept closed up proceeding up Communication Trench.

4. O.C. Coys. to report to Hd.Qrs. by telephone when their relief is completed.

5. O.C. Lewis Guns will leave for the trenches at 12-30 p.m. proceeding in small parties, at 100 yards distance from FOSSE 10.
   Guides Nos. 17, 18, 19, 20, & (21 Support Guns, 2) will meet parties at MECHANIC TRENCH at 2-30 p.m.

6. O.C. Coys. with a N.C.O. from each platoon will leave HERSIN so as to arrive at MECHANIC TRENCH by 12-30 p.m. where guides will meet them. Parties will be at 100 yards distance after leaving FOSSE 10.

- 2 -

7. R.S.M., Signallers, & Snipers, under Lt. Lavarack will leave for the trenches at 1-45 p.m.

8. One Officer per Company will see blankets rolled in bundles of ten, labelled and securely tied.

9. One officer per Company to inspect billets and see they are thoroughly clean before marching off.

10. Transport arrangements will be notified later.

11.5.16.   sd. C. Bathurst. Capt. & Adjt

OPERATION ORDERS, NO. 8,
BY
MAJOR C. G. BUCKLE, COMMANDING,
10TH (S) BATTALION, DUKE OF WELLINGTON'S (WEST RIDING) REGIMENT.

1. The battalion will relieve the 11th West Yorkshire Regt. in ANGRES (1) tomorrow.

2. "D", "C", & "A" Coys. will be in the firing line and "B" Company in Support.

3. All Companies will go up by CORON'S D'AIX Trench in the following order :-
   Headquarters. & "D" Coy.
   1 platoon "B" Coy.
   "C" Coy.
   2 platoons "B" Coy.
   "A" Coy.
   1 platoon "B" Coy.
   Leading platoon to pass Battn. H.Q. at 3-30 p.m.
   Platoons at 150 yards distance.

4. Guides will meet "B" & "C" Coys. at MECHANICS TRENCH.

5. All stores and kits to be taken up to trenches will be stacked outside Coy.H.Q. by 2 p.m.
   Blankets will be rolled and stacked outside Coy.H.Q. at 10 a.m.
   Offices valises to be ready with blankets.

6. Orders for Lewis Gunners and snipers will be issued later.

7. All billets and their vicinity will be inspected by an Officer before the battalion marches out and a report on their condition sent in to H.Q.

8. Coys. will send the following message when relief is complete:-("A") Coy correct."

              sd. C. Bathurst. Capt. & Adjt.

21.5.16.

       Issued to :- "A" Coy.
                     "B" Coy.
                     "C" Coy.
                     "D" Coy.
                     L. Gun Officer.
                     Bombing Officer.
                     Quartermaster.
                     Transport Officer.
                     R.S.M.
                     Sigs. Sergt.
                     War Diary.

Operation orders by Major C.S. Buckle

1. The battalion will be moved this afternoon by M.T. West Lancs. Rgt.

2. Companies will move with reserve line as follows:-
   A Coy - CAP a POMT.   Nos. 1, 2 & 3 platoons
          CERONS D'AIX   No 4
   B -   MOROCCO SOUTH   Nos 5, 6, 7
          R.E. 4   No 8
   C -   MECHANICS   Whole Company
   D -   CERONS D'AIX   Nos 13 & 14 platoons
          BULLY GRENAY   15 & 16

   Lewis Gunners, Bombers & Snipers & H.Q. at BULLY GRENAY

3. Rations for A Coy & 13 & 14 platoons will be dumped at CERON D'AIX
   B & C Coys at MECHANICS.
   Remainder at BULLY GRENAY
   Companies will arrange to draw their own rations from these dumps.

4. The following reports will be rendered daily as listed on above positions
   (1) Casualty Report to mide Batt'n W.O. by 9 pm.
   (2) A.A.A. Report   4 pm

5. A.C. & D Coys will each send one officer to take over their respective lines & billets.
   2/Lt. Foster will proceed to BULLY GRENAY to take over all billets.

6. H.Q under R.S.M. will march off across no-mans-land Coys. Lewis Gunners, Bombers & Snipers will form H.Q. across as advanced & will await orders to move off.
   Coys will move out by platoons at 150 yards distance. Platoon Commanders will inspect the dug-outs in their lines & report to their Coy Commdrs that the dug-outs are thoroughly clean & all loose ammunition has been collected.

26/5/th.   Col C. Bathurst
                                    Capt. & adjt.

OPERATION
ORDERS NO. 9 BY MAJOR C.G. BUCKLE,
COMMANDING,
10TH (S) BATTALION, DUKE OF WELLINGTON'S (WEST RIDING) REGIMENT.

1. The battalion will be relieved by the 2nd East Lancs Regt. tomorrow, and will move into Divisional Reserve at BOUVIGNY HUTS (R.25.d.) on completion of relief, where billets will be taken over from 1st Worcestershire Regt.

2. No trench or billet will be vacated until occupied by troops of relieving unit.

3. On relief, Companies will report to Battn. H.Q. by wire, and will march to new billets on receipt of orders from H.Q.

4. Route to be followed by Companies :—
The track from Road Junction R.10.b.6.1. to junction with main road at R.9.d.3.4. - FOSSE 10 - Road Junction at R.13.b.2½.6½. - Cross Roads at R.14.a.1.1½. - BOUVIGNY BOYEFFLES - Road Junction at Q.30.b.3½.6.

5. East of FOSSE 10, all Companies will move by sections at 100 yards intervals, thence by platoons.

6. Companies will report to Battalion H.Q. on arrival at BOUVIGNY HUTS.

7. Lt. Lavarack, C.Q.M.Sgts., 1 O.R. per Coy., 1 N.C.O. for H.Q., 1 for Transport, will proceed as billeting party.
Lieut. Lavarack will arrive at BOUVIGNY HUTS by 8 a.m. The remainder of the party will leave FOSSE 10 (Qr.Mr's. Stores) at 6-30 a.m. and will march to BOUVIGNY HUTS under the Senior C.Q.M.S. They will follow the route as laid down in para 4 of these orders. The H.Q. N.C.O. will take over billets for Lewis Gunners, Bombers, & Snipers, as well as for H.Q.

8. All billets, trenches, & dugouts, are to be carefully inspected and left clean. A report that this has been done will be rendered to Orderly Room before marching out.

9. Lewis Guns in trenches will, as soon as relieved, march down CORON D'AIX and join the other guns at that place.

10. Each Company will send one guide and the Lewis Gun Officer will send 3 guides to be at Battn. H.Q. at 10 a.m. tomorrow to guide relieving Companies to their positions.

11. Dinners will be eaten before the companies march off.

12. All kits, messes, and baggage, must be stacked as follows by 1-30 p.m. tomorrow :-
"A", "B", "C" Coys. at bottom of CORON'S D'AIX Trench.
"D" Coy. & Lewis Gun at CORON D'AIX Billets, "D" Coys. mess.
H.Q., Snipers, & Bombers, at Battalion H.Q.
Coys. will have parties held in readiness to load wagons as they arrive.
Transport is allotted as follows :—
No. 1 baggage wagon ... Officers' Kits & Coy. Messes.
No. 2 " " ... H.Q. baggage & surplus Officers' Kits.
Maltese cart .... Medical Officer.
Mess Cart .... H.Q., Bombers, and Snipers Mess Kits.
The Grenade Limber now at Battn. H.Q. will be horsed, and all above transport ready to leave BULLY GRENAY at 2-15 p.m. The Transport Officer will arrange for the remainder of Transport to join him. He will move the transport to BOUVIGNY HUTS following the same route from FOSSE 10, as laid down in para 4 of these orders. When moving from Road Junction at Q.30.b.3½.6. to the Huts transport will move with good intervals between each vehicle.

29.5.16.
sd. C. Bathurst. Capt. & Adjt

WAR DIARY or INTELLIGENCE SUMMARY

Army Form C. 2118.

June
10 West Riding
1/5th Bn. Duke of Wellington's Regiment
Vol II

Place	Date	Hour	Summary of Events and Information	Remarks and references to Appendices
BOUVIGNY HUTS.	1/6/16 to 9/6/16		During this period the weather has been indifferent, there being some rain & much wind, also colder. The Battalion has been employed in general training, care & handling of arms, careful inspection of the new clothing, equipment, iron rations &c. Everything has been thoroughly overhauled. About 8 p.m. on the 3rd inst. we received S.O.S. message from the 68th Infantry Brigade who were holding the line in SOUCHEZ. 13th Durham L.I. the enemy bombarded the trenches heavily but so far as is known no attack took place. Our artillery replied strongly and the S.O.S. were withdrawn about 8.45 p.m. Things were afterwards quiet. On the evening of the 8th we received orders to relieve the 13th Durham L.I. in the trenches. This information was only passed out to all concerned. Copy marked 'A' attached. During the early afternoon the Lewis Gun Detachment proceeded to the trenches to take over from the 13th Durhams	10 Y. 13 sheets

WAR DIARY
or
INTELLIGENCE SUMMARY.
(Erase heading not required.)

Army Form C. 2118.

Place	Date	Hour	Summary of Events and Information	Remarks and references to Appendices
			Before this work was completed the Lewis Gun Sergeant (No 11988 Sgt. W. Earnshaw. D.C.M.) was killed by a trench mortar shell, 3 others being wounded. The above named Sergeant was a very capable man & a recent disposition very popular with the Lewis Gun detachment & other ranks who new him. He joined the Battalion on its formation & worked hard for the success of the Battalion. Relief was completed about 11 p.m without sustaining further casualties.	
Trenches.	10/6/16		During the early morning Zefferino & Sevastopol traps were subjected to a heavy fire from Rifle Grenades. Zefferino trench being also a large number of trench mortar shells to contend with. We replied with 100-60pdr trench mortar shells which succeeded in quietening the enemy for a time. He soon re-commenced and continued at irregular intervals throughout the day.	

Army Form C. 2118.

WAR DIARY
or
INTELLIGENCE SUMMARY.
(Erase heading not required.)

(3)

Place	Date	Hour	Summary of Events and Information	Remarks and references to Appendices
Hurdles	11/9/16		We applied to the Artillery for assistance which was immediately given. The enemy artillery was very quiet. A thunderstorm broke out during the morning & was accompanied with very heavy rain. Dugout accommodation is very poor & consequently things are very unpleasant.	
to	12/9/16		Did not dig, a few rifle grenades were fired by both sides, otherwise nothing to report. Weather still continues bad. A few rifle grenades & trench mortar shells exchanged. We had two men wounded during the night. They were being employed on our wire. Received word from the 69 Infantry Brigade that the 93rd Division would be relieved by the 47th Division on the 13th inst.	

WAR DIARY or INTELLIGENCE SUMMARY

Army Form C. 2118.

Place	Date	Hour	Summary of Events and Information	Remarks and references to Appendices
	13/6/16		During the early morning the enemy exploded one of our mine galleries. Fortunately no material damage was done outside the shaft neither had we any casualties. In the afternoon the enemy sent over a few heavy shells and he obtained a direct hit on one of the dugouts which was occupied by the Battalion bombers. The result was 2 men killed, one man wounded, & 4 admitted to hospital suffering from shell shock. Relief by the 13th London Regt. relieving us. Relief completed without further casualties at 3 and 14 p.m. The weather during this tour in the trenches has been cold dull & very wet.	
Billets	14/6/15		In Billets at FOSSE 10. The Battalion was ordered to form up at 10-30 a.m & march to CAMBLAIN CHATELAIN, a distance of about 10 miles.	
	16/6/16		The Battalion marched via HERSIN-BARLIN and arrived about 5 p.m. The Battalion was billeted & made as comfortable as possible. Orders being issued that men were to clean themselves up as fa-	

WAR DIARY or INTELLIGENCE SUMMARY

Army Form C. 2118.

Place	Date	Hour	Summary of Events and Information	Remarks and references to Appendices
	16/6/16		as possible before proceeding to the Manoeuvre Area. The Battalion formed up at 9.45 am and marched to ENQUIN-LES-MINES as shown on attached copy marked "B". Distance about 11 miles. I may say the Battalion had had such a trying time during the last few days and that only 12 men fell out during the march, it is a very creditable performance. He arrived at 3 p.m. All ranks were directed to their respective billets & made comfortable.	
17/6/16 to 23/6/16 ENQUIN LES MINES			During this period attention was mainly directed to manoeuvres & musketry attacks, wood fighting, artillery formations. Also the men have been practiced in standing & firing musketry. Extended order drill and all movements which are necessary in the front war. The weather has been very fine & no time lost through bad weather. Orders were received on the 21st to the effect that the Brigade will be prepared to entrain on the 24th. That at BERGUETTE Station at 6 hours notice. To move to new area. All surplus stores, baggage & kits were removed to BERGUETTE	

Army Form C. 2118.

WAR DIARY
or
INTELLIGENCE SUMMARY.

(Erase heading not required.)

Place	Date	Hour	Summary of Events and Information	Remarks and references to Appendices
ENGUIN LES MINES	23/6/16		Station on 22nd & 23rd in readiness for the move. Received orders on 23rd from 69th Infy Brigade that the Brigade would march to BERGUETTE Station & entrain for LONGUEAU on 24th inst. Orders were issued for the move of the Battalion as per copy marked "C" attached	
-do-	24/6/16		The transport moved off with Convoy party at 11.45 a.m. The Battalion fell in at 2.25 p.m. & marched to BERGUETTE Station arriving at 5.30 p.m. after a stiff march against time. Distance 10½ miles & were being only 10 minutes halt during the march. By 6 p.m. the train was clear of the station. The men were in box wagons, average 45 per truck. Travelled through the night, via:- LILLERS - CHOCQUES - CALONNE RICOART - ST. POL - DOULLENS - VIGNACOURT, through AMIENS to LONGUEAU.	
	25/6/16		Detrained 2.30 p.m. The Battalion moved off again at 4 a.m. and moved through FREMONT until the Battalion took over billets at 9 a.m. the day was spent resting. On the Battalion were found to be in the vicinity	

Army Form C. 2118.

WAR DIARY
or
INTELLIGENCE SUMMARY.
(Erase heading not required.)

(4)

Instructions regarding War Diaries and Intelligence Summaries are contained in F. S. Regs., Part II. and the Staff Manual respectively. Title pages will be prepared in manuscript.

Place	Date	Hour	Summary of Events and Information	Remarks and references to Appendices
FREMONT	26/6/16		The day was spent having a complete kit-inspection & noting there were some showers during the day & very heavy rain at night.	
do	27/6/16		The day mainly devoted to Infantry Physical training & getting all ranks fit. Some heavy showers during the morning.	
do	28/6/16		Orders were received from the 69th Brigade that the Battalion would march to Hebuts & Proviers in MOLLIENS-AU-BOIS tonight & orders were issued in the morning as per copy marked "B" attached. About 3.30 p.m. a message was received from the Brigade that the Battalion would stand fast until further news. Orders were received late at night that the Brigade would not move but would carry out a route march tomorrow - distance 10 miles.	
do	29/6/16		Very fine. The route march was carried out under Brigade arrangements. The Battalion returning for dinner. The afternoon was spent in instruction in making trenches.	
do	30/6/16		Received message from 69 Inf Bde to send shelling parties to report to Staff Captain at COISY at 2 p.m. The Battalion received order to move at 4.25 p.m. to Fields & Bivouac at COISY. Tents were struck & many officers & men slept in the open.	

J.P. Hayward Col
Comdg 10th Duke of Wellington Rgt

OPERATION ORDERS NO. 12, BY LIEUT.COLONEL S.S. HAYNE,
COMMANDING, 10TH BATTALION, DUKE OF WELLINGTON'S REGIMENT.

Reference 1/40,000 Sheet B.   BOIS DE BOUVIGNY.
                                           9th June 1916.

1. The Situation on our front is reported normal.

2. The battalion will relieve the 13th Durham L.I. on the evening of the
   9th Inst. and will hold SOUCHEZ II Section as under.
       "B" Coy. SEVASTOPOL, ROTTEN ROW, KELLET.
       "C" "   SOLFERINO, KELLET, STRAIGHT.
       "D" "   Hd.Qr. Trench 2 platoons.
                 BAJOLE   " 1   "
                 BOIS SIX   1   "
                 The BOIS SIX platoon, less officers, to be attached to
                 Reserve Company BOIS SIX.
       "A" Coy. BOIS SIX.

   The battalion will march off from hutments in the following order :-
       "C" Coy. SOLFERINO Platoon.
                 KELLET.   "
       "B" Coy. ISLANDS   "
                 SEVASTOPOL   "
                 KELLET   "
                 ROTTEN ROW.   "
       "C" Coy. STRAIGHT 2 platoons.
                 & 16 H.Q. Bombers to take over bombing fronts.
       "D" Coy. Headquarters Trench 2 platoons.
       "D" Coy. BAJOLE Line 1 platoon.
                 Headquarters & remaining Hd.Qr. Bombers.

   An interval of 100 yards between platoons will be maintained until
   Communications Trenches are reached.
   Leading platoon to pass Headquarters at 8 p.m.
   ROUTE - Via track from R.32 central to AIX NOULETTE - EASTERN EXIT
   AIX NOULETTE.
   Guides will meet platoons at Junction of Ration - H.Q. Trench at 10 p.m.

   "A" Coy. & attached platoon of "D" Coy. will leave for BOIS SIX at 4 pm.
   Platoons to be at 100 yards distance.

3. O.C. Coys., less "B" Coy., will detail 1 N.C.O. and 19 men solely for
   work on dugouts, except in emergencies. These men will work night and
   day on all dugouts in battalion area. Work to commence at 9 a.m.
   10th Inst. and thence forward to be continuous.
   "A" Coy. party to be attached to "B" Coy.

4. The Lewis Gun Detachment will leave for the trenches in small parties
   at 200 yards distance, leading party to start at 1 p.m.
   Lewis Gun Limbers will use the following route :- Road Junction
   R.19.c.8.6. - Cross Roads R.14.c.0.9. -AIX NOULETTE - East of Cross Roads
   R.14.c.0.9., limbers to move at ½-hour intervals so as to arrive before
   detachment.
   SIGNALLERS to leave in small parties following the rear of L.Gun Party.
   Guides to meet Signallers and Lewis Gun Detachment will be at junction
   RATION - Hd.Qr Trench at 3-15 p.m.

5. Advance parties of H.Q. and Coys. will leave for trenches in small
   parties to take over trench stores. First party to leave at 3 p.m.
       "C" Coy. trench stores of 13th D.L.I. "C" Coy.
       "B" "   "   "   "   "   "   "A" "
       "D" "   "   "   "   "   "   "B" "
       "A" "   "   "   "   "   "   "D" "

6. O.C. Coys. will report to Headquarters by telephone as soon as relief
   is completed as follows :-
   "'B' Veal 11-30 p.m." which would mean "B" coy relief completed at 11-30

7. ~~Trench~~ *alt* Kits to be ready for loading by ~~2-30 p.m.~~ *4 pm*, ~~all other kit by 12 noon.~~
Transport Officer to arrange removal.

8. O.C. Coys. will ensure their billets being thoroughly cleaned out during the afternoon of relief.

9. Rations. Rations for tomorrow will be taken on the haversack.
The Transport Officer will arrange for the carts conveying the rations of the Naval Detachment meeting ours in AIX NOULETTE so that all are dumped at the same place.
They will be carried up from the dumps to Coys by "A" Coy. from BOIS SIX.
The NAVAL Detachment will send a party from the KELLET Line to the dump to bring up their rations. Party to be at ~~dump~~ ration dump at 9-30 p.m.
All down traffic to be stopped until rations have come up.

WATER. Reserve platoon BAJOLE Platoon *& Coys* "D" Coy. will bring water to junction Ration & Hd.Qr. Trench from where it will be fetched by Coys. Should more men be required they will be supplied by "A" Coy.
Headquarter Trench Anson Platoon will be responsible for water for NAVAL Detachment.
The water parties will come immediately in rear of ration parties.

9.6.16.   sd.   C. Bathurst. Capt. & Adjt.

OPERATION ORDER, NO. 15, BY
LIEUT.COLONEL S.S. HAYNE, COMMANDING, 10TH BN. DUKE OF WELLINGTON'S Rgt.

Reference 1/40,000 Sheet B.　　　　CAMBLAIN CHATELAIN.
HAZEBROUCK 5a. 1/100,000　　　　　15.6.16.

1. The battalion will march to ENQUIN LES MINES on the morning of the 16th Inst. Distance 11½ miles.

2. The order of march will be :-
    Headquarters, Snipers, Bombers.
    "B" Coy.
    "A" "
    "D" "
    "C" "
    Lewis Gun Detachment.
    1st Line Transport.
100 yards distance between Companies etc.
Company Cookers to follow immediately in rear of their respective Coys.
Route - FERFAY-BELLARY-ESTREE BLANCHE.

Starting point - Lewis Gun Detachment will be just past Road Junction I.9.a.10.8., Companies and Headquarters drawn up just in front of them. Transport immediately in rear of Lewis Gunners.

Tea will be made on the march as follows :-
"B" Company Cooker - to make tea for themselves & Headquarter Party.
"D"　　"　　"　　"　　"　　"　　"　　"　　"　& "A" Company.
"C"　　"　　"　　"　　"　　"　　"　　"　　"　& L.Gun Detachment.
Bread or biscuits & cheese will be carried in haversacks.

3. O.C. Coys. will satisfy themselves their respective billets are thoroughly clean before marching off.

4. Transport :-
Coys. will arrange to have all kits stacked and ready for loading by 8 a.m. outside Coy.H.Q. G.S. wagons, arranged for by Transport Officer, will collect same. Coys. will be responsible for loading their own kits.

Two lorries, at disposal of Quartermaster, will be at Cross Roads I.15.b.5.7. at 6 a.m. where he will arrange to have them met.

5. "A" Company will detail 1 N.C.O. and 4 men to report at Quartermaster's Stores at 6 a.m. to load lorries. They will load and unload lorries as ordered by Quartermaster.

6. 2/Lt. H. Dawson will march behind the battalion with 1 N.C.O. detailed by each Company to pick up any stragglers.

15.6.16.　　　　　　　　　　　　sd. H.W. Lester, 2/Lt. & A/Adjt.

MARCH ORDERS, NO. 16,
BY
LIEUT. COLONEL S.S. HAYNE, COMMANDING,
10TH BN. DUKE OF WELLINGTON'S REGIMENT.

Reference 1/100,000. Sheet HAZEBROUCK 5a.   ENQUIN LES MINES.
                                             23.6.16.

1. The battalion will march to BERGUETTE Station and entrain to our area on the 24th Inst.

   Starting Point – Battalion Headquarters.

   Order of March – Signallers.
                    Hd. Qr. Party.
                    Snipers.
                    Bombers.
                    Lewis Gun Detachment (less limbers).
                    "A" Coy.
                    "B" "
                    "C" "
                    "D" "

   Orders regarding how the battalion is to be numbered off for entrainment purposes will be issued later.

   O.C. Coys. and L. Gun Officer will ride their chargers to BERGUETTE Station. Chargers to be handed over to grooms at BERGUETTE Station and taken over to Lieut. Wolfe under whose supervision they will be entrained. One man from the loading party to meet horses at station.

   Route – ESTREE BLANCHE – LAMBRES – MOLINGHEM – BERGUETTE.
       Distance 9½ miles.

   Hour of starting – 2-25 p.m.

       2/Lt. J.S.A. Smith with a N.C.O. detailed from each company to march in rear of the battalion and bring along any stragglers.

2. LOADING PARTY.   Lieut. L. Hammond.
                    Hd. Qrs. 2 men.
                    1 full rank, 1 Lce.Cpl., & 10 men per Coy.
   will leave Hd. Qrs. at 11-45 a.m., proceeding to BERGUETTE Station.
   Packs of above party to be stacked outside Orderly Room by 10 a.m. from where they will be collected by a limber which will be arranged for by TRANSPORT OFFICER.
       Orders regarding loading have been issued to LIEUT. HAMMOND separately.
       The above party will also be responsible for unloading at destination.
       The loading party will be allotted a separate truck.
       Packs to be issued out to the party before loading commences.

3. O.C. Coys, will satisfy themselves their billets are thoroughly clean before marching off.

4. One Officer per Coy. to be detailed by O.C. Coy. to be on duty during train journey.

5. Probable hour of arrival of train at destination 1-30 a.m. night of 24/25th Inst.

6. All waterbottles are to be filled.

5. TRANSPORT. The battalion supply and baggage wagons and 1st Line Transport (less Cookers), Lewis Gun Limbers & Mess Cart will follow immediately in rear of loading party.

   The cookers will leave at 1-45 p.m. in charge of SERGT. G. SMITHAMS who will select the most convenient place for the issue of tea on the LAMBRES — MOLINGHEM Road W. of MOLINGHEM. Tea to be ready for issue on arrival of battalion. This must be done without delay and the cookers proceed as quickly as possible to BERGUETTE Station.

   Arrangements are to be made for the making of tea in cookers as soon as cookers are detrained.

   LIEUT. WOLFE is responsible for the entrainment of all horses and mules. Breast rope to be tied in front of each line of 4 animals after entrainment.

   LIEUT. PHILLIPS to assist LIEUT. HAMMOND in loading luggage and vehicles.

   Mess baskets to be ready for loading by 10-30 a.m. The Mess Cart will collect these at Coy. Hd.Qrs.

   1 N.C.O. from Hd.Qr. Party and 1 N.C.O. per Coy. will parade at Headquarters at 2-15 p.m. and proceed to BERGUETTE Station in charge of the senior N.C.O. These N.C.O's will ride bicycles, which will be handed over to LIEUT. HAMMOND at BERGUETTE Station. This party to report to Major BUCKLE their arrival.

   R.S.M. to parade this party and make certain they know the route.

   sd. H.W. Lester 2/Lt. & A/Adjt.

OPERATION ORDERS, NO. 17,
BY
LIEUT.COLONEL S.S. HAYNE, COMMANDING,
10TH BATTALION, DUKE OF WELLINGTON'S REGIMENT.

Reference 1/100,000 Sheet 17.   FREMONT. 28.6.16.

1. The battalion will march to billets and bivouacs in MOLLIENS AU BOIS on the night of 28/29th. Distance 8 miles.
The battalion to be formed up ready to march off at 7-50 p.m.

    Starting Point:- Western Exit FREMONT; rear of battalion opposite Battalion Orderly Room.

    Order of march -   Headquarters.
                             Signallers.
                             Snipers.
                             Bombers.
                             "B" Coy.
                             "C" "
                             "D" "
                             "A" "
                             Lewis Gun Detachment.

10 yards distance between companies.

ROUTE:- COISY - RAINNEVILLE - MOLLIENS-AU-BOIS.

    Transport, Supply, and Baggage wagons to follow immediately in rear of battalion.

2. Lieut. Lavarack with :- 1 N.C.O. & 3 men from H.Q.
                             1 N.C.O. & 4 men per Company.
to parade outside Orderly Room at 2 p.m. and march to MOLLIENS-AU-BOIS.
Lt. Lavarack to report to the Staff Captain at 6 p.m. outside the Church, MOLLIENS-AU-BOIS.

3. All Spare kit to be dumped outside Orderly Room ready for loading by 3 p.m.
Mess Baskets <u>only</u> at the same place by 5 p.m.

4. 2/Lt. J.C.W. Redington and 1 N.C.O. from each Company to march in rear of the battalion to pick up any stragglers.

5. Tea to be ready for issue from cookers on arrival at destination.

6. O.C. Coys. are to satisfy themselves their respective billets are thoroughly clean before marching off.

28.6.16.   sd. H.W. Lester. 2/Lt. & A/Adjt.

69th Inf.Bde.
23rd Div.

10th BATTN. THE DUKE OF WELLINGTON'S (WEST RIDING REGIMENT).

J U L Y

1 9 1 6

Attached:

Appendices "A" to
"E" (Reports on
Operations).

WAR DIARY.

Army Form C. 2118.

WAR DIARY
or
INTELLIGENCE SUMMARY

10th Batt. Duke of Wellingtons Regt

Vol 12

Place	Date	Hour	Summary of Events and Information	Remarks and references to Appendices
COISY.	1-7-16		Fine Day. A little training being done, received orders from Bde that the Battn would be prepared to move at 6 hours' notice. Definite orders soon followed and the Battn moved off at 8 p.m.	
BAIZIEUX.	2-7-16		Arrived at Baizieux at 2 a.m. The Battn was rested by the best means at disposal About 7.30 received orders that the Battn would move at 8.25 p.m. to N.W. of Albert. The place was reached at midnight and Battn was bivouced in a field.	
BÉCOURT	3-7-16		Received orders that the Battn would move into Bécourt Wood. We formed up at 11am. and arrived at 4 p.m. There we stayed the night.	
	4-7-16		Still at BÉCOURT Wood. During the day there was a heavy downpour of rain so a consequence things were not comfortable. During the evening orders were received to capture and consolidate certain positions.	
TRENCHES.	5-7-16		A copy of the operations carried out is attached marked "A". This is the first time that the Battn has been employed on attack, and it is a great pleasure for me to say that all ranks worked magnificently. The Battn is composed of the real material. The men worked well under the guidance of their Officers. Many deeds of valour were performed by both Officers and men. Our casualties read as follows :- 4 Officers Killed. 2 Officers wounded. 13. O.R. Killed. 66. O.R. wounded.	

ORDERLY ROOM.
No. W.R. 815
5 AUG. 1916
10th (SER) Bn. DUKE of WELLINGTON'S WEST RIDING REGT.

Army Form C. 2118.

WAR DIARY or INTELLIGENCE SUMMARY (CONT.)

1st Batt. Duke of Wellington's Regt.

(Erase heading not required.)

Place	Date	Hour	Summary of Events and Information	Remarks and references to Appendices
BÉCOURT.	5-7-16 (cont.)		Discipline played an important part in the operations and the training of the past 10 months in this country has not been work in vain. There was much individual effort and intelligence shewn. The Batt⁸. was relieved by the 8ᵗʰ Yorks. Regt., the Batt⁸. returning to BÉCOURT Wood – the relief complete at 10 p.m. The undermentioned officers were lost to the Batt⁸. and are greatly missed – they were popular with all ranks. CAPT. H.M.S. Carpenter killed. Lieut. A.K. Laverack " " L. Hammond " 2ⁿᵈ Lt. W.B. Taylor " " C. Sulet Wounded. " W. C.G. Merryweather "	
	6-7-16		Fine day which was spent easily, the men cleaning themselves up and relating to each other their past recent experiences. At 7 p.m. orders were received for the Batt⁸. to move to a field for the night S. of Albert. Arrived there at 8-30 p.m. A good square meal was provided for all ranks.	
LOZENGE.	7-7-16 to 8-7-16		Reveille 4 a.m. received orders to issue two days' iron rations to the Batt⁸. Moved off at 6 a.m. marched via Bécourt Wood to the captured trenches on the left of LOZENGE Wood. Rain began to fall	

Army Form C. 2118.

WAR DIARY
INTELLIGENCE SUMMARY (CONT.)

(Erase heading not required.)

10th Battn. Duke of Wellington's Regt.

Place	Date	Hour	Summary of Events and Information	Remarks and references to Appendices
TRENCHES.	9.7.16.		heavily at 9 a.m. and continued throughout the day. The rest of Bn. Ble. attacked Horse Shoe Trench & Shelter alley. About 8 p.m. the Battn. moved to the dump at Lozenge Wood where they were at once instructed to dig themselves in & sustained a few casualties during this process. Artillery is moving forward. In the late evening C & D. Coys. were filled up with all requirements for an attack & they were accompanied by about 50 of the R.E.'s & proceeded to the front line system of defences, to the left rear of Peake Wood. A & B. Coys. moved to the right of Sunken Road and dug themselves in whilst H. Qrs. proceeded to the German Bakery on the left of the same road. This bakery is a substantial construction and is about 20 feet below the surface & has two tunnel staircases. It is at present being used by our men as an advanced dressing station. It is quite proof against shell fire. Beyond heavy artillery fire there is nothing to report. About 6 p.m. A & B Coys. moved up to the trenches occupied by C & D Coys. and just at this point the enemy placed a heavy barage on the ridge and heavily shelled the now crowded trenches causing many casualties. C & D Coys. advanced on Contalmaison and were followed later by A.B. Coys. As will be seen by the attached copy of operations marked "B" the attack on the village by the 69th Brigade was a great success. Our H. Qrs.	
CONTALMAISON	10.7.16.			

WAR DIARY (CONT.)
INTELLIGENCE SUMMARY

Army Form C. 2118.

10th Batt. Duke of Wellington's Regt.

Place	Date	Hour	Summary of Events and Information	Remarks and references to Appendices
	10-7-16 (cont.)		assisted by a carrying party of the Duke of Lancaster's Own carried stores, ammunition, bombs etc. straight by the road to Contalmaison and assisted in the consolidation of the captured positions. A large quantity of 4.2 shells & stores of other descriptions were found in dugouts, they having been abandoned by the enemy in his flight. Our artillery kept up a continuous barrage & we held the position.	
	11-7-16		About 3 a.m. our machine guns were in action against a small party of the enemy, who it is thought were coming to surrender. Our men did not leave anything to chance, as the light was but their intention could only be assumed. They however returned. Judging from the appearance of the captured village, the enemy did not intend to leave this position and was probably under the impression that it was impregnable. The artillery worked magnificently; they were called upon to make a great effort & responded to it. It is impossible to speak too highly of that branch of the service. The Battn moved into a field N.W. of Albert bivouaced for the night.	
FRANVILLERS.	12-7-16		Moved to FRANVILLERS where we stayed one night only. Nothing to report.	

Army Form C. 2118.

WAR DIARY
(CONT.)
INTELLIGENCE SUMMARY

(Erase heading not required.)

10th Batt. Duke of Wellington's Regt.

9421/8/3

Place	Date	Hour	Summary of Events and Information	Remarks and references to Appendices
MOLLIENS AU BOIS.	13-7-16 to 20-7-16		Moved to Molliens au Bois arriving there about 3 p.m. During this period the Battn. was exercised in general training, Handling of arms, Musketry Practices, Short Route Marches etc., generally organising for a further effort. A draft of 154 O.R. joined us on the 19th inst. The weather has been good & the Battn. looks much better after the change. On the evening of the 20th received orders to move on the 21st inst. Battn. moved off at 9.25 a.m. prior to which the G.O.C. presented military medals to the undermentioned N.C.O's. a/C.S.M. G.F. McKill.. 13233 L/C. Davis (m/g Sec.) 13588.	
MILLENCOURT.	21-7-16 to 25-7-16		Marched to Millencourt where we were bivouaced until the morning of the 21st inst. The weather during that period was good; training was carried on as well as possible. The 8th Batt. Yorks Regt. organised sports whilst there, which consisted of foot-racing, boxing, throwing cricket ball etc. and a race for the transport mules. These Sports were thoroughly enjoyed by all ranks. On the 22nd inst. a further draft of 42 other ranks joined us. Nothing of an exciting nature transpired. On the evening of the 23rd received orders from the Bde. Hd. Qrs. that the Battn. was to Held itself in readiness to move at short notice. This embargo was eventually	

Army Form C. 2118.

WAR DIARY (CONT.)
INTELLIGENCE SUMMARY

(Erase heading not required.)

10th Batt'n Duke of Wellington's Regt.

943f

Place	Date	Hour	Summary of Events and Information	Remarks and references to Appendices
BÉCOURT.	26-7-16		On the evening of the 25th received orders to move on the morning of the 26th inst. Orders were issued to all concerned. Copy marked "C" attached.	
	27-7-16		Left for Divisional Reserve which was in trenches in front of BÉCOURT Wood. Nothing to report beyond the usual artillery activity.	
	28-7-16		Still in BÉCOURT Wood. Received orders to move into front line system of trenches through Contalmaison.	
	29-7-16		Arrived in front line system of trenches as ordered. We sustained some casualties. The enemy was shelling the main road through village and was very near to doing some serious damage. (As will be seen by the enclosed copy of operations marked "D" the Batt'n was soon again in action. We sustained somewhat severe casualties which read as under:—	
			2 Officers Killed. 31 O.R. Killed.	
			4 " Wounded. 124 " Wounded.	
			1 " Missing. 13 " Suffering from "Shell Shock".	
			30 " Missing.	
			I also attach a further list of Officers, N.C.O's men who distinguished themselves marked "E" & a copy of a message received from	

Army Form C. 2118.

WAR DIARY (CONT.) of
INTELLIGENCE SUMMARY
10th Batt'n. Duke of Wellington's Regt.

(Erase heading not required.)

Place	Date	Hour	Summary of Events and Information	Remarks and references to Appendices
TRENCHES	30-7-16 to 31-7-16		Lieut. E.K. McCULLOCH of 17th Battn. 5th Inf. Bde. A.I.F.	948f

The Battn. was relieved by the 9th Yorks. Regt. about 6 p.m. and took up position in reserve in Scots' Redoubt and whilst here we had no casualties.

The weather throughout the month has been fairly good.

During the time the Batt. was in the trenches (reserve) the enemy sent over a considerable number of gas shells & without causing casualties he created some discomfort.

Our casualties for the whole month were read as under:—

```
        Officers Killed in Action   7        O.R. Killed in Action   55
           "     Wounded    "      8           "   Wounded    "     284
           "     Shell Shock        1           "    "    at Duty     2
           "     Wounded at Duty    4           "   Shell Shock      35
           "     Missing            1           "   Missing          43
                        total      21                        total  419
```

Military Medals were also awarded to :—

Army Form C. 2118.

WAR DIARY (CONCLUDED)
INTELLIGENCE SUMMARY

(Erase heading not required.) 10th Battn. Duke of Wellington's Regt.

Place	Date	Hour	Summary of Events and Information	Remarks and references to Appendices
			13050 L/C. Leigh	
			12257 Sgt. B. McAvan	
			13551 Pte. Jas. Atkinson	
			11351 L/C. M. Kenefick	
			15228 L/C. Simpson A. was promoted to the rank of Sergeant for gallantry in the field.	

C.J. Hayne Lt. Col. Commanding
10th Battn. Duke of Wellington's Regt.

9495
813

A P P E N D I C E S "A", "B", "C",
"D" & "E".

Reports on Operations.

Headquarters,

69th Infantry Brigade.

Map Reference
57.D. S.E.
Sheet 2.
1/5,000.

During the night of 4th/5th orders were received to capture and consolidate the following line : X.21.b.7.4. - X.22.a.0.4. - X.22.a.3.3.

At 2-30 a.m. on the morning of the 5th two companies of the battalion paraded in BECOURT WOOD and marched to point X.21.d.5.6. under Major C.C. Buckle.

On arrival at point X.21.d.5.6. "A" party, consisting of half a company, a party of bombers, and two Lewis Guns, were sent to attack towards X.22.a.3.3. and X.22.a.5.6. and found 9th Duke of Wellington's were being heavily counter-attacked and had been driven back from 5.6. past 3.3.

Our bombers proceeded to bomb down the trench. It was then observed that the enemy was attacking across the open from point 0.4. and the direction of 3.0.

Lt. Hammond immediately took a party across the open and counter-attacked. He was successful, with the assistance of fire from Lewis Gun in bringing the assault to a standstill but in doing so he was killed and all his party became casualties.

A block was made in the trench just beyond 3.3.

Several bombing attacks were subsequently made but the situation remained unchanged until the afternoon.

This party having suffered severe casualties I sent up the remaining half of the company to reinforce it.

As soon as the block at 3.3. was established, PEAK WOOD, into which a large party of the enemy had been seen to retire was heavily bombarded by our own 4.5. Howitzers; the flanks of the wood being covered by Lewis Gun fire.

"B" Party, consisting of some bombers and "D" Company, proceeded up 2.7. towards 7.4. and found the enemy holding the trench about 70 yards S. of 7.4. The enemy was attacked by our bombers under Lieut. Lavarack and driven back about 20 yards. They strongly counter-attacked both across the open and down the trench and before a block could be established Lieut. Lavarack and 2/Lieut. Taylor, commanding the blocking party were both killed and most of the bombers rendered casualties. We were driven back about 50 yards at which point the retirement was stopped by the Company Officers and 2/Lieut. Tribe made a temporary block which was held throughout the day.

At about 2-45 p.m., having been reinforced by a Lewis Gun, this party again attacked under Lieut. Phillips and fought up to 20 yards of their original foremost position; this attack was repelled by hostile counter-attacks from three sides and a barage of rifle grenades, and fell back to the temporary block.

At 6 a.m., realising the serious state of affairs, the third third company and two more Lewis Guns were sent for and the reserve Company were ordered to "stand to".

At about 9 a.m. Colonel Barker, Commanding 11th West Yorks, reported that he had been heavily attacked at a point 3.5. and been compelled to retire on SCOTTS REDOUBT. He asked if we could assist him by sending reinforcements. A Company, party of Bombers, and two Lewis Guns, took up a position holding SCOTTS REDOUBT in the neighbourhood of X.21.Central.

— 2 —

At 12-30 p.m. our artillery were seen to be heavily bombarding the line OO - 51 - 80 - 21 and at the same time Major Lintott of the 52nd Machine Gun Company informed me that the 23rd Division were expected to be attacking and the artillery fire was to cover their advance. I immediately ordered "A", "B", & "C" Parties to attack their objectives. "A" Party crossed their barricade and made slow but steady progress by incessant bombing until they retook 33. and eventually X.22.a.5.6.; from 5.6. they attacked O.4. in conjunction with a Stokes Gun which we borrowed from the 52nd Brigade; this gun rendered most valuable assistance.

At 5-30 p.m., by going across the open from 5.6., a firm footing was established at O.4. and the enemy were driven down the trench towards point 7.4.

Two more attacks were delivered by "B" Party, which, though inflicting heavy losses on the Germans, failed to gain ground. At 5 p.m. this party was reinforced by a platoon from "A" Company and one Lewis Gun.

At 5-45 p.m., as they developed their final attack, a German came over and intimated that his comrades would surrender; 73 of which passed through our hands and the remainder through 11th West Yorks. This party surrendered as they had suffered heavy casualties from "A" Party and their line of retreat was cut off.

Having been informed by O.C. 11th West Yorks that his troops would be unfit for any further offensive movement that day, I allotted their objectives, namely, Point X.21.b.5.6. to "C" Party.

"C" Party, having been reinforced by half a company, on receipt of orders to attack, pushed on and drove the enemy as far as 3.5. where they established a block at 4-30 p.m. At 5 p.m. they were ordered to take point X.21.b.5.6. at 5-45 p.m. and to cover this attack an intense artillery bombardment on the TRIANGLE and communication trenches was asked for and received. At 5.55 p.m. they gained their objectives.

"A", "B", & "C" Parties having all established touch with each other, the battalion advanced as the artillery fire was lifted and the points were reached - 5.1. - 7.1. - 8.0. - 1.2. - 2.1. - 3.0. - O.8.

"C" Party took 49 more prisoners which were handed over to 9th Yorks.

"A" Party directly they obtained possession of O.4. commenced joining up O.4. & 5.6. from both points and started consolidating the line 5.6. - O.4. - 7.4.

We were then relieved by the 8th Yorks.

At 10-30 a.m. Lt.Colonel Hayne arrived at point X.21.d.5.6. and made Headquarters there.

During the final attack the reserve Company was brought up and utilised in the course of these operations.

The battalion took the following prisoners :-
         81 sent under our own escort.
about - 49 handed over to 9th Yorks.
         11 handed over to 11th West Yorks.
        141

Many automatic rifles were captured but owing to the vital necessity of pushing forward and consolidating and the large number of men required for taking back prisoners they were left in the German trench.

Headquarters,

69th Infantry Brigade.

Report on Operations carried out by 10th Duke of Wellington's Regiment from 12 noon July 10th till midnight 10th/11th.

PHASE 1.   On the evening of the 9th I received orders to move the battalion from the vicinity of LOZENGE WOOD and take over trenches from 1st Worcestershire Regt. On taking over the battalion was disposed as under :-
One Company and three platoons and 2 Lewis Guns in SHELTER ALLEY between junctions SHELTER ALLEY - QUADRANGLE TRENCH and point X.22.c.7.6.;
One platoon, a bombing party, one Lewis Gun and 6 snipers at junction QUADRANGLE TRENCH and SHELTER ALLEY; this party had orders to capture the following points X.16.d.6.0. and X.16.d.4.1. and X.16.d.2.4.

The Bombing Party proceeded down QUADRANGLE TRENCH bombing as they went and having successfully bombed the enemy out of point X.16.d.6.0. occupied this point. The next objective being commanded by 6.0. I gave orders for point 6.0. to be consolidated and cancelled any further advance. Point X.16.d.6.0. was shelled intermittantly throughout the day which became intense from 4-30 p.m. onwards when the attack on CONTALMAISON commenced. Point X.16.d.6.0. on the attack being launched was of the greatest value in assisting the advances, as it was possible to bring a very telling enfilade fire on the German position.

During the attack enemy machine gun and snipers were located at X.16.d.9.3. but owing to the excellent work done by our snipers and lewis gun, the enemy were unable to cause serious losses to our advancing troops, and eventually were compelled to abandon this gun. This gun was later captured by the attacking battalion. The excellent work done by our Snipers and Lewis Gun may be judged by the fact that when we advanced we found 15 dead Germans shot through the head at point 9.3.

The magnificent behaviour of all ranks during the attack when under intense artillery barrage and machine gun fire was beyond all praise.

PHASE 2.   At 8 p.m. on the 10th I received orders to move up my two advance Companies to CONTALMAISON at 8-30 p.m.; two advance Companies moved up across the open under intense artillery shell fire to CONTALMAISON. The remaining two Companies in support in the SUNKEN ROAD immediately moving up and occupied trenches recently vacated by Advance Companies.

At 10 p.m. I received orders for the remainder of the battalion to proceed at once to CONTALMAISON and to arrange for 6 platoons of 10th Gloucestershire Regt. to occupy my trenches.

The advance to CONTALMAISON was carried out with the utmost gallantry. Several parties during the advance were encountered who stated that we had evacuated CONTALMAISON and orders had been given for retirement. Some of these we were able to rally and take with us and during the advance the men never wavered, proceeding straight to CONTALMAISON under galling fire.

— 2 —

PHASE 3.   On entering CONTALMAISON the battalion took up dispositions as under :-
2 platoons and 1 Lewis Gun N.W. of CHATEAU.
1 platoon in Support.
1 Company S.E. Exit of Village.
1 Company S.W. of village.
Remainder of battalion in support.

Night and day was taken up in consolidating position won.

The behaviour of all ranks during these operations was magnificient and I wish to bring forward the names of ~~the~~ Officers, N.C.Os. and men ~~on attached lists~~ who specially distinguished themselves.

Lieut. Colonel.

Commanding,

10th Bn. Duke of Wellington's Regt.

14.7.16.

CAPTAIN JAMES CHRISTOPHER BULL.

    Displayed great gallantry and devotion to duty when in Command of his Company which occupied SHELTER TRENCH and Point X.16.d.6.0. During the attack on CONTALMAISON when his Company was under intense artillery fire constantly walked up and down the trench setting a magnificent example of coolness and personal ability.

2/LIEUT. HENRY KELLY.

    Was in charge of the platoon, snipers, and lewis gun at point X.16.d.6.0. This garrison was exposed to accurate sniping and heavy shell fire throughout the operations. He displayed the greatest gallantry throughout and handled his garrison so well that the enemy had to abandon a machine gun at point 9.3. He undoubtedly saved many casualties by the prompt way in which he dealt with the hostile machine guns.

CAPTAIN JOHN ATKINSON.

    Commanded his Company in SHELTER TRENCH and when under very heavy artillery fire with the greatest coolness and devotion to duty. By his example he inspired his Company with the greatest confidence and although unable to lead his company in the advance on CONTALMAISON through being buried by a shell, he joined the battalion at CONTALMAISON as soon as he had been dug out.

2/LIEUT. FRANK HUBERT CANDWELL REDINGTON.

    Displayed great coolness and bravery during the confusion caused by the retirement of certain parties. He continually rallied men of the battalion and brought them on with his platoon. He set a fine example to his men and rendered very valuable assistance throughout the advance.

2/LIEUT. & A/ADJT. HUGH WILLIAM LESTER.

    Rendered the most valuable service throughout the operations. He continually went forward to ascertain the situation under heavy fire, displaying the utmost disregard for personal safety.

2/LIEUT. ROBERT CLEMENT PERKS who, when his Company Commander had been wounded, gallantry led his Company forward to CONTALMAISON. By his coolness and devotion to duty, he set a fine example to his Company during the advance.

NO. 13700 SERGT. THOMAS HENRY EDMONDSON.

    Assisted 2/Lt. F.H.C. Redington in rallying the men and pulling them together. He displayed the utmost gallantry and coolness throughout the advance.

NO. 12199 CORPORAL CHARLES WRAGG.
NO. 16512 PRIVATE LEONARD PANKHURST.
NO. 14980 PRIVATE ARTHUR GILL.

    The above men showed the greatest bravery when under heavy artillery barrage in continually digging out men who had been buried by shell fire. No. 14980 PTE GILL having himself been buried. These men by their gallantry and devotion to duty were responsible for saving several lives.

NO. 13581 PRIVATE JOHN WILLIAM ATKINSON.

Did invaluable work as stretcher bearer. He continually carried back wounded regardless of his own safety. The work of the stretcher bearers was magnificient and I select him as being the senior.

NO. 13888 LCE/CORPORAL JOHN DAVIS who was in charge of the Lewis Gun at X.16.d.6.0. He handled his gun with great ability and coolness and throughout showed the greatest gallantry, setting a magnificient example to the remainder of the team. The work of this gun undoubtedly saved our advancing troops heavy casualties.

NO. 11808 PRIVATE RAYNER SUTCLIFFE.
NO. 14562 LCE/CORPORAL DAN FRETWELL.
NO. 12318 PRIVATE CHARLES BURNS.

Of the Battalion Snipers, did consistently good work throughout the day in locating and silencing the enemy snipers. They occupied an exceedingly shallow trench and were subjected to heavy sniping and machine gun fire before the advance and intense artillery fire after the advance had been launched. These men continued sniping the enemy with great success throughout the operations although the casualties among our snipers were very heavy.

NO. 13233 SERGEANT DAVID FREDERICK MCKRILL.

Displayed the greatest bravery and coolness under exceedingly heavy artillery fire. He continually went up and down his platoon steadying the men and by his example and assistance greatly assisted in keeping an unbroken line during the advance on CONTALMAISON.

NO. 11839 PRIVATE ENOCH RHODES.

A stretcher bearer. Rendered the most efficient work as a stretcher bearer. He carried out his duties with an absolute disregard of all danger and was responsible for getting a considerable number of wounded carried back.

NO. 15327 PRIVATE JOHN WILLIAM HAWKRIDGE, who was one of a Lewis Gun Team although six of the team had become casualties, continued with great coolness and bravery to work the gun with the remaining man.

NO. 10897 PRIVATE WILLIAM RAWNSLEY.

During the advance, on several occasions went through intense artillery barrage with messages to Companies. He invariably delivered the messages without delay, having to return through the artillery barrage to bring back information.

MOVEMENT ORDERS BY
LIEUT.COLONEL S.S. HAYNE, COMMANDING,
10TH BATTALION, DUKE OF WELLINGTON'S REGIMENT.

Ref. 57.D. S.E. 1/20,000								In the Field.
												25.7.16.

1. The battalion will relieve the Loyal N. Lancs Regt. in O.B.2. Squares X.20.X.26. Guides will meet Battalion at BECOURT Chateau at 11 a.m.

2. The Battalion will fall in ready to march off at 8-20 a.m.
Steel helmets to be worn.
Packs will be carried. Caps to be packed with the pack.

3. Order of march — Hd.Qrs.
Snipers.
"A" Coy.
"B" "
"C" "
"D" "
Lewis Gun Detachment.
Pack mules will not follow companies.
Interval of one minute to be maintained between companies as far as ALBERT; from ALBERT the battalion will march by platoons.

4. The following transport will follow immediately in rear of battalion:
Lewis Gun Limbers.
Cookers.
Watercarts.
Mess Cart.
Maltese Cart.
Remaining Transport will pass Brigade H.Q. at 9-30 a.m. and proceed to Transport Lines. Interval of 100 yards between each group of 5 vehicles to be maintained.

5. Tents will be struck ready for loading at 6 a.m.
O.C. "C" Coy. will detail two Sergeants and 45 men to report to R.S.M. at 5-45 a.m. to strike and load tents.
Transport Officer to provide transport to carry tents to Brigade Hd.Qrs. at 6-45 a.m. and stack them in yard.

6. Officers kits to be ready for loading at 7-30 a.m.
Mess baskets at 7-45 a.m.

7. Bivouac ground and latrines to be left clean.

sd. H.W. Lester. 2/Lt. & A/Adjt.

25.7.16.

REPORT ON OPERATIONS CARRIED OUT
BY
10TH BATTALION, DUKE OF WELLINGTON'S REGIMENT,
ON THE NIGHT OF 28/29TH JULY 1916.

Orders having been received to bomb up MUNSTER ALLEY as far as possible consolidate on the night of 28/29th, I issued orders to "D" Company to carry out this operation.

No. 13 platoon, under Lieut. F. Hird, formed the attacking party, No. 14 platoon followed to carry out the work of consolidating the position, the operation covered by two Lewis Guns.

An advance was made about 12-45 a.m. preceded by a bombing party of 8 men with Lieut. Hird in rear, followed at a distance of 20 yards by the remainder of No. 13 platoon.

Little opposition was met with for about 60 yards at which point the enemy vigorously attacked with bombs with men concealed in shell holes on either side of the trench and a party in the trench.

Six of the bombing party were wounded and Lieut. Hird killed at this point and the remainder of No. 13 platoon were driven back to their original barricade, some 20 yards in rear of Point 41.

The enemy here launched a vigorous bombing attack which lasted for half an hour but were driven back from our barricade.

About 2 a.m. 2/Lieut. H.H.O. Stafford with a bombing party endeavoured to again advance, but were forced to submit after having advanced about 20 yards owing to the enemies bombs.

A barricade was then erected, our bombers continuing to bomb the enemy during its construction.

This compelled the enemy to abandon his original barricade and put up another one some yards further back, from which position he opposed our further advance vigorously for about one hour.

There is little doubt he wished to drive us out of MUNSTER ALLEY as his bombers came into the broken ground in front of his barricade and continued until it was quite light to throw bombs with great determination. Fortunately supplies of bombs, S.A.A., and filled sandbags, were sent up with great regularity and in this we received great assistance from the 17th Battalion AUSTRALIAN Contingent, who prolonged our chain of supplies and did us great service in this respect.

In connection with this operation I beg to draw attention to the fact that prior to this attack we were not in possession of Point 41 but a point 20 yards in rear behind O.G.2. which was thought to be Point 41, the mistake occurring on account of O.G.2 at and near Point 41 having been obliterated by shell fire.

In connection with this operation I wish to bring the names of the following Officers, N.C.Os., and men to your notice.

2/LIEUT. ROBERT CLEMENT PERKS. Honour for which recommended – MILITARY CROSS.
No previous Honour received.

This Officer was in charge of a party of "B" Company, which had been brought up by mistake to Point 61. He was wounded in the face about 1 a.m. and was for a time insensible but on recovering continued to throw bombs until wounded seriously in the hand, foot, and face again. He throughout the operation showed the greatest gallantry and by his magnificent example was largely responsible for our being able to hold and consolidate the point gained in MUNSTER ALLEY

2/LIEUT. HENRY HERBERT OWEN STAFFORD. Honour for which recommended – MENTION IN DESPATCHES.
No previous honour received.

Was at the head of all our bombing parties at the barricade. His bravery and exceedingly cheerful spirit was of the greatest value in cheering on the bomb throwers when under exceedingly heavy bomb fire.

NO. 13605 SERGEANT ALBERT EDGAR PALMER. Honour for which recommended – MILITARY MEDAL.
No previous honour received.

On Lieut. Hird being killed, immediately took command of No. 13 Platoon, and having re-organised it, remained throwing bombs for several hours, being under heavy bomb fire throughout.

NO. 11967 SERGEANT WILLIAM JONES. Honour for which recommended – MILITARY MEDAL.
No previous honour received.

Personally built up the greater part of the barricade, and although several men near him were killed and wounded, continued to work with greatest bravery and coolness until his work had been completed.

NO. 11585 PRIVATE ENOCH RHODES. Honour for which recommended – DISTINGUISHED CONDUCT MEDAL.
No previous honour received.

Has in every engagement shewn the most wonderful devotion to duty. At CONTALMAISON on the way to the trenches a shell killed his partner and he was thrown over a cart. Though badly shaken he at once tied up a man who had had his hand blown off and then proceeded to the trenches. During the night of 28/29th July he attended to at least 50 wounded men, always under intense artillery fire.

NO. 14165 PRIVATE TOM FEATHER.   ) Honour for which
NO. 13357 PRIVATE JOHN WILLIAM BEAVER.) recommended – MENTION IN DESPATCHES.
No previous honour received.

Both these men carried many messages with speed and regularity regardless of shell fire. Pte. Beaver was afterwards admitted into hospital suffering from shell shock.

30th July 1916.

From .. Lieut. E.K. McCulloch. 17th Bn. 5th Inf. Bde. A.I.F.
To .... The Adjutant, 10th West Riding Regiment.

    I beg to congratulate you on the excellent work done by your Signal Section during the 28th, 29th, and 30th July. The way they have maintained telephone communication under heavy shell fire is grand, repeatedly going out on the lines while the wires were being out and in this connection I must mention two names, that of Corporal Dean and L/C Walker. It is no exaggeration on my part to say your lines were broken on an average of once an hour and immediately the operator reported any one of your companies out of "call" the above two men went out and repaired the break. Altogether these two men have laid over three miles of wire, the whole of it under shell fire.

    On the 28th the front of your signal dugout was blown in, wrecking all wires and smashing two telephones. One of your section was killed and the cool way your Signal Sergeant and his men set to work to clear the debris and restore the wires excitedmy admiration and their subsequent work has been a revelation to me.

    I am in a position to criticize the work done by your section because I have been standing by your telephones for the past three days keeping up communication with our Brigade through yours and I trust you will excuse me in taking this opportunity of congratulating you on such and a fine section.

    With regard to Cpl Dean and L/Cpl. Walker, these two men must have taken enormous risks in maintaining your wires and I feel it xxxxxxxx my duty to specially mention their names.

                              sd. E.K. McCulloch. Lieut.
                            O/C Sigs. A.I.F. 17th.

69th Brigade.
23rd Division.

1/10th BATTALION

THE DUKE OF WELLINGTON'S REGIMENT

AUGUST 1 9 1 6

Army Form C. 2118.

WAR DIARY
INTELLIGENCE SUMMARY
(Erase heading not required.)

1. August 1916.
10th Bn. Duke of Wellington's Regt.

VOL 13

Place	Date	Hour	Summary of Events and Information	Remarks and references to Appendices
SCOTS REDOUBT.	1-8-16		There is the usual artillery activity without anything of a more exciting nature. At 5 p.m. we were relieved by the 8th Yorkshire Regt., relief completed without casualties. The Battalion occupied billets in Albert. The enemy has sent a few shells into the town without doing much damage.	
ALBERT.	2-8-16		The enemy fired one or two heavy shells into Albert and in one instance caught the 68th Brigade Headquarters killed two staff officers and wounded one. Whilst here we found working parties taken advised to bury general horses which had become casualties as a consequence of the enemy shells. Weather fine. Nothing further to report.	
SCOTS REDOUBT.	3-8-16		During the day there was the usual artillery activity. The Battn. relieved the 8th Yorks regiment in Scots Redoubt, leaving Albert at 2 p.m. Relief complete about 5 p.m. Copy of operations marked "A" attached. In the evening A & B coys were employed as working and carrying parties to the front line. We sustained the following casualties 1 O.R. killed, H.Q.R. wounded and 2 O.R. missing.	"A"
	4-8-16		C & D coys. were ordered to Contalmaison to reinforce the 10th N.F. and late in the evening C Company were ordered up to the front line. Our artillery made a terrific bombardment on the enemy trenches and defences. We had 1 O.R. wounded.	
	5-8-16		The usual artillery activity is maintained, both sides sending large numbers of shells. Albert has been in receipt of a good many from the enemy. C & D Coys. reported to the Battn. about noon. In the afternoon received orders to relieve the	

Army Form C. 2118.

WAR DIARY
INTELLIGENCE SUMMARY
(Erase heading not required.)

August 1916.
10th Battn. Duke of Wellington's Regt.

Place	Date	Hour	Summary of Events and Information	Remarks and references to Appendices
PEAKE WOOD.	5-8-16 (cont.)		8th Yorks. Regt. in Peake Wood. This relief was carried out without sustaining casualties	
	6-8-16		Nothing further to report.	
			A Company found carrying parties during the morning, the remainder of the Battn. resting and cleaning themselves up. After tea hour a fatigue party were also ordered to reinforce the 8th Yorks. Regt. Very heavy shelling is taking place, both sides very busy, we had no casualties.	
	7-8-16		Still at Peake Wood. Received advice that the 69th Brigade would be relieved by the 45th Infantry Brigade, tomorrow the 8th inst. The 13th Battn. Royal Scots Regt. relieving us at 10 a.m. Beyond the usual artillery activity there is nothing to report. Copy of 69th Inf. Bde. Order marked "B" is attached.	"B"
	8-8-16 to 9-8-16		Relief carried out without losses. The Battn. marched to BRESLE, arriving there about 3-30 p.m. They were rested and utilized their time in cleaning their clothes, equipment etc. On the evening of the 9th received orders from the 69th Bde. Office that the Battn. would move to BUIGNY-L'ABBÉ. Copy marked "C" attached	"C"
BRESLE.	10-8-16		This information was duly passed to all concerned. Nothing to report except that instead of moving on the 11th inst. received urgent orders to be ready to march away on the evening of the 10th. These orders were duly complied with. We entrained from MERICOURT at 12 midnight.	
	11-8-16 to 12-8-16		Arrived at PONT REMY at 6-50 a.m. and marched to BUIGNY-L'ABBÉ at 9-30 a.m., the distance being about 6 kilometres. The Battn. was bivouaced and billeted. Hereto rested the remainder of the day. During this period various inspections were held to ascertain the state of the	40.

Army Form C. 2118.

WAR DIARY
INTELLIGENCE SUMMARY
(Erase heading not required.)

3. August 1916.

10th Battn. Duke of Wellington's Regt.

Place	Date	Hour	Summary of Events and Information	Remarks and references to Appendices
BUIGNY L'ABBÉ.	12-8-16 (cont.)		news kits. All deficiencies were made good. A little musketry practice, handling arms was performed. On the evening of the 12th received orders from Bde Office that the Battn would move to BAILLEUL. These orders were issued to all concerned. Copy marked "D" attached.	"D"
	13-8-16 to 16-8-16		Preparations for the move of the Battn. in progress. The Battn. formed up at 6 p.m. and marched to PONT REMY station, entrained, the train leaving at 8.45 p.m. arrived at BAILLEUL at 5.30 a.m. where it formed up and marched to METRIEN a distance of 7 kilometres, where we arrived at 10 a.m. Some little training was done the whole of the battalion each had a bath and a change of clean clothing. Nothing further to report except that we received orders to move into trenches in STEENWERCK. This information was passed to all concerned. Copy marked "E" attached.	"E"
METRIEN.	17-8-16		marched to STEENWERCK arriving there about 3 p.m. the distance being about 8 miles. Here we stayed the night. During the evening received orders from the Brigade Office that the Battn would relieve the 32nd Battn. Royal Fusiliers in Reserve trenches in PLOEGSTEERT. This	"F"
	18-8-16		information was passed to all concerned. Copy marked "F" attached. The Battn. formed up at 6 a.m. marched to reserve trenches relieving the 32nd Battn R.F. at 10 a.m. During this period we are finding large working parties for the front line and communication trenches. There has been some rain. It is very quiet in comparison to ALBERT, the whizz-bangs and machine gun fire only firing a few rounds per day. There are occasional bursts of rifle and machine gun fire. During the night of the 19th and 20th insts. two or three enemy aeroplanes came over our lines and dropped about 15 bombs in	
	19-8-16 & 20-8-16		STEENWERCK & BAILLEUL. There is no report of serious damage. There have been a few showers of rain otherwise the weather has been very good. On the 20th inst. we received orders that the Battn. would dig a trench commencing from PROWSE POINT and leading easterly for a distance of 400 yards. This enabled us to make an advance of between	

4.4.

WAR DIARY

INTELLIGENCE SUMMARY

Army Form C. 2118.

August 1916.

10th Bn. Duke of Wellington's Regt.

Place	Date	Hour	Summary of Events and Information	Remarks and references to Appendices
PLOEGSTEERT	21-8-16 to 22-8-16		250 and 300 yards and brought us into closer contact with the enemy. On the night of the 21/22nd inst. the party of 350 other ranks and 12 officers proceeded to the place of action and successfully accomplished the task at 3-30 a.m. on the 22nd inst. without alarming the enemy. We had the following casualties: 2 O.R. killed, 1 O.R. & two 2nd Lieuts. + O.R. wounded and 1 O.R. wounded at duty. (Total 8). The above casualties were caused by stray bullets. Major R.M. Gill was in charge of the party, Capt. M.G. Ramshill was supervising officer. The trench has been named the West Riding Trench. On the 23rd inst. we received notice that the Battn. would change position with the 11th West Yorks. Regt. on the 23rd inst. This information was duly passed to all concerned. Copy marked "G" attached.	G
RUE DU SAC	23-9-16		The change was successfully completed without incident at 5-30 p.m. The Battn. is being practised in musketry, handling of arms, inspection of arms, equipment, haversacks and iron rations. The weather still continues fine.	
	24-9-16		Baths for the Battn. have been arranged and take advantage of. Some physical training has also been indulged in. Received orders to relieve the 8th Bn. K.O.Y.L.I. in the front line trenches tomorrow the 25th inst. The information was duly passed to all concerned. Copy marked "H" attached.	H
	25-8-16		The Battn. was marched from its rest billets at 3 a.m. all relief reported complete at 6 a.m. The weather proceeding as per the copy marked "H" deters not. The weather is fine. Our field guns fired intermittently throughout the day. During the day the enemy was very quiet, but as darkness came along he was somewhat busy with machine gun and rifle fire, all partial panic leisurely overhead. The new trench previously mentioned is at present held by a part of the battalion.	
NEW TRENCH	26-9-16		Day very showery. Our artillery continued registering during the morning. The enemy artillery is not actually quiet. He has sent a few trench mortars in and about	47.

Army Form C. 2118.

WAR DIARY / INTELLIGENCE SUMMARY

(Erase heading not required.)

August 1916

10th Bn. Duke of Wellington's Regt.

Place	Date	Hour	Summary of Events and Information	Remarks and references to Appendices
TRENCHES PLOEGSTEERT	27-8-16		Trench no. 125. The only damage produced was to a small dugout, which at the time was unoccupied. We are employing a working party of 3 Officers and 120 other ranks every day to the Royal Engineers. The enemy fired this morning about twenty 77 m.m. shells at a working party of the 9th South Staffords, doing a certain amount of damage, particulars as to the extent are not to hand. Our to the trench mortars repairers this morning. The enemy retaliated with a few trench mortars all along the line we were holding. There was also considerable enemy rifle and machine gun fire last night and early this morning. The day has been showery.	
	28-8-16		Very dull day. There has been no hostile shelling on the front line, but about six howitzer shells fell in the neighbourhood of Battn. Headquarters during the late afternoon. Enemy aircraft has been unusually active during the day. The usual machine gun and rifle fire was indulged in by the enemy during the night. Much progress has been made in wiring the new trench.	
	29-8-16		Very little to report, during most of the day there was much heavy rain. According to report the enemy is working particularly hard improving his trenches, he was also heavier most persistent in rifle and machine-gun fire during late night and early morning. It was intended that a gas attack entitled with raiding parties on the enemy trenches should have taken place today. As per attached copy marked "I" this could not however be carried out, owing to the wind changing and to our disadvantage. The operation was therefore postponed. A very wet day. Everything particularly quiet. The wind veered round to the west in the afternoon and the postponed gas attack was ordered to take place at 1-30 a.m. in the morning.	"I"
	30-8-16			
	31-8-16		The gas liberated from our right went straight over to the enemy lines was apparently successful. The gas liberated on our right sector of the division passed over a portion of the new trench causing us 3 casualties, one of whom has since died. This has happened in spite of the most rigorous precautions. Gas helmets inspection was held in the morning and	51.

Army Form C. 2118.

WAR DIARY
OR
INTELLIGENCE SUMMARY
(Erase heading not required.)

Place	Date	Hour	Summary of Events and Information	Remarks and references to Appendices
			August 1916	
			10th Bn. Duke of Wellington's Regt.	
TRENCHES.	31-8-16 (cont.)		and all ranks in the front line had their helmets adjusted before 1-30 a.m. A noticeable feature of the gas attack was the entire absence of any noise or commotion in the enemy line. No Strombos horns, bugles or balls of any kind were heard. On the other hand a number of red very lights were sent up by the enemy. His artillery fire in retaliation to ours was almost ineffective. He seemed only to be doing damage to the actual front line trenches, the repairing of which has been carried out today. His machine-gun and rifle fire was apparently. It is thought that a certain number of his guns on our right became temporarily jammed from the effects of our gas. Since the operation, the enemy has been very quiet. The day is fine.

On the evening of the 22nd inst we received the following message from B.O.C. 69th Inf. Bde. "The Brigadier is much pleased to learn of the excellent work done by the Batt'n. last night in digging the new trench in front of the line." Copy of same received from G.K. Inf. Bde. dated 23-8-16. "Following telegram received from Division begins aaa Please convey my congratulations to all those who under your orders carried out the good work of digging and wiring the new trench in front of trenches 127 and 126 night of 21st and 22nd. aaa ." | 57. 58 |

W. Payne Lieut. Colonel.
Commanding 10th Batt'n. of Duke of Wellington's Regt.

MOVEMENT ORDER BY LIEUT. COLONEL S.S. HAYNE, COMMANDING, 10TH BATTALION, DUKE OF WELLINGTON'S REGIMENT.

1. The battalion relieves the 8th Yorks Regt. at SCOTTS REDOUBT today.

2. Starting Point: 2 p.m. Cross Roads RUE BAPAUME - RUE DAUSSY.
Route: BEECOURT WOOD - SAUSAGE VALLEY.
Dress: Full marching order, packs will be carried.
Order of march: "A" Coy.
                  "B" "
                  "C" "
                  "D" "
                  L. Gun Det.
                  H.Q.
                  Cookers and watercarts to follow in rear at intervals of 50 yards.
By platoons at 200 yards interval.

Mess baskets and officer's kits to be dumped by 1-30 p.m. outside Battalion H.Q. or Orderly Room. The Transport Officer will make necessary arrangement for collecting same and sending up to SUNKEN ROAD.
Advance party of 1 N.C.O. and 3 men from H.Q. and 1 N.C.O. & 4 men from each Company will parade outside Orderly Room at 1 p.m., under Lieut. Bolton, to take over bivouacs.
Each Company will take over same bivouacs as before and Advance Party will meet battalion on arrival.

3.8.16.

sd. H.W. Lester. 2/Lt. & Adjt.

69TH INFANTRY BRIGADE.   Copy No. 4
ORDER NO. 75.

7/8/1916.

1. The 69th Infantry Brigade less 69th Machine Gun Company and 69th Trench Mortar Battery will be relieved in the left Brigade area by 45th Infantry Brigade on August 8th 1916.

2. On relief, the Brigade will march to billets at BRESLE, via BECOURT - XALBERT - MILLENCOURT - LAVIEVILLE.

3. Reliefs will take place as per attached table. One guide per platoon and one for each Battalion Headquarters will be sent.

4. Certificates will be obtained from relieving Units as to satisfactory state of trenches or billets on handing over.

5. Units will send billeting parties in advance and representatives should meet the Staff Captain at 3 p.m. at the Town Major's office (if no Town Major, at the Mairie). BRESLE

6. All Transport lines, Quarter Master's store etc., are to be cleared by 4 p.m.
Transport not required to march with Units, will move under orders of Brigade Transport Officer.

7. Brigade Headquarters will close at CONTALMAISON at 5.30 p.m. and reopen at BRESLE at the same hour.

ACKNOWLEDGE.

X Troops will use emergency routes to SE of Town

Capt.,
Brigade Major,
69th Infantry Brigade.

Copy No. 1. 11th West Yorkshire Regt.
2. 8th Yorkshire Regt.
3. 9th Yorkshire Regt.
4. 10th West Riding Regt.
5. 69th Machine Gun Company.
6. 69th Trench Mortar Battery.
7. Brigade Signal Officer.
8. 192 Company A.S.C.
9. 23rd Division.
10. 45th Infantry Brigade.
11. 46th Infantry Brigade.
12. 12th Australian Brigade.
13. 69th Field Ambulance.
14. War Diary.
15. War Diary.
16. File.

MARCH TABLE.

Position.	Unit.	Relieved by.	Guides.
"A" Battalion.	8th Yorkshire Regt.	6/7th Royal Scots Fusiliers	ROUND WOOD at 1.30 p.m.
"B" Battalion.	11th West Yorkshire Regt.	11th Argyll & Sutherland Highrs.	BECOURT WOOD (X.25.d.5.5.)at 11 a.m.
"C" Battalion.	10th West Riding Regt.	13th Royal Scots	BECOURT WOOD (X.25.d.5.5.)at 10 a.m.
"D" Battalion.	9th Yorkshire Regt.	6th Cameron Highlanders	BECOURT WOOD (X.25.d.5.5.)at 9 a.m.

NOTE :- An Officer from each Unit should be detailed to accompany guides.

MOVEMENT ORDER BY LIEUT.COLONEL S.S. HAYNE,
COMMANDING,
10TH BATTALION, DUKE OF WELLINGTON'S REGIMENT.

1. The battalion moves on the 11th Inst. from MERICOURT to PONTREMY by train and from there it will march to billeting area, VAUCHELLES VAUCOURT - BUSSUS - BELLANCOURT - BYNGNY L'ABBE.

2. The whole of the transport will leave here tomorrow at 3 p.m. for ALLONVILLE via QUERRIEU in charge of Capt. J. KELSALL, Commanding 192nd. Coy. A.S.C.
On 11th at 8-30 a.m. the transport will move to billeting area, VAUCHELLES - VAUCOURT - BUSSUS - BELLANCOURT - BINGNY L'ABBE via ARGOEUVRES and FLEXICOURT.

3. All L. Gun and Signalling apparatus will be loaded on the two Lewis Gun limbers tomorrow morning.
The L.Gun section under 2/Lt. CLARKSON of 69th Trench Mortar Battery will leave here with all battalion handcarts (empty) at 3 p.m. tomorrow for POULAINVILLE. They will leave POULAINVILLE at 5 a.m. on the 11th for BOUCHON via ARGOEUVRES and FLEXICOURT.

4. Transport and L. Gun Section will carry unexpired portion of rations for 10th and rations for 11th.

5. All Officers valises and spare kits will be dumped tomorrow morning by noon at Q.M. Stores.
Mess baskets and small trench kits may be kept but it is pointed out that Companies must make their own arrangements for getting them to the station as no transport is available. Negotiations are proceeding for the hire of a French cart but this cannot be relied on.

6. O.C. Coys. will inspect their Companies at 9 a.m. tomorrow and send all men with clothing requiring changing or any deficiencies of helmets, waterproof sheets, etc. to Q.M. Stores under an Officer.
There will be a voluntary C. of E. Service at 10-30 a.m. tomorrow in the field behind L. Gun billets, followed by Celebration of Holy Communion at 11 a.m.

9.8.16.   sd. H.W. Lester. 2/Lt. & Adjt.

MOVEMENT ORDER BY LIEUT.COLONEL S.S. HAYNE,
COMMANDING,
10TH BATTALION, DUKE OF WELLINGTON'S REGIMENT.

1. The battalion will move today by train from PONTREMY to BAILLEUL. Train leaves at 8.28 p.m. tonight and arrives at 5.09 a.m. tomorrow morning.

2. The battalion will be drawn up at the Southern Exit of the village at 6 p.m. tonight.

3. Order of march - Hd. Qrs.
   Snipers.
   "B" Coy.
   "C" "
   "D" "
   "A" "

4. The Transport will leave the village at 4 p.m. for PONTREMY to entrain.
   Major Gill and 20 O.R. detailed by "A" Coy. will accompany transport to assist in entrainment and detrainment.

5. Mess baskets and Officers' kits will be dumped outside Q.M. Stores at 3 p.m. and will be loaded on Motor Lorry. Q.M. and other Stores to be dumped outside Q.M. Stores at 2 p.m. to be loaded on G.S. wagons.
   Sergt. Cook and 4 Pioneers to accompany Lorry to Station.

6. L. Gun Section will join the battalion on arrival at PONTREMY.

7. Dixies can be loaded on Motor Lorry at 5 p.m. which will enable the Battalion to have tea after transport leaves. Dixies to be packed in lots of six.

13.8.16.   SD. H.W. LESTER.   LIEUT. & ADJUTANT.

E

MARCH ORDERS BY LIEUT.COLONEL C.C. HAYNE,
COMMANDING,
10TH BATTALION, DUKE OF WELLINGTON'S REGIMENT.

Map Reference - 27 S.E.)
        28 S.W.) 1/20,000.
        36 N.W.)   16.5.16.

1. The battalion marches tomorrow to Bivouacs in STEENWERCK Area, A.10.A.16. and ~~Scattered~~ on the 18th to Reserve Brigade Area at CRESLOW to relieve Men 32nd R.F.

2. Starting point - Cross Roads 1,000 yards S. of Battalion H.Q. 1-30 p.m.
Route - METEREN - BAILLEUL - C.14.c.5.2. Level Crossing B.27.a.3.0.
Road Junction B.27.d.
Distance 8 miles.

3. Order of march - H.Q. Bombers, Snipers.
           "C" Coy.
           "D" "
           "A" "
           "B" "
           Lewis Gun Det.
           Transport.
2/Lt. F.H.C. Redington will be in charge of the whole of H.Q. Party.

4. Lewis Guns will be loaded on handcarts.

5. Officers' Kits will be dumped outside Battn. and Coy. H.Q. at 11 a.m. 2 G.S. wagons which will be arranged for by Transport Officer will call for them at above hour.
The Mess Cart will call at Battn. and Coy. H.Q. for Mess Baskets at 12-30 p.m.
Q.M. Stores will be loaded at 11 a.m. on L.Gun Limbers. Part of one G.S. wagon will be allotted if necessary.

6. Lt. G.R.C. Heale with one N.C.O. detailed by each Coy. and one by H.Q. and one by Transport will parade at Battn. H.Q. at 11-30 a.m. tomorrow at *illegible* and will proceed by motor bus from METEREN Cross Roads X.15.d.5.6? to 125th I.B. H.Q. B.10.a.5.5. They will report there at 2 p.m. and make themselves thoroughly conversant with all roads and localities in the part of the Reserve Brigade Area that concerns them. They will be at PONT D'ACHELLES at 6 a.m. on 18th Inst. to act as guides for the battn. Rations for 18th to be carried.

7. H.Q. and Transport Officer will each detail 1 O.R. and O.C. Coys. 1 N.C.O. to parade at H.Q. at 9 a.m. under 2/Lt. Kelly. They will proceed to STEENWERCK Area A.10. and A.16. to take over bivouacs for Battalion. Details will be issued separately.

8. Dinners will be eaten before marching off.

ROUTINE ORDERS.

O.C. Coys. and other Commands will ensure that all ranks possess at least one serviceable ~~helmet~~ gas helmet until the full complement is made up.

               sd. H. W. Lester. Lieut. & Adjt.

Major A.H. Gill.

March Orders by Lt. Col. S.S. Hayne
Commanding 10° Duke of Wellington's Rgt.
In the Field
17.8.16.

Map Ref.
36 NW } 1/20 000
28 SW }

1. The Batt. relieves the 32nd Royal Fus. in reserve trenches in PLOEG STEERT District. — Distance about 8 miles
2. Starting Point — A.10 central
   Time — 6-15 am
   Distance between Coys. 200 yds.
   Coys are responsible for keeping in touch with Company immediately in front of them.
   Order of march — H.Q, SNIPERS, BOMBERS
   "A" Coy
   "B" "
   "C" "
   "D" "
   Transport.
   2 L.B. to be allotted to each Coy & will march with respective Coys.
3. Guides will meet the Batt. at PONT d'ACHELLES
4. Officers kits & mess baskets will be dumped ready for loading at 5-45 am Transport officer will arrange for

2

2 G.S. wagons & Mess Cart to collect same.

4. G packs to be carried on hand-carts

5. Breakfast 5.15 am.
Orders with regard to dinners will be issued later.

__Routine__

1. Commencing tomorrow Battalion Bombers will be rationed & billeted with H.Q. party.

sd. H.W. Lester Lt & Adjt

SECRET.

With reference to working party for tomorrow night consisting of 350 men, it will be supplied and officered as follows :-

Major R.H. Gill - In charge.
Capt. H.G. Tunstill - Supervising Officer.

1.	2.
2/Lt.H.HARRIS.	2/Lt.F.H.C.REDINGTON.
5 N.C.Os.	5 N.C.Os.
50 men.	50 men.

"A" Coy. & Bombers.

3.	4.	5.	6.	7.
2/LT.D.L.EVANS.	2/LT.E.G.COSTELLO.	2/LT.HODGKINSON.	2/LT.H.KELLY.	2/LT.STAFFORD.
5 N.C.Os.	5 N.C.Os.	5 N.C.Os.	5 N.C.Os.	5 N.C.Os.
50 men.	50 men.	50 men.	50 men.	50 men.

"C" Coy. "B" Coy. "D" Coy. & L.Gunners.

Capt. Tunstill will see that the first two parties are complete.
Capt. Atkinson, Capt. Bull & Capt. Pereira, will arrange together for parties 3,4,5,6,7, completing the last party with L. Gunners.
As far as possible Officers should have men of their own company under them.
Each Officer will have a roster of his party.
Parties to be arranged by 10 a.m. tomorrow.
Major Gill with Capt. Tunstill will inspect parties at 11 a.m.

sd. H.W. LESTER LIEUT. & ADJT.

20.8.16.

MARCH ORDERS BY LIEUT.COLONEL S.S. HAYNE, COMMDG.,
10TH BATTALION, DUKE OF WELLINGTON'S REGIMENT.

Map Ref. 28.S.W.) 1/20,000
" "   36 N.W.)
                                                                     22.8.16.

1. The battalion will be relieved by the 11th West Yorks Regt. at 4 p.m. this afternoon, and proceed to huts at RUE DE SAC.

2. H.Q., O.C. Coys. & L. Gun Det. will each detail an N.C.O. to parade at Battn. H.Q. at 1-30 under Lt. Bolton and proceed to RUE DE SAC as an Advance Party.

3. There will be two dumps for Officers' kits and Mess baskets - Battn. H.Q. and LE TOUQUET BERTHE. G.S. Wagons and Mess Cart will be at these dumps at 2 p.m. when everything will be ready for loading.

4. As soon as relieved O.C. Coys. will notify H.Q. as follows :- D.10.
                                                                                time (4.10
                                                                                          p.m
                                                                               "A" Coy.

and will wait for orders to move off.
Distance between platoons 100 yards.

5. Steel Helmets to be worn.

6. Teas on arrival at RUE DE SAC. Cookers will proceed there as soon as horses arrive.

22.8.16.   sd. H.W. Lester. Lieut. & Adjt.

OPERATION ORDERS BY LIEUT. COLONEL S.S. HAYNE,
COMMANDING, 10TH BATTN. DUKE OF WELLINGTON'S REGIMENT.

Map Ref. 28 S.W.4. 1/10,000   In the Field.
                                                                                24.8.16.

1. The battalion will relieve 8th K.O.Y.L.I. in the front line on 25th Inst. and will hold trenches 122 - 127 between U.21.b.7.9. and U.14.b.8.5. The line will be held "A" "B" "C" "D" - 4 Coys. in the front line.

2. Route - Romarin ROMARIN - PLOUGSTEERT Road - New Road from T.30.d.5.6. to U.25.a.5.3. Guides will meet the battalion at U.25.a.5.3.

3. Order of march -   L. Gun Det.
                         "A" Coy.
                         "D"   "
                         "B"   "
                         "C"   "
                         Hd.Qrs.
L. Gun Det. to leave H.Q. at 3 a.m.
Distance 200 yards between ½ Coys.

4. All the Snipers and 16 of H.Q. bombers will rejoin their Coys. and will be rationed by their respective Coys. tomorrow.

5. O.C. Coys. & L. Gun & Bombing Officer, together with one N.C.O. from each Command will be at PROWSE POINT at 2 p.m. this afternoon to inspect the line and take over trench stores.
A copy of Lists of Trench Stores taken over to be rendered to Orderly Room by 6 p.m. this evening.

6. Mess Cart and a limber will call at Battn. & Coy. H.Q. at 2 a.m. for Mess baskets, Officers' trench kits.
These will be dumped at HYDE PARK CORNER and Officers can send their servants on ahead to carry them up.
Remainder of Officers' kit will be dumped outside Battn. & Coy. H.Q. by 6 p.m. this evening. Transport Officer will arrange to collect it and take to Q.M. Stores.

7. O.C. Coys. will arrange for tea for all ranks at 2 a.m.

24.8.16.   sd. H.W. Lester. Lieut. & Adjt.

OPERATION ORDERS BY LT. COLONEL S.S. HAYNE,
COMMANDING,
10TH BATTALION, DUKE OF WELLINGTON'S REGIMENT.

1. Wind permitting Gas will be liberated from trenches 96 to 104, 113 to 117, and 121 to 124.
Smoke will be interspersed along the front line from LT TOU/682 to 124.
The gas will last from zero to zero plus 20 and then cease altogether.

2. At zero plus 4 the Artillery and T.Ms. will bombard hostile trenches until zero plus 38.

3. Raiding parties of this Brigade (not this Battn) will go out after the gas has ceased from :-

   (a). U.21.B.60.57.
   (b). Between U.21.B.75.55 and U.21.B.9.7.
   (c). U.15.A.5.7.

A raiding party will also go out from the battalion on our left. O.C. "D" Coy. will be advised in due course of this.

4. Zero time will be 1.30 a.m. on 30th Inst.
This will be confirmed according to wind conditions at 10 p.m. today by telephone, thus :-
   (a). If the wind is favourable by   - "YES".
   (b). If the wind is not favourable by - "NO".

Should the wind change after "YES" has been sent the word to cancel will be - ("The answer is now "NO").

Everything else concerning this operation will be by Code or Runner.

5. When Gas is being discharged all troops in front line system will wear Gas Helmets.
The bays in which the cylinders are situated will be evacuated during the discharge and the men kept in the traffic or support trench close behind. The trenches from which only smoke is being discharged need not be evacuated.

6. A Vickers Gun will be in trench 124 in charge of 2/Lt. MARSH and it will co-operate in every way with Infantry Officer in charge of trench.

7. Helmets will not be taken off until an Officer or N.C.O. who has been through a Gas School course has been consulted and they will then be worn in the "Alert Position".

8. Two Stokes Guns will fire on FACTORY FARM from zero plus 15 to zero plus 30 and two guns on U.19.B.5.3. at above time.

29.3.16.   sd. H.W. LESTER, LIEUT. & ADJT.

WAR DIARY or **INTELLIGENCE SUMMARY**

Army Form C. 2118.

September 1916. 10th Batt. Duke of Wellington's Regt.

Place	Date	Hour	Summary of Events and Information	Remarks and references to Appendices
Front line Thiepval	1/9/16		Operations – Gas attacks and raid were being carried out by the 26th Division who are on our left commencing at 1-30 A.M. The first warning signal received by the enemy were two whistle blasts and came from the direction of BARRICADE AVENUE at 1-45 A.M. immediately afterwards Very lights and flares were sended and their sent to search (it is generally thought that these alarms were sent) from some distance behind their front line system. There was the usual amount of Machine gun fire during the night from the enemy who also sent about 20 T.M. shells at our line without doing damage. The day is dull but there has been no rain. The enemy is using more trench mortar shells than usual. Our artillery have at intervals during the day opposite our immediate front, have appeared to be answerd at in our rear lines.	

Army Form C. 2118.

WAR DIARY
or
INTELLIGENCE SUMMARY

(Erase heading not required.)

55.

Place	Date	Hour	Summary of Events and Information	Remarks and references to Appendices
	7/9/16		Received orders from the 69th Inf Bde, regarding a relief the 11th West Yorks Regt. Coming to relieve us at 9. a.m. We remove to the reserve trenches in PLOEGSTEERT WOOD: which had been occupied by the beforementioned Batt. This information was passed round to all Coates Copy marked "A" attached. The night passed very quietly. Relief completed at 10 a.m. There was some aeroplane activity during the afternoon. Our Casualties during his tour in the trenches was as follows:- 2 O.R. Killed 2 O.R. Died of wounds >1 " wounded 1 " accidently wounded	

WAR DIARY or INTELLIGENCE SUMMARY

Army Form C. 2118.

Place	Date	Hour	Summary of Events and Information	Remarks and references to Appendices
RESERVE TRENCHES	3/9/16		Dull day. Artillery on both sides quiet. Whilst in our present position we find working parties of 160 men strong who are under the supervision of R.E's. Received orders during the afternoon that the Brigade (69th) women, we relieved by the 56th Inf Bde (19 Donnan) on the 4th inst. Orders regarding move of the Battn were duly issued & all confirmed (copy marked "B" attached) to the effect that we — The Battn is to be relieved by the 7th South Lancs Regt. We have also received a notification to the effect that we shall move to the 2nd ANZAC TRAINING AREA. During the night we had 3 men wounded as a result of enemy shell fire.	5/.
	4/9/16		Dull day. Preparations for relief were carried out as per above mentioned order marked "B". Relief commenced at 5 p.m. The Battn marched to its new billets in Comprise, the last company reporting its arrival about 9 p.m. During the late afternoon and evening	

WAR DIARY or INTELLIGENCE SUMMARY

Army Form C. 2118.

Place	Date	Hour	Summary of Events and Information	Remarks and references to Appendices
	4/9/16 cont.		here were a comfort train. Nothing further to report.	
	5/9/16		Received orders to make ready for a further move to billets at EPERLECQUES on the 6th inst. These orders were duly carried out as ordered. Copy marked "C" attached. The remainder of the day the men were engaged in cleaning, making preparation for the move. During the night the guns were busy, nothing further to report.	
	6/9/16		The Batt. formed up at 9 am and marched to BIALUEL station, entrained, and arrived at SS OMER at 10's am. A march of about 7 miles brought us to our destination at EPERLECQUES at 3pm. The whole Batt. was comfortably billeted, nothing further to report.	
	7/9/16 to 9/9/16		During this period the Batt. has been practised on the miniature range. The companies on an average firing 300 rounds. Musketry practice and handling of arms. Allirbon that also been part	

WAR DIARY or INTELLIGENCE SUMMARY

Place	Date	Hour	Summary of Events and Information	Remarks and references to Appendices
	1st/9/16 to 11/9/16		to cleanliness of all equipment and improvement as far as possible to general smartness, short route marches (am) physical training has also been indulged in. The weather has been good. (Received) orders that the Battn would hold itself in readiness to move to the army of the Line on the 10th inst. On the evening of the 9th a definite order was received for the move. Were would copy marked "D" attached. Still day. Preparation for move proceeding, we leave EPERLECQUES as per orders of mine preceding day, arrived at LONGEAU at 6.30 am 11th inst. The Battn formed up and was marched to Hells at COISY a distance of 8 miles. Received orders from the 69th Inf Bde that the Battn would proceed to HEMENCOURT WOOD tomorrow the 12th inst. This information was duly passed to all Coys. Copy marked "E" attached	
	7/9/16		The Battn formed up and marched to HEMENCOURT the distance being 10 miles, we arrived at Hulls at 3pm The Battn marches well, only a	

WAR DIARY or INTELLIGENCE SUMMARY

Army Form C. 2118.

Place	Date	Hour	Summary of Events and Information	Remarks and references to Appendices
	13/9/16 to 14/9/16		a few cases of men falling out on the line of march are reported. The N.C.O's and men are billeted in huts/tents, the officers in bell tents. Dull and rainy. The artillery can be heard in the distance. The Batt. has been subjected to a thorough inspection of arms, equipment, ammunition and gas helmets. Some physical training has been practised. During the 14th we received orders to hold ourselves ready to move at short notice.	
	15/9/16 to 17/9/16		Dull day. Orders were received about 12 noon that the Batt. would move as soon as possible. This order was amended to why the Batt. being formed up within the hour, and marched to MELLINCOURT arriving there about 7 p.m. During this period nearer information have been had. The Batt. doubtful have been practised in turning live bombs. During the evening of the 17th we received orders to move the Batt. on the morning of the 18th. The 23rd Division to relieve the 15th Division at O.L.I. releiving the 8/10 Gordons in the support trenches accordingly. Orders were issued accordingly.	

WAR DIARY or INTELLIGENCE SUMMARY

Army Form C. 2118.

Place	Date	Hour	Summary of Events and Information	Remarks and references to Appendices
	18/9/16		The day has turned out very wet and cold, by the time our situation was reached all ranks were in a sorry condition. The relief was completed by 7 pm. There is little urgent accommodation. Consequently the Battn is placed in a comfortable position. Much good work was done to improve things during our stay in these trenches.	
	19/9/16		The enemy shelled our position during the day causing a few casualties. The wet weather is still maintained. The enemy is also dull.	
	20/9/16		The weather has become much brighter, the Aeroplanes from both sides were soon at it, we found carrying parties for no front line during the day.	
	21/9/16		Much aeroplane activity. The enemy sent a few shells into our position causing us a few casualties. Received orders that the Brigade would be relieved by the 6'8'3 Brigade, we being ordered to move back to SHELTER WOOD and chocolate wallah. We have supplied a burying party for the burial of 2 British & 21 German soldiers. Relief was worked completed about 7 pm.	

2449 Wt. W14957/M90 750,000 1/16 J.B.C. & A. Forms/C.2118/12.

Army Form C. 2118.

WAR DIARY
or
INTELLIGENCE SUMMARY

(Erase heading not required.)

Instructions regarding War Diaries and Intelligence Summaries are contained in F. S. Regs., Part II. and the Staff Manual respectively. Title Pages will be prepared in manuscript.

Place	Date	Hour	Summary of Events and Information	Remarks and references to Appendices
	25/9/16		Fine day and much warmer. The usual artillery in the air, and nothing of importance is happening in our present sector.	
	26/9/16		Weather still continues fine. Our heavy artillery is very busy. The lighter guns can fire to hand in the air have. We found a working party of 750 strong, men being employed on road repairing.	
	27/9/16		Arrangements have been made for the whole of the Batt. to bathe, all men were appropriated some new tunics & clean underclothing. Our heavy guns are very active during the afternoon and early evening. An enemy shell in vicinity of Batt. Headquarters. It is enemy shell in replying to our battery generally. Thought we who shell very close to the H.Q.'s. Men he sent one heavy shell very close [...] killed and one man who he would that he was wounded.	
	28/9/16		The good weather is maintained. The enemy artillery is unusually quiet. Received orders from the 69th Brigade to relieve a Batt. of the 70th Brigade tonight. Orders were duly issued	

WAR DIARY
or
INTELLIGENCE SUMMARY

Army Form C. 2118.

Place	Date	Hour	Summary of Events and Information	Remarks and references to Appendices
Front	26/9/16		1. All Enemies Copy marked "J" attached. Our Artillery has again been active throughout. Have but Artillery has nothing to report.	
	27/9/16		Weather good, we found a working party of 150 men who were employed until he guidance of the R.E. Airplane still active in both sides, some rain fell during the evening.	
	28/9/16		Day fine, he usual aeroplane activity, also artillery. Otherwise nothing to report.	
	29/9/16		Weather fine. Enemy moved cool. Our artillery carried out a bombardment on a large scale commencing during the early part of the day and continuing throughout the night. We found a party of 150 men for road repairing.	

Place	Date	Hour	Summary of Events and Information	Remarks and references to Appendices
	30/9/16		Weather somewhat improved, still cold, no rain. Received orders from the 69th Bn Bde to move up to GOURLEY TRENCH in the morning. This information was duly passed to all concerned copy marked "G" attached.	
	1/10/16			

(Sgd) W D Dunn
Lieut Colonel
Commanding 1st Battalion
Duke of Wellingtons Regt

MOVEMENT ORDER BY LIEUT. COLONEL S.S. HAYNE,
COMMANDING,
10TH BATTALION, DUKE OF WELLINGTON'S REGIMENT.

1. The battalion will be relieved by the 11th West Yorks Regt. tomorrow at 9 a.m.

2. A, B, C, & D Coys. will be relieved respectively by A, B, C, & D Coys. 11th West Yorks and will proceed to reserve trenches occupied at present by those Coys. Lewis Gunners will proceed with the Coys. to which they are at present attached.

   The new positions for Coys. are as follows :-

   "A" COY.   ST. ANDREW'S DRIVE.
   "B" "   HUNTER'S AVENUE. (DEAD HORSE CORNER).
   "C" "   Just beyond GLOSTER HOUSE.
   "D" "   GLOSTER HOUSE.

3. Guides will be provided as follows :-

   "A" COY.   4 guides at ST. ANDREW'S AVENUE at 9 a.m. to report to O.C. "A" Coy. 11th West Yorks.

   "B" COY.   4 guides at DEAD HORSE CORNER at 9 a.m. to report to O.C. "B" Coy. 11th West Yorks.

   "C" COY.   4 guides at DEAD HORSE CORNER at 9-20 a.m. to report to O.C. "C" Coy. 11th West Yorks.

   "D" COY.   4 guides at PROWSE POINT at 9 a.m. to report to O.C. "D" Coy. 11th West Yorks.

   1 guide from each Lewis Gun to be at DEAD HORSE CORNER at 8-30 am. in charge of Sergt. Roberts to conduct the Lewis Gunners of 11th West Yorks.
   Lewis Gunners, when relieved, will immediately rejoin the Coy. to which they are attached and move out with that Coy.
   O.C. Coys. and L.Gun Sergeant will ensure that guides are fully cognizant of the route to be taken.

4. Companies, on being relieved, will obtain guides from the respective Coys. of the West Yorks which have relieved them and proceed by half-Coys. at 100 yards distance, without further instructions to the new positions. O.C. Coys. to telephone H.Q. before moving off.

5. Care will be taken that trenches are left clean and that all water tins are full when handing over.

6. The West Yorks Rxegt. will leave 1 N.C.O. per Coy. and 1 N.C.O. for H.Q. to hand over stores, etc., to this battalion on arrival. After handing over they will rejoin their regiment.

7. Officers who require additional kit may send their servants to Q.M. Stores. A limber will be provided for bringing it up and will leave Q.M. Stores at 3 p.m. tomorrow.

sd. H.W. LESTER. LIEUT. & ADJUTANT.

1.9.16.

MARCH ORDERS BY LIEUT.COLONEL S.G. HAYNE,
COMMANDING,
10TH BATTALION, DUKE OF WELLINGTON'S REGIMENT.

Ref. Map 36.S.W. 1/20,000.   In the Field.
     36.N.W. 1/20,000.   3.9.16.

1. The battalion will be relieved tomorrow by 7th South Lancs. Regt. and proceed to billets in C.27. at present occupied by 13th D.L.I.

2. Four guides per Company and one from H.Q. will be at Road Junction U.29.a.6.3. at 6-40 p.m. to meet the incoming battalion.

3. On being relieved O.C. Coys. will telephone H.Q. and wait for orders to move off.
   Distance 200 yards between half-companies as far as PONT D'ACHELLES where the battalion will close up to 100 yards between Coys.

4. All Officers' spare kits will be dumped at G.P.R. terminus at 11-30 am. Mess baskets at the same place at 6-15 p.m.
   Transport Officer to arrange for necessary transport, including Maltese cart at 6-15 p.m.
   Officers' servants may be sent on with Mess Cart and will be marched to new billets by Sergt: Cooke. (H.Q.)

5. Transport Officer will arrange to have all transport, including Mess and Maltese Carts, at new billets by 5 p.m.
   Quartermaster will have tea ready for battalion on arrival.

6. Advance Party, consisting of 1 N.C.O. from H.Q., 1 N.C.O. from each Coy. who can ride bicycles, will parade at bottom of STRAND at 8 a.m. under Mr. R. Colton and proceed to billets where they are due at 9 a.m.
   N.C.O. in charge of Signallers will see that 5 bicycles are at the bottom of the STRAND at 8 a.m.

7. All maps 1/10,000 FLORENBURGE will be handed over to incoming Unit. Receipts for all trench stores etc. to be obtained, a copy to be returned to Orderly Room by 8 p.m. This also applies to Quartermaster and Transport.

8. Officers' chargers will be at the bottom of STRAND at 5 p.m.

9. All water tins to be left full.

10. L.Gunners will march out with Coys. they are at present attached to.

3.9.16.   sd. H.V. LISTER, LIEUT. & ADJT.

"C"

MARCH ORDERS BY LIEUT.COLONEL. S.S. HAYNE,
COMMANDING,
10TH BATTALION, DUKE OF WELLINGTON'S REGIMENT.

MAIN

1. The battalion will march to BAILLEUL Station tomorrow and entrain for ST. OMER. From ST. OMER it will proceed to billets at STERLACQUES.

2. Reveille will be at 6 a.m.
   The battalion will be drawn up in mass on Parade Ground facing S.E. at 8 a.m.

3. Train leaves BAILLEUL at 9-28 a.m. and arrives at ST. OMER at 10-48 am

4. Cookers, Mess Cart, Water Carts, 1 G.S. Limber, containing L.Gunners packs, will leave Transport Lines under Corpl. Brown at 8-15 a.m. and proceed to entrain at BAILLEUL WEST Station. Train leaves there at 11-28 a.m. and arrives at ST. OMER at 12-49 p.m.

5. Lewis Gun handcarts will accompany battalion.

6. Mess baskets will be dumped outside H.Q. Mess at 7-30 a.m.
   Orders about Officers' kits will be sent on later.

7. O.C. "A" Coy. will detail two men to act as M.F.P. and one sanitary man to report to Capt. GRIMSHAW, 11th West Yorks, at MAIN BAILLEUL Station at 8-25 a.m.
   O.C. "B" "C" & "D" Coys. will each detail 4 men and "B" Coy. 1 N.C.O. in addition to parade outside Orderly Room at 7-30 a.m. and proceed to BAILLEUL WEST Station and report to Lieut. KNOWLES, 11th West Yorks Regt., to act as entraining party for cookers, mess cart, etc.

8. O.C. Coys. will inspect all packs before parade and see that nothing is carried outside ordinary kit. All parcels etc. must be sent by Lorry which will be provided for Officers' kits.

9. Haversack rations to be carried and water bottles full.

10. Major R.H. GYL will proceed this afternoon and inspect approaches to station and will be at MAIN Station tomorrow morning one hour before arrival of battalion to arrange entrainment.

sd. H.W. LESTER, LIEUT. and ADJT.

5.9.16.

MARCH ORDERS BY LIEUT. COLONEL S.S. HAYNE,
COMMANDING,
10TH BATTALION, DUKE OF WELLINGTON'S REGIMENT.

Map Ref. 27.a. N.E.   In the Field.
1/20,000.   9.9.16.

1. The battalion will march tomorrow to AUDRUICQ and entrain there for LONGNEAU. Train leaves AUDRUICQ at 10-39 p.m.

2. Starting Point: "A" Coy. H.Q. on the GANSPETTE - OUEST MONT Road.
   Time: 6-55 p.m.
   Order of march: H.Q., Bombers, Snipers.
                   "A" Coy.
                   "B" "
                   "C" "
                   "D" "
                   L.Gun Det. with handcarts.
                   Quartermaster.

   Route: OUEST MONT, Cross Roads in FORET D'EPERLECQUES - MUNCQ NIEURLET- POLINCOVE BLANC BOUILLON.

3. Transport will leave EPERLECQUES at 5-10 p.m. for AUDRUICQ and follow the above route. Breast ropes for horse trucks must be supplied by Transport Officer.

4. O.C. Coys. to detail 7 men per Coy. and "A" & "B" Coys. one N.C.O. per Coy. in addition to march under 2/Lt. J.E.L. PAYNE with the Transport to AUDRUICQ to help to entrain it. They will parade ready to march off at 5 p.m. outside "A" Coy. H.Q. and will meet the Transport at the Cross Roads at OUEST-MONT. 2/LT. PAYNE will obtain from the Orderly Room at 4-30 p.m. Battalion Entraining State which he will hand over to R.T.O. on arrival at AUDRUICQ.

5. Officers' kits and mess baskets will be dumped outside respective H.Q. at 3-30 p.m. ready for loading. Transport Officer to arrange for G.S. wagons and mess cart to call for it.

6. Rations for 10th will be carried on the man.
7. Officers' chargers to accompany battalion to station.
8. 2/Lt. J.K. SNOWDEN will march behind the battalion with one N.C.O. detailed from each Coy. to prevent stragglers.

9.9.16.
                                    sd. H.W. LESTER. LIEUT. & ADJUTANT.

ROUTINE ORDERS.

Orderly Officer for tomorrow ... 2/Lt. W.C. Evans.

1. Sick Parade 9 a.m.

2. **CHURCH PARADE.** R.Cs. will parade outside "A" Coys. Mess at 9-45 a.m. and will be marched to EPERLECQUES Church by the Orderly Officer.

   C. of E. Service at 12 noon in Orchard behind "A" Coy. H.Q. Capt. J.C. Bull will command the parade and two subalterns per Coy. to attend.

3. All Estaminets will be "out of bounds" after 1 p.m. tomorrow.

9.9.16.
                                    sd. H.W. LESTER. Liuet. & Adjt.

MARCH ORDERS BY LIEUT.COLONEL S.S.HAYNE,
COMMANDING,
10TH BATTALION, DUKE OF WELLINGTON'S REGIMENT.

REF. MAPS. AMIENS 17. 1/100,000.
ALBERT 1/40,000.

1. The battalion will march to HENENCOURT WOOD tomorrow. Distance about 12 miles.
   Starting Point: On Road South of Y in COISY.
   Time: 8-20 a.m.
   Route: RAINNEVILLE - Cross Roads North of M in MOLLIENS - Cross Riads ½ mile North of G in MONTIGNY - HENENCOURT - BAIZEUX - HENENCOURT.
   Order of March: H.Q., Bombers, Snipers, "B", "C", "D", "A", L.Gun Det. Transport 1st & 2nd Line.

2. Advance party consisting of 1 N.C.O. from H.Q., 1 N.C.O. from each Coy. will parade under 2/Lt. KELLY at H.Q. at 8 a.m. and proceed to on bicycles to HENENCOURT WOOD and meet the Staff Captain at the entrance of the WOOD on the HENENCOURT WARLOY Road about V.26.b.

3. Officers' kits, mess baskets, and stores, will be dumped outside Battn.H.Q., Coy. H.Q. & Q.M. Stores by 7-15 a.m. TRANSPORT Officer will arrange to collect same.

4. Dinners will be en route.

5. Baggage wagons will proceed to new billets; the horses will then proceed to the Train Lines at BRESLE.

6. All N.C.O's. and men who do not carry packs will be dressed in "fighting order", i.e., haversack on the back.

11.9.16.　　　　　　　　　　sd. H.W. LESTER. LIEUT. & ADJUTANT.

"A" Form.
MESSAGES AND SIGNALS.

Army Form C.2121 (in pads of 100).

TO: Operation Order by Lt Col S.S. Hayne Comg 10th Duke of Wellington Regt

Day of Month: 18th

AAA

1. The Battn will march out of MILLENCOURT this morning and relieve 8/10th Gordon Highlanders in left support trenches tonight.
Starting point E. end of MILLENCOURT.
Time 10.10 am   Route ALBERT BEECOURT CONTALMAISON
Order of march HQ SNIPERS, BOMBERS A.B.C.D. L.G.
The Battn will halt for dinners & tea beyond BEECOURT

2. Transport Cookers, water cart, mess cart, maltese cart and French kit limber will follow Battn. Remainder of transport proceeds to E.3.C.2.2.

3. Mess baskets & Officers trench kit must be outside Battn and Coy H.Q. by 9.30 am. Transport Officer to collect same.

4. Officers not proceeding to trenches will join Transport lines here at 9.45 am.

5. 200 yds distance to be maintained between Coys from start.

From:

"A" Form.
MESSAGES AND SIGNALS.

Army Form C.2121 (in pads of 100).

Prefix	Code	m. Words	Charge	This message is on a/c of:	Recd. at .... m.
Office of Origin and Service Instructions.		Sent		.... Service.	Date ....
		At .... m.			From ....
		To			
		By		(Signature of "Franking Officer.")	By ....

TO

Sender's Number.	Day of Month.	In reply to Number.	
*			A A A

6. Steel Helmets can be carried on the pack until after Kit.

Toronto
Adj.

From			
Place			
Time			

Operation order by Lt Col SS Hayne
Commdg. 10th Duke of Wellingtons.

In the field
26.9.16

1. The Brigade moves into support tonight and the Battn moves to PEAKE WOOD at 6 pm.

2. Two L.G. will be attached to each Coy before moving off.
   A Coy will leave present quarters at 6 pm
   B   "   "   "   6.10 pm
   C   "   "   "   6.20 "
   D   "   "   "   6.30 "

   OC Coys will synchronise watches with H.Q. at 5.30 pm & will notify H.Q. on moving off.

3. Trench kits only will be taken by Officers & valises will be stacked outside C.Coy. H.Q. at 5 pm. Ration limbers will take them back to Transport Lines.
   One limber will take mens baskets & trench kits at same hour to new quarters.

4. The following officers will return this evening to Transport Lt R BOLTON, 2Lt F W MILLWARD 2Lt D L EVANS 2Lt G S ISAACS. Before doing so they will remain in present quarters with one NCO per Coy until incoming unit has taken over & they will obtain receipts for all kits and tarpaulins from incoming unit which NCOs will ~~return~~ bring to Batt HQ.

5. Packs will be carried and steel helmets worn

6. Cookers & watercarts will accompany Battn to PEAKE WOOD

8. Movement to new quarters will be by platoons at 200 yds distance

Leslie
Lt
Adjt.

Operation Order by Lt Col S.S. Hayne
Commanding 10th (S) Batt West Riding
Regt.

In the Field
30.9.16

1. The Batt proceeds at 9 am to GOURLAY TRENCH.

2. A Coy will leave present quarters at 9 am
   B Coy   -"-   9 am
   C Coy   -"-   9.20 "
   D Coy   -"-   9.30 "

Distance 200yds between platoons.
Watches will be synchronised with
Batt HQ at 8.30 am.

3. Advance party of 1 2.Co from HQ
& 4 2 COs per Coy will parade
at Batt HQ under 2nd Lt PAYNE
at 7.30. am & proceed to GOURLAY
TRENCH. They will meet the
Batt at 9 am at the CUTTING.

4. L.G. will proceed with Coys.

5. Steel hats will be worn & pack carried.

~~French kit & mess baskets will be dumped at Batt HQ or A Coy HQ ready for loading at 8.30 am.~~

6. One officer and one N.C.O. per Coy will remain in present quarters until incoming Batt takes over. Receipts for kits, tarpaulin to be obtained & returned to Orderly Room.

7. French kits & mess baskets will be dumped at 8.30 am as follows:-
   B Coy & HQ at Batt HQ
   A, C, & D Coys at A Coy HQ.

   [signature]
   Adj.

To
    Headquarters, 69th. Infantry Brigade.

    Herewith please find War Diary for the 10th. Battalion Duke of Wellington's West Riding Regiment for the month of October, 1916.

                                      Lieut.-Colonel
                                            Commanding
            10th. Battn. Duke of Wellington's Regiment.

.11.1916.

Army Form C. 2118.

WAR DIARY

INTELLIGENCE SUMMARY

1/ 10th Bn. Duke of Wellington's Regt.
October 1916.

(Erase heading not required.)

Instructions regarding War Diaries and Intelligence Summaries are contained in F. S. Regs., Part II. and the Staff Manual respectively. Title Pages will be prepared in manuscript.

Place	Date	Hour	Summary of Events and Information	Remarks and references to Appendices
GOURLEY TRENCH	1-10-16		The Battalion left PEAKE WOOD for GOURLEY TRENCH in the morning. During the afternoon a heavy bombardment was carried out by our guns in preparation for an attack by the 70th Brigade. Word was received later that they had gained their objectives. Day fine.	
	2-10-16 to 4-10-16		Orders received from Brigade that Battalion would proceed to front line on 2nd inst., the 69th. Infantry Brigade relieving the 70th and our battalion relieving the 8th K.O.Y.L.I. Orders were issued to Companies as per attached copy marked "A". The relief was very much delayed owing to congestion in the trenches and was not complete until just before daybreak.	"A"
	5-10-16		Orders were received on the morning of the 5th that the latter would be relieved by the 11th West York. Regt. and orders were issued as per copy marked "B" attached. It took until the early hours of	"B"
	6-10-16		the morning to complete the relief. On the 6th inst. the news reached as much as possible but a few carrying parties had to be found for the front line.	
LE SARS			Late at night orders were received that the battalion would proceed to support the 11th West Yorks. Regt. in the attack on LE SARS.	
	8-10-16		On the night of the 8th. the 15th. Division relieved the 23rd Division, our battalion being relieved by the 6th Cameron Highlanders. The battalion on relief proceeded to ROUND WOOD.	
ROUND WOOD.			Reports on operations carried out by the Battalion from 1st to 8th October are attached marked "C" and "D". Our total Casualties for this period are:- Officers - 3 killed, 4 wounded, 1 Shell Shock. O.R. - 38 killed, 104 wounded, 10 Missing, 21 Shell Shock.	"C" "D"
ALBERT	9-10-16		1st of 23rd Division Special Order of September attached. The battalion moved to fifth of August attached. Received a warning order from 69th Inf. Bde. that the Division is to be temporarily transferred to the 10th Corps and move to	

Army Form C. 2118.

WAR DIARY
INTELLIGENCE SUMMARY

10th Bn. Duke of Wellington's Regt.

October 1916.

(Erase heading not required.)

Place	Date	Hour	Summary of Events and Information	Remarks and references to Appendices
ALBERT.	10.10.16		AILLY - LE - HAUT CLOCHER area on the 11th and 12th inst. 69th Brigade will probably move by tactical train on the 11th inst and 68th and 70th. on 12th. inst. Transport will move by road probably the day before. Further that the division would send advance billeting parties to POPERINGHE in preparation for the move of the division to that area on the 15th. inst. The day spent quietly, the men resting as much as possible. Each man had a bath and a clean change of clothing. Received orders late at night that the Transport would move by road tomorrow, also that a billeting party of one officer and 14 O.R. would proceed by train tomorrow to BUIGNY L'ABBÉ.	
	11.10.16		Very fine. The Brigade were inspected in the morning by General Sir H. S. Rawlinson Bart. K.C.B., K.C.V.O. commanding Fourth Army. Received orders from Brigade that the Battalion would entrain tomorrow at ALBERT for LONGPRÉ and proceed to BUIGNY - L'ABBÉ immediately after detrainment. Orders as per copy marked "E" were issued to companies. During the morning orders were also received that the Battalion would move from BUIGNY - L'ABBÉ to YVRENCH tomorrow and orders as per copy marked "F" were issued to companies. It was nearly 7 p.m. before all the Battn. got away from ALBERT and it was found that there was a great congestion on the railway and no one seemed to know exactly what was the cause. All trains were very much delayed and it was 8 a.m. on the 13th. inst. when "A" & "B" Companies arrived at LONGPRÉ and almost 2 a.m. on the 14th when "C" & "D" Companies and Headquarter party arrived there. On the 13th. inst. C, D & Headquarters had no rations so everything was rushing them at their destination. Owing to this delay it was decided to take the Battalion straight to YVRENCH and motor buses were at the Station waiting to take the Battalion there.	"E". "F".
LONGPRÉ	12.10.16			

Army Form C. 2118.

Instructions regarding War Diaries and Intelligence Summaries are contained in F.S. Regs., Part II. and the Staff Manual respectively. Title Pages will be prepared in manuscript.

WAR DIARY
INTELLIGENCE SUMMARY

(Erase heading not required.)

10th Bn. Duke of Wellingtons Regt.

October 1916.

Place	Date	Hour	Summary of Events and Information	Remarks and references to Appendices
YVRENCH.	14-10-16.		The day was spent quietly resting, and orders for our move to the Northern area were issued as per copy marked "G" attached.	"G"
POPERINGHE.	15-10-16.		The Battalion entrained up to time and HOUPOUTRE was reached about 3 p.m. The Battalion marched into POPERINGHE where billets were occupied.	
	16-10-16. 17-10-16.		The day was spent cleaning up & inspection of equipment, clothing &c. In the morning the Battalion was inspected by the Brigadier-General who afterwards gave a short speech congratulating the Battalion on its fine work on the SOMME front. He also spoke of the work which was to be done in the trenches we are about to take over.	
	18-10-16.		A wet day. During the morning the Battalion was placed at the disposal of Company Commanders for drill, inspection &c. After dinner the men were at liberty to do as they pleased.	
	19-10-16 to 22-10-16.		Nothing particular was done during these days. The weather was very fine but cold. A new Gas respirator was issued to all ranks, who were daily instructed in the use of same. Received orders on the 22nd that the 69th Brigade would relieve the 68th Brigade in the line on the night of the 23rd. Orders for the relief were issued to all concerned as per attached copy marked "H"	"H"
TRENCHES (YPRES SALIENT).	23-10-16. 24-10-16.		Left POPERINGHE rather later than schedule - at about 7 o'clock - owing at YPRES very quickly. There was some little delay in leaving the Station we were further delayed by the darkness & difficulty of the track. We relieved the 13th Battalion Durham Light Infantry & completed relief about 1.30 a.m. The men were comfortable in the shelters & dugouts in the trenches. These are very good shelters, but, generally, not too well protected in the event of any heavy shelling. The Sector is, however, remarkably quiet with only an occasional shell passing over & an exchange of a few machine gun & rifle bullets each night.	
	25-10-16.		Nothing of a serious nature has transpired. Since we arrived here the weather has been generally dull & soft. Wind generally S.S.W. to S.S.E. Our men have done very much work in strengthening the parapets, draining trenches & strengthening the wire in front line trenches. Several dumps & portions of the parapets & trench sides have fallen in, but all have been repaired.	

59

Army Form C. 2118.

WAR DIARY
INTELLIGENCE SUMMARY

(Erase heading not required.)

10th Bn. Duke of Wellington's Regiment

October 1916.

Place	Date	Hour	Summary of Events and Information	Remarks and references to Appendices
TRENCHES - YPRES.	26-10-16		Wind veered round to N.N.W. The "wind dangerous" was taken off. Our 18 pounder battery fired several times during the day. Our patrols have been out each night & have found the ground very marshy & in places impassable. These patrols have only occasionally been fired at & have sustained no casualties.	
	27-10-16		Everything still very quiet. An enemy observation balloon was seen floating about this morning, but it went away north into its own territory.	
	28-10-16		Nothing unusual to report. Work of clearing up the trenches and making them as far as possible into a workable condition continued. Weather still wet. Our usual nightly patrols went out but found nothing of particular interest to report.	
	29-10-16		In the afternoon an artillery test was carried out on the German front line opposite to the line occupied by the battalion. This was timed and observed by us and duly reported. We were relieved by the 11th Batt. West Yorkshire Regt., and we occupied the hutts which they had left at the Barracks Ypres. Copy of orders attached marked "J."	"J"
BARRACKS YPRES.	30-10-16		The day was spent by the men cleaning up clothing, equipment, rifles etc. In the afternoon Lt. Colonel S.S. Thwayne relinquished command and left the Battalion, which was taken over by Lt. Colonel R.R. Raymer D.S.O. In the evening we supplied four working and carrying parties to the R.E. consisting of 200 men in all.	
	31-10-16		Each day whilst here the battalion has had instruction and practice in the use of the new small box respirator. We again supplied working parties to the R.E. similar to those sent yesterday. During the last week several men have been sent away from the battalion to attend courses in various subjects viz: signalling, sniping, repairing of guns, bombs & gas. The weather during the month has been rather wet but not very cold for the season.	60

Williamson
Lt. Colonel
Commanding
10th Bn. Duke of Wellington's Regt.

Orders
Operations by Lt. Col. Col. J.S. Hayne
Commdg 10th West Riding Regt.
In the Field
2nd Oct 1916

A.

1. The Battn will relieve 8th K.O.Y.L.I in the line this afternoon as follows.
   A & C Coys in O.G.1 FLERS LINE
   B Coy DESTREMONT FARM
         and TRENCH
   D Coy 26th AVENUE
   Battn H.Q. M 26. 6 8.4.

2. Starting point between CONTALMAISON VILLA and O.G.1
   Time 3.45 pm
   Order of March   B Coy
                    C Coy
                    A Coy
                    D Coy
                    H.Q.
   Distance 200 yds between platoons
   Guides will be at M 33 a 3.5.

3. Two Sandbags per man will be carried. All Coys will carry Coy tools and

A C & B Coys will carry up 200 bombs per Coy.
Great Coats will be worn rolled up on the back & waterproof sheets worn.
170 rounds SAA will be carried by each man.
L-G Handcarts will be left at CONTALMAISON VILLA.

OC Coys are reminded that they must advise H.Q. when relief is complete.

[signature]
Adjt.

~~Report~~
~~"A"~~

In the Field,
4.10.1916.

This morning at dawn two strong bombing parties proceeded up the sap leading from M.22, b.2.9¾ and up sap from point 93; at the same time a platoon went over the top from the left of point 93. The bombing parties were allowed to proceed up these saps, which are not more than about 3 ft. deep, until quite close to O.G.2. when heavy machine gun fire was opened on both parties and hostile bombing attacks were at the same time made from arrow heads, at ~~M~~ O.G.2. The remnants of both bombing parties were forced to retreat to O.G.1.; the platoon which went over the top only advanced about 10 yards when all except three privates were rendered casualties.

From a very careful inspection of O.G.2. with the aid of periscope and glasses it is apparent that it is very strongly held. The trench has been considerably deepened and sentries in "niches" in the parapet may be seen every eight or ten yards. There is still a good deal of uncut wire in front close to the road and I am of opinion that the trench and wire should be dealt with by the artillery; owing to the depth of the trench 18 pdrs. ~~lbs.~~ would be of very little use unless a direct enfilade can be obtained. There is undoubtedly a machine gun at or about M.15.,d.7.0. Considerable sniping goes on from the houses in LE SARS two snipers ~~of whom~~ are thought to occupy the chimney which is still standing at about M.15.d.

(Signed) H.W.LESTER,

Lieut. and Adjutant,

10th. Battn. Duke of Wellington's Regt.

12 noon
4.10.16.

"B"

OPERATION ORDERS BY LIEUT.-COLONEL HAYNE, COMMANDING 10TH. BATTALION DUKE OF WELLINGTON'S REGIMENT.

===

1. The Battalion is being relieved this afternoon by 11th. Battalion West Yorkshire Regiment and will occupy reserve trenches at present occupied by 11th. Battalion West Yorkshire Regiment to the N.W. of MARTINPUICH.

2. Guides and advance parties have been arranged for. Advance party will meet the Battalion at Battalion Headquarters to guide it to new trenches.

3. The Companies in the front line will come over the top as far as possible to Battalion Headquarters as the 8th. Battalion Yorkshire Regiment are being relieved to-night by the 9th. Battalion Yorkshire Regiment and 26th. Avenue will be congested.

4. Lewis Gunners will stay with Companies.

5. As soon as relieved Companies will move out sending an Orderly to report to Battalion Headquarters on the way. O.C. Companies please take special care to do this.

(Signed) H.W.LESTER,
Lieut. and Adjutant,
10th. Battn. Duke of Wellington's Regiment.

5.10.1916.

Report on Operations carried out by 10TH BATTALION DUKE OF
WELLINGTON'S REGIMENT from 4th to the 8th October 1916.

On the evening of the 4th orders were received to attack
O.G.2. from M.21.b.5.8 to M.15.d.2.3. At 6.03 p.m. the attack
was launched by 2 companies in three waves 80 yards distance
between waves. The Advance waves went forward right under our
barrage but on the barrage lifting it was found that owing to
the wet state of the ground the progress was exceedingly slow.
The enemy, therefore, were enabled to bring an intense M.G. and
rifle fire on to our troops with the result that a few men only
were enabled to reach the enemy's trench and eventually we were
compelled to retire. The enemy then launched an immediate
counter-attack which was repulsed with heavy loss to the enemy.
The two companies which took part in the attack behaved with the
utmost gallantry, 6 out of the 8 officers becoming casualties,
but owing to the state of the ground and the enemy's wire
being uncut in several places the task was impossible.

The battalion was relieved on the night of 5/6th and
proceeded to MARTINPUICH.

On the evening of the 6th orders were received to proceed
to 26TH AVENUE, 70TH AVENUE, and DESTREMONT FARM on the following
morning to support 11th WEST YORKS in the attack on LE SARS.
The battalion was in position by noon and was heavily shelled
on the way to take up this position. Orders having been
received by the Brigade, I placed one Company at the disposal
of 11TH WEST YORKS from 1 p.m. on. The first attack on O.G.2.
having failed this Company was ordered up to O.G.1. by O.C. 11TH
WEST YORKS to be prepared to launch a second attack. Shortly
after this Company was in position the enemy finding himself
taken in flank and rear surrendered to a bombing attack of 11TH
WEST YORKS and enabled my Company to occupy O.G.2. without
opposition. O.C. 11th WEST YORKS having notified me that he
required two further Companies in the front line I ordered this
to be done immediately and moved my reserve Company to DESTREMONT
TRENCH and establishing H.Q. in the DESTREMONT LINE. I
then took over command of the line from O.C. 11TH WEST YORKS
and finding that there were only 61 of the 11TH WEST YORKS
remaining in the trenches I sent up a further two platoons of
my battalion and applied to Brigade H.Q. for two Companies of
the YORK & LANCS to be sent up to 26th AVENUE & 70TH AVENUE in
support. I then ordered MAJOR R.H. GILL to proceed to the front
line to clear up the situation and inform me as soon as possible
of the position.

At 4 a.m. the situation was as follows:- My battalion and
11th WEST YORKS held O.G.2. up to M.15.a.8.3., North side of
Triangle to apex and had pushed out patrols right up to 9.2. and
had got in touch with 9TH YORKS at M.15.d.6.3., all points being
blocked and consolidated; the enemy were found to be by our
patrols in O.G.1. at M.15.a.4½.4½. Both communication trenches
between O.G.1. and O.G.2. were deepened during the night and
put in a state of defence. At 4-30 a.m. two Companies of
YORK & LANCS passed through my line in O.G.1. and O.G.2. and
bombed down to the track in M.15.a. capturing the
enemy who had been cut off in O.G.1. and got into touch with the
Canadians who had attacked at dawn and captured O.G.1. & 2. on
my left flank. At 3 a.m. the enemy made a heavy counter-attack
on the Canadian Division on our left flank, compelling it to
withdraw to its original line, but were unable to force back my
left flank, which I held on to until relieved by 6TH CAMERON
HIGHLANDERS. The relief was complete at 3-35 a.m.

REPORT ON OPERATIONS S.W. & W. of LE SARS
from 4th to 9th OCTOBER, 1916
by
Major R.H. GILL, 10th Bn. W. RIDING REGT.

Map Ref: GUEDECOURT
57.c. S.W. 1.
1/10,000

In the Field,
October 11th 1916.

4.10.16   At dawn on 4.10.16 the 10th W. Rid. Regt. occupied O.G.1 from main ALBERT - BAPAUME road to M.15.c.75.45 with Bde H.Q. in 26th Avenue. Two strong bombing parties attacked up communication trenches to O.G.2 and were repulsed with heavy loss. (see report signed by Adjt marked "A" and attached hereto.)

In the afternoon I received verbal orders to attack O.G.2 with two companies 10th W. Rid.Regt. from M.21.b.5.8. to M.15.d.25.30. I at once proceeded to O.G.1 and issued Operation Order No.1 (attached hereto and marked "B")

At 6.3 p.m. both companies went over the top and crept up under our barrage until it lifted at 6.8 p.m. They then advanced under intense rifle fire and traversing fire from at least three machine guns. The ground was so heavy that it took them ten minutes to cover 50 yards. Some got to the German wire(which was practically intact) others as far as the enemy's parapet which was fully manned and where the enemy had no difficulty in dealing with them in their exhausted condition. 2nd Lieut. H. Kelly, C.S.M. O'Shea and two men alone succeeded in entering the German trench remaining there bombing and fighting down it until enemy reinforcements arrived overland, killed one man. and wounded the C.S.M. 2nd Lt. Kelly then retired carrying the C.S.M. back to our own lines. Here with the assistance of part of "C" Coy he repelled a German counter-attack. These two companies behaved with the utmost gallantry but their task being an impossible one they failed to take the trench and were decimated.

5.10.16   The 10th W. Rid. Regt continued to hold O.G.1 until relieved by the 11th W. Yorks Regt on the night of the 5th Oct. when it
6.10.16   withdrew to MARTINPUICH, arriving there at 4 a.m. on the 6th.

7.10.16   On the 7th Oct. the 10th W.Rid. Regt was ordered to support the 11th W. Yorks Regt in an attack made in conjunction with the Brigade and Division on our right and at 12 p.m. was in position in DESTREMONT FARM, 26th Avenue and 70th Avenue, with Bde H.Q. in 26th Av. The attack took place at 1.45 p.m. before which the W. Yorks Regt had already absorbed one Coy of the W. Rid. Regt. The latter in compliance with requests from O.C. West Yorks continued to reinforce until only two weak platoons of "A" Coy remained. O.C. 10th W. Ridings then received orders to move his H.Q. to DESTREMONT TRENCH (the H.Q. of West Yorks Regt) and did so at 7.15 p.m. There I received orders from O.C. my own Bn. and O.C. 11th W. Yorks to proceed to O.G.1 to take command of the West Yorks and West Rid. Regts in O.G.1 and O.G.2, to reorganize them, the West Yorks to hold O.G.2 and the West Ridings O.G.1, blocks on left flank of the linees and if possible to take and hold N. S of triangle in M.15.d. and trench up to M.15.b.9.2. As the West Yorks Regt had only 61 other ranks in the trenches I found this inexpedient so garrisoned O.G.1 with "D" Coy W. Rid. Regt, O.G.2 with "B" Coy, 2 platoons of "A" Coy of W. Rid, Regt. and the 61 West Yorks Regt. I gave "C" Coy the task of occupying trenches to W of LE SARS. This it did without difficulty getting into touch with the 9th Yorks Regt on the road at M.15.a.7.7. where the R.E. constructed a strong post and another at apex of triangle at M.15.d.5.5. The trench marked on map as running from the road to Point 92 was patrolled and found to be a natural ditch about 2 feet deep useless to either enemy or ourselves so I ignored it. Finding that O.G.2 was unoccupied for some distance to its left the West Yorks Regt extended over the ridge M.15.central there

cutting off Germans who were sending up flares in O.G.1, in
M.15.d. In the meantime the West Riding Regt had deepened the
trench from O.G.1 to the apex of triangle and made it defensible
and had also improved shallow communication trench from O.G.1
to O.G.2 (M.15.d.2.o to 3.2) so that it afforded adequate cover.

8.10.16 At dawn two companies of the York & Lancs Regt passed through
my lines and bombed along O.G.1 and O.G.2 from the blocks on our
left flanks to the track in M.15.a capturing the enemy whom we had
cut off in O.G.1. They then said they were instructed to act
under my orders so I ordered them to hold and consolidate the
ground from my left flank to that track. I now occupied about 1,300
yds of O.G.1, the same of O.G.2 with a composite force of about
400 men in both lines. The Canadian Division on my left had also
attacked at dawn and taken O.G. 1 and 2 in continuation of the
left flanks of the York and Lancs companies.

Except for heavy shelling the situation remained normal until
about 3 p.m. when the enemy made a heavy counter-attack on the
Canadian Division on my left and drove it back to its original
lines. Communication with my Bn H.Q. was difficult and no
telephone wire lasted more than a few minutes under the continual
shelling and messages by runner took from 1 to $1\frac{1}{2}$ hours each way.
I gave the Canadians what support I could with oblique machine
gun fire and also sent them the bombs they asked for replenishing
my supply from the 9th Yorks Regt on my right in anticipation
of counter-attack on me. I received a message from my C.O.
offering me reinforcements.but replied that I hoped to hold my lines
without as my left flank was well protected by Stokes guns,
bombing parties, Vickers and Lewis guns.

9.10.16 At 12.30 a.m. the 6th Cameron Regt. arrived to relieve us
and the last coy of my command left the trenches at 3.35 a.m.

            sgd. R. H . . GILL,
                Major
            10th West Riding Regt.

Movement orders by Lt. Col. S.S. Hayne
commanding 10th Duke of Wellington's Regt.

Map Ref. ABBEVILLE 14.
        LENS   11

In the field
12.10.16

1. The Battn including Transport will march tomorrow to billets at YVRENCH.

2. <u>Starting point</u>   E. end of BUIGNY

   <u>Time</u>   9 am.

   <u>Route</u>   ST RIQUIER — ONEUX.

   <u>Order of march</u>   H.Q.
                            A
                            B
                            C
                            D

L.G. will remain with Coys.

3. Officers kits, mess baskets & stores will be dumped outside Q.M. stores at 8.15 a.m. Transport officer will arrange to collect same. Half the space of one motor lorry will be at disposal of the for his stores.

MOVEMENT ORDERS
BY
LIEUT.-COLONEL S. S. HAYNE,
COMMANDING 10TH. BATTALION DUKE OF WELLINGTON'S REGT.

Map Ref. LENS 11.   REVEILLE 4 a.m.   BREAKFAST 4.30 a.m.

1. The Battalion will march to CONTEVILLE STATION to-morrow morning and entrain for, probably, MONTCOUTRE.

2. Starting Point - N.W.Exit of village on CONTEVILLE ROAD.
   Time - 5.15 a.m.
   Order of March - Headquarters, A., B., C., D. Coys., Lewis Gunners with handcarts

3. The whole of the Transport will leave here for CONTEVILLE STATION at 5 a.m.
   Lieut. PHILLIPS will leave with the Transport taking with him entraining state of Battalion.

4. Mess baskets and officers' kits will be dumped outside Q.M.Stores at 4.30 a.m. Transport Officer will arrange to collect same.
   One servant per Company will march with mess cart and arrange for officers' rations for the journey.

5. Rations for 15th. will be carried on the man.

6. Officers' chargers will accompany Battalion to Station.

(Signed) H.W.LESTER,
Lieut. and Adjutant,
14.12.1916.   10th. Battn. Duke of Wellington's Regiment.

OPERATION ORDERS BY LIEUT.- COLONEL G.S.HAYNE
COMMANDING
10TH. BATTALION DUKE OF WELLINGTON'S REGIMENT.

1. The Battalion will entrain at POPERINGHE Station to-night at 6 p.m. and will proceed in the train which is drawn up nearest the YPRES Road.
The Battalion will relieve the 13th.D.L.I. in the trenches this evening.
"A", "B" and "C" Coys. in the front line. I.17.4 - I.18.4.
3 platoons of "D" Coy. in the front of HALF-WAY HOUSE.
1 platoon of "D" Coy. at LEINSTER FARM.
Headquarters at HALF-WAY HOUSE.

2. Guides will meet the Battalion at YPRES Station.

3. Companies will parade outside their billets at 5.15 p.m. and will move off in the order "C", "B", "A" and "D" Coys., and Headquarters. Companies at 100 yards intervals.

4. Lewis Gunners and all handcarts will be at POPERINGHE Station at 5.30 p.m. There will be three flats on each train for handcarts. Handcarts will form up at the YPRES end of the platform.
On arrival at YPRES Station Lewis Gunners will rejoin their Companies.

5. Two snipers will parade with "C" Company for duty at the CULVERT. The remainder of the snipers will parade with Headquarters.

6. To-morrow's rations will be carried on the man. Packs will be taken into the trenches.

7. One officer's servant per company will join the Transport at YPRES and will proceed with it to the Dump near HELL FIRE CORNER where they will remain until their respective companies' kits have been collected.

8. Transport and Q.M.Stores will remain in their present positions. Cookers will go to the Transport Lines. One cook per company will remain with their respective cookers.

9. Officers' valises will be dumped at Q.M.Stores by 2 p.m. Trench kits and mess baskets will be ready outside respective Company H.Q. by 3 p.m. Sergt.Gibson will arrange to collect these.

10. Blankets will be rolled in "tens", securely tied, labelled and dumped at Q.M.Stores by 1 p.m.

11. 2/Lieut.EVANS will be at POPERINGHE Station by 5 p.m. and will find out the arrangements for the entraining of the Battalion. On arrival at YPRES he will join "A" Company.

12. List of trench stores and gum boots taken over to be sent to Battalion H.Q. by 9 a.m. to-morrow.

(Signed) L.R.PHILLIPS,
Lieut. and A/Adjutant.

23.10.1916.

Army Form C. 2118.

WAR DIARY
or
INTELLIGENCE SUMMARY
(Erase heading not required.)

10TH (S) Battalion DUKE OF WELLINGTON'S Regt

Vol 16

Instructions regarding War Diaries and Intelligence Summaries are contained in F. S. Regs., Part II and the Staff Manual respectively. Title Pages will be prepared in manuscript.

Place	Date	Hour	Summary of Events and Information	Remarks and references to Appendices
YPRES	Nov. 1st to 3rd		The Battalion was in the Infantry Barracks at YPRES in Divisional Reserve. 200 men were supplied for working parties each night and small working parties during the day. All officers and men were practiced in the use of the new tube respirator and had them tested with lachrymatal gas.	
	4th	5.0pm 8pm	The Battalion was relieved at 5.0 pm by the 8th KINGS OWN YORKSHIRE LIGHT INFANTRY and left YPRES marching to VLAMERTINGHE marching thence to WINNIPEG CAMP H.19.d.2.3. The transport and 2 m.g. teams joined the Battalion from their quarters in POPERINGHE. The Battalion was in CORPS Reserve.	
WINNIPEG CAMP I 19.A.2.3 MAP 1/40000	5th to 8th		The Battalion was exercised in Physical Training, Arms drill, Bayonet fighting, and Box respirator drill very heavy rain fell on the 9th. The transport lines were flooded. On the 10th the west parade was held and inspections of arms, rations, equipment and ammunition made preparatory to going into the trenches.	
	9th 10th			
	11th	4.0pm 5.0pm	The Battalion marched out of camp at 4.0 pm and left VLAMERTINGHE at 5.0 pm by train for YPRES. From YPRES the Battalion marched to the trenches and relieved Trenches at I.24.d.3.9.A to I.24.d.7.2 and relieved the 12th DURHAM LIGHT INFANTRY. The sector taken over was the left sector of the right Brigade of the Front occupied by the 23rd Division. The Battalion held one of the Companies as a yellow line. B Company & D Company in the line. A Company at MAPLE COPSE I.23.b.7.m. and C Company at ZILLEBEKE BUND I.15.d.1.3.	
Trenches YPRES Salient I.24.d.3.9.A to I.24.d.7.2 MAP 1/10000	12th		The relief was completed at 9.15 pm The trenches and front lines throughout the sector were found to be in a very bad condition. Work was at once begun to repair the trenches. The enemy in front of this sector was found to be in a very bad condition and intermittent working parties were formed under 2nd Lieut. E. DIXON and work begun on the wire. Work and Patrolling was carried on during the night.	
	13th		The enemy were active with their trench mortars during the afternoon but ceased upon our retaliating with rifle grenades. The Lewis gun posts except for a few Trench mortars shots and occasional bursts of M.G. fire at night. The Battalion Patrols were very active and considerable work was done. A Company relieved B Coy in the front line and B Company patrolled to MAPLE COPSE I.23.b.7.m in the evening.	
	14th		The Battalion relief of D Company in the front line took place during the night C Company relieved D Company in the front line and D Company proceeded to ZILLEBEKE BUND I.15.d.1.3.	
ZILLEBEKE BUND I.15.d.1.2 to I.15.b.1.2h2 MAP 1/10000	15th 16th		The Sector was quiet and working of an extensive scale took place.	
	17th 18th 19th 20th		The Battalion was relieved by the 11th WEST YORKSHIRE REGT. and moved back into Brigade Reserve at ZILLEBEKE BUND I.15.d.1.2 to I.21.b.1.2h2 MAP 1/10000 Sheet 28 NW I NE3. Working parties were supplied to the RE. 200 men working each night. The period was quiet, the days very foggy and observation bad. Operation orders were issued, and day attacks marched A and the Battalion racking party proceeded to the Front Line to carry out the raid under the Command of Captain KELLY. A report of the operation is attached marked 'B'	'A' 'B'

2449 Wt. W14957/M90 750,000 1/16 J.B.C. & A. Forms/C.2118/12.

WAR DIARY
INTELLIGENCE SUMMARY

Army Form C. 2118.

10TH (S) Battalion DUKE OF WELLINGTON'S REGT

(Erase heading not required.)

Instructions regarding War Diaries and Intelligence Summaries are contained in F. S. Regs., Part II. and the Staff Manual respectively. Title Pages will be prepared in manuscript.

Place	Date	Hour	Summary of Events and Information	Remarks and references to Appendices
Trenches YPRES Salient ZILLEBEKE BUND	Nov 20th		The Battalion casualties were 2nd Lieut: L.T. MILLWARD wounded and 11 O.R wounded and 1 O.R died.	
	22nd		The Battalion was relieved by the 11th SHERWOOD FORESTERS and proceeded to YPRES siding and entrained for VLAMERTINGHE arriving at WINNIPEG Camp at 9.30 p.m. Captain C. BATHURST rejoined the Battalion and took over the duties of Second in command.	
Winnipeg Camp I.19.A.2.3	23rd to 28th		The period was spent in resting. The annual Battalion and Company Parades took place and every other day 45 O.R's were drafted to the R.E. 2/5 as working parties. At 11 am on the 29th the Corps Commander presented the ribbon of the V.C. to Captain HEELY. The Battalion and the 9th YORKSHIRE REGT Paraded for the ceremony.	
Trenches YPRES Salient I.18.a.5.7 to I.18.c.4.7 MAP MOOR 28NW4 9 NE 3	29th		The Battalion relieved the 13th DURHAM LIGHT INFANTRY in the left sector of the left Brigade, 23rd Division. The Battalion left WINNIPEG Camp at 3.30 pm entrained at VLAMERTINGHE at 4.45 pm detrained at YPRES siding at 5.20 pm and marched to the Trenches. The dispositions of the Company were "A" Company on the right. "B" Company in LEINSTER Trench and "C" Company on the left.	
Map 1/10000 sheet 28NW4 9NE3	30th		The relief was complete at 12 midnight. 29th - 30th. The day was mostly and very quiet. A good deal of work was done in improving the trenches and wire.	

Casualties during the month:—
1 Officer wounded
13. O.R wounded
2. O.R died of wounds
1. O.R killed in action

Winchester Shepard
LIEUT: COLONEL
COMMANDING THE 7TH 10TH DUKE OF WELLINGTON'S REGT.

ORDERLY ROOM.
No. W.D. 75
5 DEC.1916
10TH DUKE OF WELLINGTON'S REGT.

"A"

OPERATION ORDERS NO.51   Copy No.
BY
LIEUT.-COLONEL R.R.RAYMER, D.S.O.,
COMMANDING 10TH. BATTN. DUKE OF WELLINGTON'S REGT.

Map Ref.   19.11.16.
    ZILLEBEKE
    1/10,000
    Edition 3E.
    and attached sketch.

1. The Battalion will carry out a raid on the night of November 20th/21st. against the enemy sap at J.19.c.00.35 opposite CROSS STREET (I.24.2). The sap is marked "A" in sketch.

2. The object of the Raid is to capture as many as possible of the enemy forming posts at the sap and at the sap junction.

3. The Raiding Party will leave our trenches from the Listening Post in CROSS TRENCH at I.24.d.90.57 (marked "L" in sketch).

4. Our Wire. O.C. 11th. WEST YORKS.REGT. has arranged to clear a passage through our wire as soon as possible after dark on the evening of Nov.20th.

5. Enemy's Wire. A gap will be cut through the enemy's wire by firing a Bangalore torpedo which will be placed in position after dark on the evening of 20th. as soon as the necessary passage has been cleared through our wire. The torpedo will be fired at zero hour. Arrangements for placing and firing the torpedo will be made by O.C. 128th. Coy. R.E.

6. The Raiding Party under the command of Capt.H.Kelly will be formed as follows:-
    (a) A. (Assaulting)Party. 2/Lieut.J.DAVIS and 25 O.R. This party will be arranged in two columns in single file with the 4 leading files over the parapet and the remainder in the trench ready to follow. The explosion of the torpedo will be the signal for the party to dash forward into the enemy's sap, each man proceeding to the task allotted him.
        On reaching the sap junction they will divide as detailed along the three enemy trenches which meet there. Care must be taken to bomb all dug-outs.
        Nine of this party will be bayonet men, and 16 bombers.
        One N.C.O. and 2 men will be specially detailed to secure prisoners, and two men to secure identification marks and papers from enemy dead.

    (b). B.(Communicating) Party. 2/Lieut.F.W.MILLWARD and 6 O.R. As soon as "A" Party is clear of the parapet "B" Party will move forward and be extended from the enemy's parapet to our own. They will act as communicating files to pass up bombs and to pass down prisoners and if necessary will reinforce the Assaulting Party. The Officer will take post on the enemy's parapet.

    (c). C. (Reserve) Party. Capt.H.KELLY and 6 O.R. This Party will be available to assist "B" Party and will immediately take their place if they go forward to reinforce. One L.G. will be with this Party to give any necessary support to their retirement.

-2-

      (d). D. (Flanking) Party - 3 O.R. - will occupy our sap at I.24.d.85.60 marked "K" on sketch and be supported by one L.G. 11th. WEST YORKS. in readiness to stop any enemy counter attack along the sap.

7.   A prolonged whistle blast given by O.C. Raid and repeated by the other two officers will be the signal for the Assaulting Column to retire. They will return by the same route as they entered. Three men previously detailed will act as rear guard to cover retirement and evacuation of our wounded.

    As soon as O.C. "B" Party is satisfied that "A" Party is clear he will order "B" Party to retire. All parties, unless otherwise ordered, will proceed to dug-outs in CRAB CRAWL, where they will be assembled for rest and refreshment.

8.   Prisoners on reaching our trench will be handed over to an Officer and escort detailed by O.C. 11th. WEST YORKS. After being searched they will be conducted to Brigade H.Q. in YPRES.

9.   Two bombing parties have been detailed by O.C. 11th. WEST YORKS, to be in readiness to deal with any counter attack.

10.   <u>DRESS AND EQUIPMENT</u>. Men taking part in the Raid will remove any identification marks from their uniform and will leave behind all letters and papers and personal property. Bombers will wear belt and bayonet and carry a bag of bombs, secured round the waist and over their shoulders. Bayonet men will carry rifle with fixed bayonet and wear a cotton bandolier. They will each carry two bombs in their pockets. Faces will be blacked.

11.   The Raid will be supported as follows:-

  (a) <u>Artillery</u> support as per programme attached.
  (b) <u>Trench Mortars</u>. One medium trench mortar will enfilade the enemy trench J.19.c.04.30 to 24-33.
  (c) <u>Stokes Mortars</u>. One Stokes Mortar, 69th.T.M.B., will fire on the trench junction J.19.c.25.47 and another on the enemy machine gun emplacement J.19.c.00.15.
  (d) <u>Lewis Guns</u>. The L.G. in Sap "K" (I.24.d.90.62) and another L.G. of 11th. WEST YORKS. at I.24.d.90.62 will sweep the German parapet immediately opposite, taking care not to traverse North and South respectively of and EAST and WEST line through their positions.

    The placing of the torpedo will be covered by bursts of L.G. fire from our trenches.

12.   <u>TIMETABLE</u>. Zero - Torpedo fired and attack starts.
                Zero + 2 Lewis Guns open fire.
                Zero + 5 18-pdrs., Trench Mortars and Stokes Guns open fire.
                Zero + 10 Howitzers open fire.
                Zero + 15 Recall signal given.
                Zero + 35 Artillery, mortars and Lewis Guns cease fire.

13.   A temporary Dressing Station will be established in Company H.Q. in CRAB CRAWL.

-3-

14.   O.C. 10th. WEST RIDING REGT. will establish H.Q. in CROSS STREET. He will assume command of the Left Battalion Sector (trenches I.24.1.2.3) at 8 p.m. on Nov.20th. and will hand over again to O.C. 11th. WEST YORKS. REGT. as soon after completion of the Raid as the tactical situation permits.

15.   Zero time will be at   p.m.

                              (Signed) H.W.LESTER,

                                      Lieut. and Adjutant.
                         10th.Battn.West Riding Regiment.

Issued at 8 p.m.

Copies
- 1.)
- 2.) 69th. Brigade.
- 3.)
- 4.   O.C. 11th. WEST YORKS.
- 5.   Major GORDON.
- 6.   O.C. 128th. Coy.R.E.
- 7.   Capt.H.KELLY.
- 8.   O.C. 69th.T.M.B.
- 9.)
- 10.) File.

SECRET CODE FOR USE BETWEEN CREDIT AND CASTLE.

	Code Word.
Torpedo successfully placed	bat.
Torpedo not yet placed. Enemy have spotted it and opened fire..	ball
Further attempt to place torpedo again stopped by enemy...	base
All parties in position and everything ready	band
Enemy quiet..	bowl
Enemy active.	box
Enemy's working parties busy	brick
Torpedo successfully exploded and attack launched	cow
No retaliation yet from enemy	cat
Enemy retaliating with T.M's on	camp
" " " " field guns on	cox
" " " " howitzers on	cub
Enemy prisoners come in	cool
Total prisoners..........	crawl
Still held up by failure to place torpedo..	crank
All going well	crib
Attack checked by	crack
All raiding party returned..	crow
Casualties nil	cable
All raiding party returned except	dawn
Killed and missing	dog
Wounded	doll
Wounded seriously	drink
Wounded slightly	dump
All party back in dug-outs in Crab Crawl...	dry
I have taken over command...	drag
Command resumed by O.C. 11th. West Yorks...	duck
.....prisoners under escort left for Brigade H.Q.	drift
.....prisoners wounded	drop
.....prisoners detained for evacuation to dressing station	dirt.

REPORT ON OPERATIONS AGAINST ENEMY SAP AT J.19.c.00.35
ON NIGHT OF 20TH./21ST. NOVEMBER, 1916.

—x—x—x—x—x—x—x—x—x—x—x—x—x—x—x—x—x—

Map Reference
ZILLEBEKE 1/10,000
Edition 3E.

1. OBJECTIVE.- Enemy's sap at J.19.c.00.35 opposite listening post in CROSS TRENCH (I.24.2) at I.24.d.90.57. The head of the sap, which has two horns curling slightly to North and South respectively, is from 30 to 35 yards from our parapet and is protected by a belt of thick wire from 20 to 30 feet deep. An examination of this wire on the night of the 19th./20th. showed that it had been extended outwards within the last day or two by a light apron about 7 feet deep.

2. METHOD OF ATTACK.- To make a passage through the enemy's wire the 128th. Coy. R.E. used a Bangalore torpedo of about 3" diameter and made up of three lengths of 10 feet each, fired electrically from the trench.
    A detachment, consisting of 3 officers and 40 O.R. 10th. Battn. WEST RIDING REGIMENT under Capt. H.KELLY, was detailed to rush the sap and force an entrance into the enemy's first trenches. It was divided into an Assaulting Party (2/Lieut. J.DAVIS and 25 O.R.), a Communicating Party (2/Lieut. F.W.MILLWARD and 6 O.R.), a Reserve Party (Capt. H.KELLY and 6 O.R.), and a small Flanking Party of 3 O.R. stationed in the sap I.24.d.85.50 with one Lewis Gun 11th. WEST YORKS. REGT.

3. ARTILLERY AND OTHER SUPPORT.- The attack was supported by 18 18-pdr. guns and one Howitzer Battery R.F.A. (Right Brigade, Lowe's Group R.A.) under Major A.C.GORDON, D.S.O. Also by one medium trench mortar, 23rd. Division; two Stokes Mortars, 69th. T.M.B.; and two Lewis Guns, 11th. West Yorks. Regt.

4. NARRATIVE.- At 6.30 p.m. the wire covering our listening post was cut by a party of the 11th. Battn. WEST YORKS. REGT., the Battalion holding the trenches, and a number of "gooseberries" (or wire balls) was placed temporarily in the gap. Sappers of the 128th. Coy. R.E. then proceeded to cut a passage through the apron of the enemy's wire. At 9.15 p.m. 2/Lieut. COPE, 128th. Coy. R.E., and two sappers commenced taking out the torpedo from a point about 30 yards South of the listening post, working obliquely towards the enemy's sap head. This movement was covered by bursts of Lewis Gun fire from our trenches. The night was still and fairly dark, and though the enemy fired a number of flares he showed no further sign of activity.
    The Attacking Party reached the trenches at 10.30 p.m. and was in position in CROSS TRENCH by 11.5 p.m. Meanwhile the placing of the torpedo proceeded smoothly but slowly until about 20 feet was through the wire. The point then appeared to meet some obstacle and when 22 feet was through it was found that further progress was impossible. As the depth of the wire was estimated to be no greater than this and it was thought that the point must have struck the enemy's parapet, the R.E. Party retired to the trench and at 11.34 p.m. fired the torpedo.

-2-

At 11.17 p.m. the gap in our wire was cleared, and at 11.18 p.m. 2/Lieut. DAVIS began to lead his party over the parapet in two columns. Immediately the torpedo exploded they dashed for the gap in the enemy's wire, but found that a barrier of some 8 feet of wire remained uncut. The leading men of the party at once endeavoured to cut a way through with their wire cutters, whereupon the enemy in the sap head attacked them with bombs. To cover the wire-cutting our bombers immediately replied. Several of the wire cutters having become casualties after making very little progress, Capt.H.KELLY at 11.39 p.m. gave the signal for recall, and at 11.43 p.m. the party had all regained the trench bringing in their wounded.

Communication with the Artillery having become interrupted it was then impossible to stop their fire which proceeded according to programme and appeared to be very well directed.

The enemy retaliated with heavy bombardment by trench mortars especially on VIGO STREET and the Northern end of VANCOUVER STREET, and in the neighbourhood of CRAB CRAWL. There was a little rifle fire but no machine gun fire and, apparently, only a little artillery retaliation from light field guns. The trench mortar fire ceased about 12.35 a.m.

5. CASUALTIES.- 11th. WEST YORKS. REGT.-
    O.R. 2 killed, 2 wounded.
    (from trench mortar retaliation).
10th. WEST RIDING REGT.-
    2/Lieut.F.W.MILLWARD severely wounded.
    10 O.R. wounded.

6. From information brought back by 2/Lieut.J.DAVIS it would seem that the point of the torpedo had been stopped by the rim of a shell hole into which it must have dipped.

I am of opinion that a torpedo of smaller bore and pushed through on some sort of cradle which would keep the point as long as possible off the ground would be more effective. All other arrangements so far as they were tested worked well and gave every promise of a successful attack had the breach in the enemy's wire been practicable.

7. Communication by wire with the rear was not re-established until 2.30 a.m. when the O.C. 11th. WEST YORKS. REGT. resumed command of his sector and the last of the Attacking Party withdrew with me to billets.

8. I consider that 2/Lieut.COPE, 128th.Coy.R.E., showed great courage and determination in carrying out a difficult task, and that the conduct of 2/Lieut. J. DAVIS and his men in their efforts to force a passage through the uncut wire is worthy of commendation.

Richmond Raymer.

LT-COLONEL,
COMMANDING 10th Bn. DUKE OF WELLINGTON'S REGT.

21.11.1916.

Army Form C. 2118.

Vol 1

10th (S) Battalion Duke of Wellington's Regt.

WAR DIARY
or
INTELLIGENCE SUMMARY

(Erase heading not required.)

Instructions regarding War Diaries and Intelligence Summaries are contained in F.S. Regs., Part II. and the Staff Manual respectively. Title Pages will be prepared in manuscript.

Place	Date 1916	Hour	Summary of Events and Information	Remarks and references to Appendices
YPRES Salient I.18.a.5.7 to I.18.c.4.7 Map Sheet 28NW	Dec 1st and 2nd 3rd		The Battalion was left Battalion Left Brigade on the 23rd Division front. The weather was rather misty and observation bad. A good deal of work was carried out and the wire improved in many places. The period was very quiet. The Battalion was relieved by the 11th West Yorkshire Regt. and took over Billets in the Infantry Barracks YPRES.	
INFANTRY BARRACKS YPRES	4th to 6th		Nothing of importance took place. 200 men worked under the R.E's each night. 25 men were attached for one month to H.Q. R.Es. (10th S.T. Coy.)	
Trenches I.18.a.5.7 to I.18.c.4.7	7th to 11th		The Battalion relieved the 11th West Yorkshire Regt. in the left sector Left Brigade on the 23rd Division front. The enemy artillery was rather more active and shelled the R.E. dump at HALFWAY HOUSE each day. The nights were long but not very much trenching to be done. Work was carried on improving the trenches and wire. On the 10th inst. Major A.A. ST HILL 1st Battalion DUKE OF WELLINGTON'S REGT reported for duty and took over the duties of 2nd in command of the Battalion. On the 11th inst the Battalion was relieved by the 11th WEST YORKSHIRE REGT. and took over their huts in the Infantry Barracks, YPRES, whilst the Battalion was in Brigade Reserve.	
Infantry Barracks YPRES	12th		200 men worked under the R.E's each night.	
WINNIPEG CAMP H.19.A.2.3 MAP I/20000	13th 15th 16th		On the night of the 15th the Battalion was relieved by the 8th KING'S OWN YORKSHIRE LIGHT INFANTRY and left YPRES arriving at 7.30 p.m. by tram from VLAMERTINGHE marching 3 kms to WINNIPEG CAMP.	
	17th to		4 N.C.O's and 50 men were attached to the R.E's for 8 days. 1 Officer and 4 I.O.R. went by tram to YPRES on this evening of the 17th, 18th, 19th and 20th to work under the R.E's (they returned about 2.30 am) The usual parades were held. On the 10th Reinforcements went resumed 5 Officers, 20 trained men and 52 untrained men. The officers were as follows:— 2nd Lieuts A.P. GARRATT, J.R. DICKINSON, A. C. TETLEY, W.G. WADE, H.M. HANDS. On the 21st the 52 untrained men were sent to the Brigade School for further instruction. On the 22nd the Commander in Chief, Sir DOUGLAS HAIG inspected the Battalion at 12.20 pm on the VLAMERTINGHE OUDERDOM Road. This day was very wet. On the night of the 23rd the Battalion relieved the 11th NORTHUMBERLAND FUSILIERS (68th of 9 Brigade), in the right Battalion front of the right Brigade of the 23rd DIVISION FRONT. The relief was complete at 9.45 pm. Three Companies were in the frontline, one Company in Support and Batt. H.Q. at RUDKIN HOUSE.	
YPRES Salient I.24.d.6.6 to Y.30.c.2.8	23 24th to 26th		The period was fairly quiet. On the 26th there was a good deal of Trench Mortar activity on the part of the enemy. WINNIPEG St. was a good deal knocked about, otherwise not much damage was done.	2 files

2449 Wt. W14957/Mgo 750,000 1/16 J.B.C. & A. Forms/C.2118/12.

Army Form C. 2118.

WAR DIARY
INTELLIGENCE SUMMARY 10TH (S) Battalion DUKE OF WELLINGTONS REGT.

(Erase heading not required.)

Instructions regarding War Diaries and Intelligence Summaries are contained in F. S. Regs., Part II. and the Staff Manual respectively. Title Pages will be prepared in manuscript.

Place	Date 1916	Hour	Summary of Events and Information	Remarks and references to Appendices
The HOSPICE YPRES	Dec: 29th		The Battalion was Relieved by the 11th WEST YORKSHIRE REGT and moved into billets at YPRES Batt HQ and one Company at the HOSPICE two Companys at the Cathedral and one Company at the Cavalry Barracks. The relief was complete at 8 p.m. The whole of the Battalion was employed every day on working parties, either on the line or at YPRES. The enemy shelled the square each day.	
	30th		On the 30th a 5.9" shell burst in the Court-yard at the HOSPICE killing one man.	
	31st		The Battalion Relieved the 11th WEST YORKSHIRE REGT in the right Battalion front of the 23rd Division Front. The Relief was complete at 9 p.m.	
			Casualties for the month	
			1 O.R Killed	
			7. O.R Wounded	
			1. O.R Accidentaly wounded.	

AO. Neill MAJOR

for O.C. 10TH (S) Battalion DUKE OF WELLINGTONS REGT.

ORDERLY ROOM.
WR: 1477
4 JAN. 1917
10TH BATT. DUKE OF WELLINGTONS
(RIDING REGT.)

Headquarters,
69th Infantry Brigade

Enclosed please find War Diary of this Battalion for the month of January 1917.

L Phillips Capt & A/Adjt
for OC. 10 Bn. West Riding Regt.

2/2/17.
WR 1706

Army Form C. 2118.

WAR DIARY
or
INTELLIGENCE SUMMARY

10th (S) Battalion Duke of Wellington Regt

Vol / 8

(Erase heading not required.)

Place	Date	Hour	Summary of Events and Information	Remarks and references to Appendices
Trenches YPRES Salient Trenches I.24.d.7.M6 to I.30.a.4.0 MAP 1/5000	Jan 15th 1917		The Battalion was the right Battalion of the right Brigade on the 23rd Divisional front I.24.d.7.M6 - I.30.a.4.0. Three Companies were in the front line and one Company in support in HALIFAX St. Between 5pm and 6.30pm the enemy opened heavy trench mortar fire on the front line and artillery fire on the trenches behind. All telephone wires were cut. The trenches were badly damaged and the Battalion suffered a few casualties. On the 2nd Lieut Colonel R.R. Raynor D.S.O. took over temporary command of the 69th Infantry Brigade and Major A.A. St Hill was left in command of the Battalion.	
YPRES Bluffs	4th		Lieut & Adjt H.W. LESTER was awarded the Military Cross on the New Years Honours List. From the 2nd to the 4th the enemy was fairly quiet except for a little trench mortar fire on the front line. The Battalion was relieved on the evening of the 4th by the 11th Battalion of the WEST YORKSHIRE Regt and went into billets at YPRES as follows:- H.Q. & 'A' Coy at the HOSPICE; B & 'C' Coys at ST PETER'S CHURCH and 'D' Coy at the CAVALRY BARRACKS. YPRES was shelled by the enemy artillery. One shell fell in ST PETER'S CHURCH and caused a large number of Casualties. ST PETER'S CHURCH was broken up as a billet and 'C' Coy went to the INFANTRY Barracks and B Coy to ZILLEBEKE BUND.	
	5th to 8th		On the 6th and 7th the enemy shelled the City but the bombardment was not so heavy as on the 5th. On the 8th YPRES was again heavily bombarded. Several shells fell in the HOSPICE but nobody was hit.	
WINNIPEG CAMP H.19.G.2.3 MAP 1/20000	9th to		The Battalion was relieved by the 8th KINGS OWN YORKSHIRE LIGHT INFANTRY and marched to Camp at WINNIPEG CAMP H.19.G.2.3. MAP 1/20000. Specialists were trained under Specialist Officers. One Platoon in each Company was set aside for training. About 60 men per day were employed on working Parties. On the 14th the Battalion received a draft of 49 men.	
	16th		On the 15th the Battalion carried out a practice for assembling between trenches and infantry Barracks. On the 16th the Battalion relieved the 12th DURHAM LIGHT INFANTRY and proceeded by train to YPRES and went into billets in the INFANTRY Barracks.	
YPRES INFANTRY Barracks	to 20th		The Battalion received a draft of 109 O.R. During the four days at YPRES 160 O.R. were employed on working Parties each night. Specialists trained under their respective officers. The last four new drafts were given instruction in Arms Drill.	

Army Form C. 2118.

10(th)(S) Battalion DUKE OF WELLINGTON'S Rgt.

WAR DIARY
INTELLIGENCE SUMMARY

(Erase heading not required.)

Place	Date	Hour	Summary of Events and Information	Remarks and references to Appendices
YPRES SALIENT Trenches I 24.d.2.7/2.8/4 to I 24.d.8/4.3/4 MAP/sono Barracks YPRES Trenches I 24.d.2.7/2.8/4 to I 24.I.8/4.3/4 MAP/sono	20th to 23rd 24th to 27th 28th to 31st		The Battalion was the right Battalion of the Left Brigade on the 23rd Divisional front. Two Companies were in the Front line. One Company in WELLINGTON CRESCENT. One Company in RITZ STREET. Battalion H.Q. at the TUILERIES. The weather was very cold and the ground so hard that little work could be carried out for the improvement of the Trenches. A good deal of wire was put out each night. There was a little enemy shelling and the Battalion suffered a few casualties. The Battalion was relieved by the 11th WEST YORKSHIRE Regt and went into billets at the Infantry Barracks, YPRES. About 200 men were employed each day on working parties. The period was quiet. The Battalion relieved the 11th WEST YORKSHIRE Regt on the right Battalion of the Left 89th Brigade of the 23rd Divisional Front. Relief was complete on the night of the 28th at 8.20 pm. The enemy was rather more active than they were previously. The period was quiet in this sector. The Battalion suffered no casualties.	

Casualties for the month
11 O.R. Killed
35 O.R. Wounded

O.N.Will Major
Commanding 10th(S) Battalion DUKE OF WELLINGTONS Regt.

WAR DIARY
INTELLIGENCE SUMMARY

Army Form C. 2118.

10TH (S) Battalion DUKE OF WELLINGTON'S REGT.

Instructions regarding War Diaries and Intelligence Summaries are contained in F.S. Regs., Part II. and the Staff Manual respectively. Title Pages will be prepared in manuscript.

(Erase heading not required.)

17.4
2 sheets

Place	Date 1917	Hour	Summary of Events and Information	Remarks and references to Appendices
YPRES Salient Trenches I.24.d.8½.3½ I.24.b.2.8½ MAP 1/5000	Feb 1st		The Battalion was the right Battalion of the left Brigade of the 23rd Divisional Front. The Battalion was relieved by the 8th York and Lancaster Regt. On the evening of the 1st and marched to WINNIPEG Camp. Got eight days Rest — in Corps Reserve.	
WINNIPEG Camp H.19.b.2.3 MAP 1/20000	2nd to 9th		The Relief was complete at 9.40 pm on the 1st and arrived at Camp at 1 am on the 2nd. The Battalion carried out a Programme of training and a few working parties were supplied to the R.E.s. The weather was very fine but very cold.	
YPRES Salient Trenches I.24.C.7.1 to I.24.C.8.6 MAP 1/50000	9th & 13th		On the evening of the 9th the Battalion relieved the 11th NORTHUMBERLAND FUSILIERS as the left Battalion in the right sector of the 23rd Divisional Front. Battalion H.Q. at VALLEY COTTAGES, two and a half Companies in the front line I.24.C.7.1 to I.24.C.8.6. One Company in Support. Two Platoons were lent to the Battalion on the right. A draft of 29. O.R.'s was received from the Base. The Relief was quiet.	
ZILLEBEKE BUND I.24.a.1.5 MAP 1/5000 Trenches I.24.C.7.1 to I.24.C.8.6 MAP 1/50000	10th 17th	8.30 pm 2.50 am	On the evening of the 13th the Battalion was relieved by the 11th WEST YORKSHIRE Regt. and went into Brigade Reserve. Battalion H.Q. and two Companies at ZILLEBEKE BUND I.24.C.1.5, two Platoons in MAPLE COPSE I.24.C.1.9 & four Platoons in STAFFORD STREET I.24.C.3.5. The Relief was complete at 8.30 pm on the 13th. Working Parties were supplied to the R.E.'s each day. On the evening of the 17th the Battalion relieved the 11th WEST YORKSHIRE Regt as the left Battalion in the right sector of the 23rd Divisional Front. The Relief was complete at 8 pm on the 17th. On the 18th a fighting patrol of 12 O.R. under 2nd Lieut. P.H. MORRIS went out from our trenches to try to get a prisoner. The patrol encountered a large party of the enemy and after a bombing fight retired to our line, without suffering any loss. It is thought that several casualties were caused to the enemy.	
	20th		On the 20th between 3 pm and 8 pm there was very heavy artillery bombardment on both sides. The Battalion suffered four casualties, little damage was done to our trenches.	
ZILLEBEKE BUND I.21.a.1.5 MAP 1/5000	21st		The Raw Section and the Trenches became very wet. The Battalion was relieved by the 11th West Yorkshire Regt and went into Brigade Reserve. The Relief was complete at 8 pm on the 21st. Working Parties were supplied each day to the R.E.'s.	
WINNIPEG Camp H.19.b.2.3	25th 26th		On the night of the 25th The Battalion was relieved by the 12th Royal Sussex Regt. and marched to WINNIPEG Camp H.19.b.2.3 MAP 1/2000. The Relief was complete at 12.45 am on the 26th. WINNIPEG Camp at 4.15 am on the 26th. The 26th was spent in cleaning up march on the following day.	
Camp Z F.2.S.C. Sheet 27	27th		(39th Division) The Battalion arrived at The Battalion marched to Camp Z F.2.S.C. Sheet 27 in the HOUTKERQUE area.	

Army Form C. 2118.

WAR DIARY
INTELLIGENCE SUMMARY 10th (S) Battalion DUKE OF WELLINGTON'S REGT

(Erase heading not required.)

Instructions regarding War Diaries and Intelligence Summaries are contained in F. S. Regs., Part II. and the Staff Manual respectively. Title Pages will be prepared in manuscript.

Place	Date	Hour	Summary of Events and Information	Remarks and references to Appendices
Camp Z F.2.5.C.Ment'y	Feb 1/17	28th	The Battalion marched to BOLLEZEELE via WATOU, HOUTKERQUE, HERZEELE, WORMHOUDT ESQUELBECQ and ZEGGERS CAPPEL.	
			Casualties during the month	
			Killed in action — 3 O.R.	
			Wounded in action — 12 O.R.	
			Accidentally wounded — 1 O.R.	

Matthews Haynes.
Lieut. Colonel
Commanding 10th (S) Batt. DUKE OF WELLINGTON'S REGT.

Army Form C. 2118.

WAR DIARY
INTELLIGENCE SUMMARY 10TH (S) Battalion DUKE OF WELLINGTON'S Regt.

(Erase heading not required.)

Vol 20

Place	Date 1917	Hour	Summary of Events and Information	Remarks and references to Appendices
BOLLEZEELE	March 18th		The Battalion left BOLLEZEELE at 8 a.m. and marched to EPERLECQUES via WULVERDINGHE, WATTEN-BRIDGE and GANSPETTE	
EPERLECQUE to BOLLEZEELE	19th		The Battalion was in billets at EPERLECQUE and was occupied in platoon, company, Battalion and Brigade training	
			On the morning of the 19th the Battalion marched to BOLLEZEELE via GANSPETTE, WATTEN-Bridge and WULVERDINGHE	
HOUTKERQUE	20th		On the morning of the 20th the Battalion marched to HOUTKERQUE via ZEGGERS CAPPEL, WORMHOUDT and J. MERZEELE	
Camp L LSC Sheet 27 1/40000	21st to 31st		The Battalion marched to Camp L (L.S.C Sheet 27 1/40000) via WATOU and S.JAN to BIEZEN was in a good sad state and at work on improving the Camp which. On the 28th General Sir H.C.O PLUMER g.C.M.g., K.C.B, A.D.C commanding the 2nd Army inspected the Battalion on the Parade Ground.	1 O.R. died from broncho. pneumonia.

Murchin Hay..
LIEUT. COLONEL
COMMANDING 10TH DUKE OF WELLINGTON'S Rgt.

ORDERLY ROOM.
No. 6/R.20/3
4 APR 1917
10th (SERV) DUKE of WELLINGTON'S W. RIDING REGT.

Army Form C.2118.

WAR DIARY
INTELLIGENCE SUMMARY
(Erase heading not required.)

10TH (S) Battalion DUKE of WELLINGTONS Regt

Vol 21

Place	Date	Hour	Summary of Events and Information.	Remarks and references to Appendices
L.Camp. POPERINGHE L.3.C Sh.27 1/40000	April 1st–5th		The Battalion was still occupied in training, including Special Course in Bayonet Fighting under an Army Instructor. & Special instruction in the use of the LEWIS AUTOMATIC RIFLE by an Instructor from the School at Etaples.	
	6th		The Battalion left L.Camp at 10 a.m. & marched to SCOTTISH CAMP (G.23.C.0.8 Sheet 28.N.W.)	
SCOTTISH CAMP G.23.C.0.8 Sh.t 28. N.W.	7th 8th 9th		The Battalion was occupied in training & in cleaning Camp which was in a very dirty condition. N.C.O.s received special training under Major Bathurst. 2 Officers & 75 O.R. attached to 2nd Canadian Tunnelling Coy for duty.	
	10th 11th 12th	11.50 pm	B Coys Officers' Mess (Nissen Hut) burned. Training continued as for 7th 8th 9th. On the 11th Capt. Harrison proceeded to the ZILLEBEKE BUND with a party of 340 Officers & men to provide working parties to repair the trenches on the HILL 60 (subsector)	
HILL 60 (sub-sector) I.34.b & 35.a. Sh.t 28. N.W.	14th		The Battn. relieved the 8th Bn. York & Lancs Regt in the HILL 60. sub-sector. A.Coy (Capt Botting) & C.Coy (Capt Harrison) going into the Front Line. (I.34.716) B.Coy in Close Support in the SUNKEN Rd I.28.d.32 and D.Coy. in reserve 2 platoons being at S.P. 9 (I.28.a.64) + 2 platoons in the RAILWAY DUGOUTS I.28.d.99	
	15		B+D Coys relieved A+C in the Front Line on the evening of the 18th. Working parties to repair trenches carried on by every available man.	
SCOTTISH CAMP G.23.C.0.8 Sh.t 28 NW	22nd to 29th		The Battn. was relieved by the 8th/13th KOYLI on the evening of the 22nd + marched to SCOTTISH CAMP G.23.C.0.8 Sheet Finding Guards I.35/J.6.2 etc.t.c. 28 NW. The Battalion was occupied in training and route marching from the 23rd to 29th.	
STEENVOORDE K.31.d.3-4 Sheet 27. 1/40000	30th		The Battalion marched to billets at STEENVOORDE via ABEELE on the afternoon of the 29th. The 2 Officers & 75 O.R. who were attached to the 22nd CANADIAN TUNNELLING COMPANY on C.9th rejoined the Battalion. The day was spent in Training and route marching.	

Casualties during the month
2nd Lieut J. CROCKER Wounded.
1.O.R. accidentally Wounded
6.O.R. Wounded in action
1.O.R. Killed in action.

No.11644 Pte A. FOSTER was awarded the MILITARY MEDAL for bravery during a bombardment with gas shells at YPRES on the night of 9.11th–15th February. Authority LONDON Gazette 26/3/17.

[signature]
LIEUT COLONEL
COMMANDING 10TH DUKE OF WELLINGTON'S REGT.

ORDERLY ROOM
1/R.22.39
2 MAY 1917
10TH (SERVICE) BN. DUKE OF WELLINGTON'S REGT

Army Form C. 2118.

YC 22
20 Y
2 sheet
cont d.

WAR DIARY
for Month of MAY 1917
INTELLIGENCE SUMMARY
(Erase heading not required.)

10TH (S) BN DUKE OF WELLINGTON'S REGT

Instructions regarding War Diaries and Intelligence Summaries are contained in F. S. Regs., Part II. and the Staff Manual respectively. Title Pages will be prepared in manuscript.

Place	Date	Hour	Summary of Events and Information	Remarks and references to Appendices
STEENVOORDE (K.31.d) 27 N.E. 1:20000	1st May		Battalion in training.	
	2nd "		Inspected by Major General Sir J.M. Babington K.C.M.G. who presented the M.Medal to 11644 Pte A. Foster, C. Coy.	
	3rd "		" in training.	
	5th "			
HALIFAX CAMP (H.14.c.3.5) 28 N.W. 1:20000	6th "		" moved from STEENVOORDE to HALIFAX CAMP	
CHIPPEWA CAMP M.6.a. Central	8th "		" to CHIPPEWA CAMP owing to HALIFAX CAMP being shelled.	
	9th "		" Supplied working parties amounting to a total of nearly 500 Officers and O.R. for the construction of the Water Pipe from ZILLEBEKE BUND and DICKEBUSCH LAKE towards Front Line and also on G.H.Q. 2nd Line Trenches at night.	
	12th "			
SCOTTISH CAMP (G.23.b.0.5) 28 N.W. 1:20000	12th "		" moved from CHIPPEWA CAMP to SCOTTISH CAMP taking over from 8th K.O.Y.L.I. A draft of 59 O.R. arrived from the Base, most of them being Territorials who had seen previous Service in FRANCE with the 6th Bn. D. of W's Rgt	
	13th "			
	15th "		" Supplied same working parties as far 9th to 12th inst each night.	
	17th "			
HILL 60 subsector 18th (Verbrandenmolen) T.28.d.7.5 28 N.W. 1:20000	18th "		" relieved the 10th N.F. in the HILL 60 sub-sector — H.Q. at S.P.9 — Front Line held by B. Coy. on right and D. Coy on left. C. Coy in Support in Sunken Road & A. in Reserve at S.P.9. Major Bathurst in Command owing to illness of Lieut Colonel RAYMER D.S.O Capt J.C. Bull 2nd in Command. On night of 22nd inst Coys C and A relieved B. and D. Much work was done during this tour to improve the trenches and large ammunition, bomb, ration and water stores were formed in view of impending Offensive Owing to enemy retaliation for our heavy bombardments the Battn suffered Casualties as under.	
	24th "			
BOESCHEPE Training Area H.Q. at K.5.d.c 27/N.E. 1:20000	25th "		" Relieved in early hours of morning by 8th Bn Y&L Regt and marched to BRANDHOEK Train to ABEELE. March to billets in the Boeschepe Training Area. H.Q. at K.5.d.c.	
	26th "		" Training for attack, using Model Trenches at enemy lines opposite our lines in Hill 60 (sub s)	
	27th "		" attended Brigade Church Parade and continued training on Model Trenches after service.	
	28th "		" Draft of 40 O.R. joined Battn from Base.	
	31st "		" in training.	

Sheet. 2.

WAR DIARY
INTELLIGENCE SUMMARY

for MAY 1917 (continued)

10TH (S) Bn DUKE OF WELLINGTON'S REGT

Army Form C. 2118.

Place	Date	Hour	Summary of Events and Information	Remarks and references to Appendices
			CASUALTIES 2/Lieut B.O. HUNT - Wounded in action - died of wounds 14 O.R. Killed in action 1 " died of wounds 30 " Wounded 1 " " accidentally J. Stewart Payne Lieut for Major COMMANDING 10th Bn. DUKE OF WELLINGTON'S REGT.	

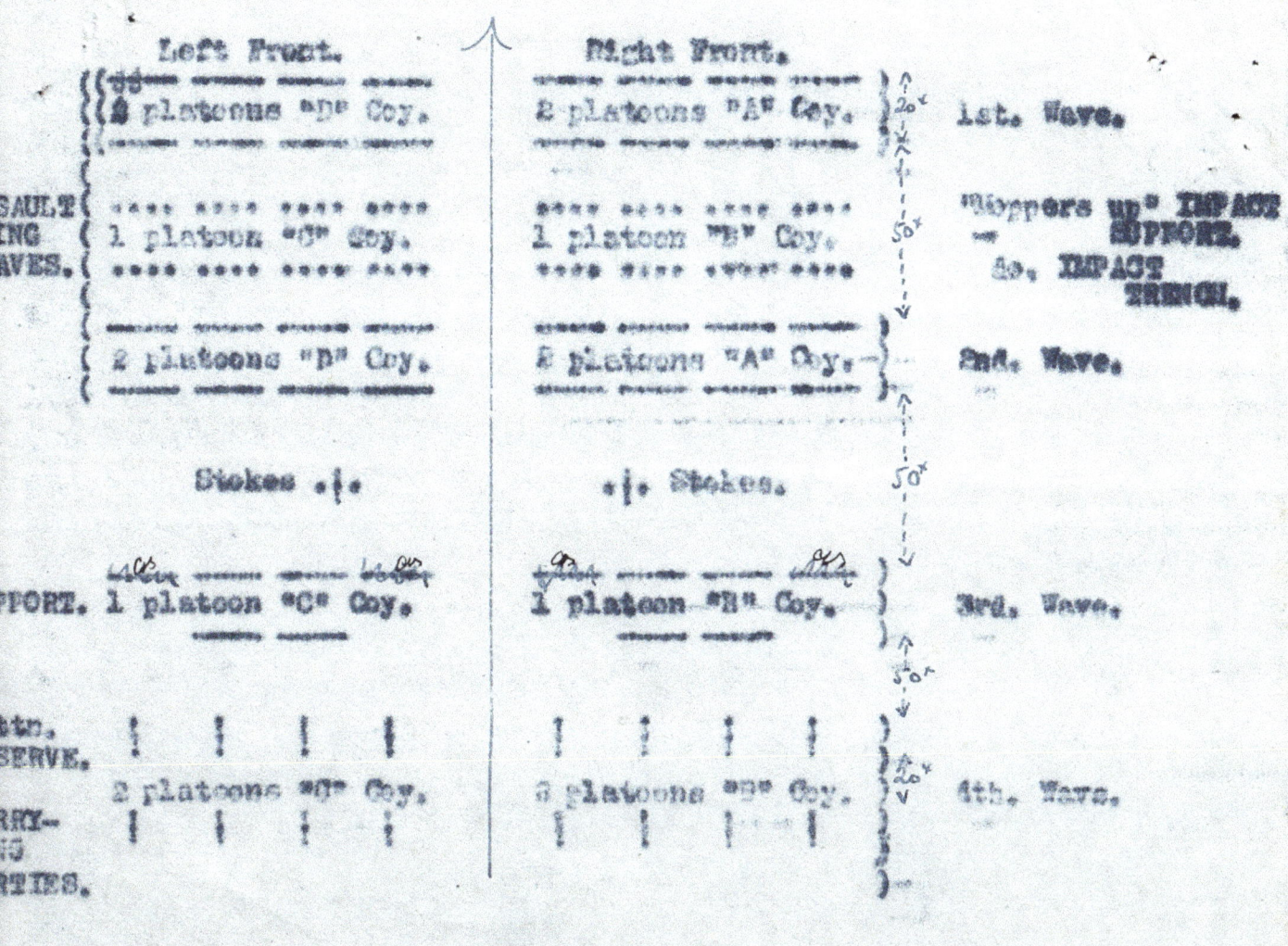

ADVANCE MOVEMENT ORDERS
BY
BY LIEUT.-COLONEL H.H.HAYNE, COMMANDING 10TH. BATTALION
DUKE OF WELLINGTON'S REGIMENT.

1. The Battalion will entrain to-morrow at ALBERT for LONGPRE and proceed immediately after detrainment to BUIGNY.

2. "A" and "B" Companies will proceed by No.7. train and "C" and "D" Companies, Headquarters and Q.M.Stores will proceed by No.8. train. Times of departure will be notified later. Lewis Gunners will accompany Companies.

3. Party which proceeds by No.7. train will be in charge of MAJOR R.E. GILL. Both train parties will leave billets 1½ hours before departure of respective trains.

4. Mess baskets and officers' kits and Company dixies will be dumped at Battalion Headquarters at a time to be notified later.

(Signed) H. W. LESTER,
Lieut and Adjutant
11.10.1916.   10th. Battn. Duke of Wellington's Regiment.

Secret. Copy No. 11

OPERATION INSTRUCTIONS
BY
LIEUT-COLONEL F. W. LETHBRIDGE,
COMMANDING 10TH. BATTALION DUKE OF WELLINGTON'S REGIMENT.
++++++++++++++++++++++++

Map References – HOOGE 1/10,000 and TRENCH OPERATION MAP 1/5,000.

1. The 23RD. DIVISION will attack and capture the line J.15.d.40.90 – J.21.b.40.10 – J.21.c.95.75 on a date and at a zero hour to be notified later. The attack will be in conjunction with simultaneous attacks on the whole 2nd. and 5th. Army Fronts.

2. The 69TH. INFANTRY BRIGADE will capture the line J.15.d.40.90 – J.21.b.40.60. The objectives and Brigade and Battalion boundaries are shown on the maps already in possession of O.C. Companies.
   The 2ND. AUSTRALIAN BRIGADE will attack on the LEFT and the 68TH. INFANTRY BRIGADE on the RIGHT, the Battalions of these Brigades detailed for the GREEN LINE being the 8TH. AUSTRALIAN INFANTRY BATTALION and the 13TH. BATTALION DURHAM LIGHT INFANTRY respectively.

3. The 11TH. WEST YORKSHIRE REGIMENT will capture and consolidate Brigade Front on the RED LINE; the 9TH. YORKSHIRE REGIMENT will capture Brigade Front on the BLUE LINE; this Battalion will capture and consolidate the GREEN LINE.

4. The Battalion, plus "D" Company 8TH. YORKSHIRE REGIMENT, will attack the GREEN LINE in two bounds.
   "A" and "B" Companies and two platoons of "D" Coy. 8TH. YORKSHIRE REGIMENT will attack and consolidate a line J.21.a.2.7. – J.15.a.95.00. "A" Coy. will be responsible for all the ground SOUTH of the track running East-South-East through VELDHOEK.
   "B" Coy. will be responsible for all the ground between that last named track and the track running East-South-East SOUTH of NORTHAMPTON FARM.
   "D" Coy. 8TH. YORKSHIRE REGIMENT will be responsible for the remainder of this portion of the Battalion's objective.
   "A" Coy. will commence the construction of STRONG POINT "N" and will construct similar strong points North and South to connect with the 13TH. BATTALION DURHAM LIGHT INFANTRY on the RIGHT and "B" Company on the LEFT.
   "B" Coy. will construct at least two STRONG POINTS about J.15.d.05.30 and J.15.d.0.5.
   "D" Coy. 8TH. YORKSHIRE REGIMENT will commence the construction of STRONG POINT "P" and will make at least one other STRONG POINT to command the VALLEY OF THE REUTELBEEK. This line will form the SUPPORT LINE.
   "C" Coy. will attack the GREEN LINE from the RIGHT BOUNDARY to the DUG OUT at the apex of the German Line at J.15.d.60.35 inclusive.
   "B" Coy. will capture the GREEN LINE from that point to a line between the CENTRE OF THE FOUR GERMAN DUG OUTS at about J.15.d.35.75.
   "D" Coy. 8TH. YORKSHIRE REGIMENT will capture the remainder of the GREEN LINE including the two left German dug outs.
   On completion of the capture of the GREEN LINE "C" and "D" Companies and half company 8TH. YORKSHIRE REGIMENT will consolidate the line – "C" Coy. being responsible for the consolidation from the RIGHT to J.15.d.45.25; "D" Coy. from that point to J.15.d.40.65 including Strong Point "O"; half company 8TH. YORKSHIRE REGIMENT will be responsible for the consolidation of the remainder of the line, including Strong Point "Q".

"B" Coy. will construct at least two STRONG POINTS - one in front of the BUILDING at about J.15.d.5.1, and another on the RIGHT FLANK to command the egress from the SCHERRIABEEK VALLEY, SOUTH of POLDERHOEK.

All coys. in the FRONT LINE will put out posts in front of the

"D" Coy. DUKE OF WELLINGTON'S REGIMENT will construct STRONG POINT "O" and at least one other STRONG POINT on their RIGHT and LEFT FLANKS to connect with "C" Coy. DUKE OF WELLINGTON'S REGIMENT and "D" Coy. 8TH. YORKSHIRE REGIMENT.

"D" Coy. 8TH. YORKSHIRE REGIMENT will construct and STRONG POINT "P".

"D" Coy. 8TH. YORKSHIRE REGIMENT and the FORWARD BRIGADE RESERVE COMPANY of the 8TH. YORKSHIRE REGIMENT will proceed direct from their Battalions to the SANCTUARY WOOD AREA to the positions which will be allotted to them later.

The jumping off position of the Battalion and the two coys. of the 8TH. BATTALION YORKSHIRE REGIMENT will be as follow:-

FORWARD BRIGADE RESERVE COMPANY 8TH. YORKSHIRE REGIMENT in NEW CUT TRENCH, N. of Jasper Lane, and JASPER LANE up to INVERNESS COPSE.

"B" Coy. Duke of Wellington's Regt. in NEW CUT TRENCH, S. of Jasper Lane, NEW CUT between JASPER LANE AND JASPER AVENUE.

"A" Coy. Duke of Wellington's Regt. EASTERN END of JASPER AVENUE.

"D" Coy. 8TH. YORKSHIRE REGIMENT, in JASPER LANE between GRID TRENCH and NEW CUT.

"D" Coy. Duke of Wellington's Regt. in LEFT HALF of GRID TRENCH

"C" Coy. Duke of Wellington's Regt. in the REMAINDER of GRID TRENCH up to JASPER AVENUE and up JASPER AVENUE as far as "A" Coy.

O's.C. Coys. will time their departure from SANCTUARY WOOD and YEOMANRY POST so as to get into these positions as soon after ZERO + 10 minutes as possible, that being the hour when GRID and NEW CUT TRENCHES will have been evacuated by the 11TH. WEST YORKSHIRE REGIMENT and the 9TH. YORKSHIRE REGIMENT.

The Battalion plus "D" Coy. 8TH. YORKSHIRE REGIMENT will commence the advance for the attack at ZERO + 3 hours, advancing in columns of half platoons in file file and will deploy for the attack, "A" and "B" Coys. Duke of Wellington's Regt. and 2 platoons 8TH. YORKSHIRE REGIMENT in front of the BLUE LINE and "C" and "D" Coys. Duke of Wellington's Regiment and two platoons of "D" Coy. 8TH. YORKS. REGIMENT immediately behind the BLUE LINE and will carry on the advance immediately on the barrage going forward at ZERO + 4 hours 13 minutes.

The deployment will be delayed as far forward as possible.

"A" and "C" Coys. will take care not to move SOUTH of JASPER AVENUE in order to give room for the various companies of the 68TH. INFANTRY BRIGADE which are moving through the SOUTHERN portion of the 69TH. INFANTRY BRIGADE AREA.

The artillery and machine gun BARRAGE will be as shown on the barrage maps to all concerned.

6. The MACHINE GUN OFFICER will arrange to place two of his machine guns at a position immediately to the EAST of STRONG POINT "P" to command the VALLEY OF THE REUTELBEEK. Two guns will be placed on the right flank of the GREEN LINE in a position to command

-2-

"C" Coy. will construct at least two STRONG POINTS - one in front of the BUILDING at about J.15.d.5.1, and another on the RIGHT FLANK to command the egress from the SCHERRIABEEK VALLEY, SOUTH of POLDERHOEK.

All coys. in the FRONT LINE will put out posts in front of the line as close as possible under the barrage.

All the consolidation will be carried out as rapidly as possible in view of the certainty of an early counter attack.

5.   At 1 p.m. on "D" Day, the Battalion will move to RAILWAY DUG OUTS by platoons at 100 yards intervals. Order of March - H.Q., "A", "B", "C" and "D" Coys. At 9.30 p.m. the Battalion will continue its march to its assembly position in the SANCTUARY WOOD AREA by sections at 100 yards intervals. Order of March - H.Q., "A", "B" and "C" Coys, Stretcher bearers, police and pioneers, and "D" Coy. The latter will proceed to YEOMANRY POST direct and report to MAJOR CRELLETT, 8TH. YORKSHIRE REGIMENT.

"D" Coy. 8TH. YORKSHIRE REGIMENT and the FORWARD BRIGADE RESERVE COMPANY of the 8TH. YORKSHIRE REGIMENT will proceed direct from their Battalions to the SANCTUARY WOOD AREA to the positions which will be allotted to them later.

The jumping off position of the Battalion and the two coys. of the 8TH. BATTALION YORKSHIRE REGIMENT will be as follow:-

FORWARD BRIGADE RESERVE COMPANY 8TH. YORKSHIRE REGIMENT in NEW CUT TRENCH, N.of Jasper Lane, and JASPER LANE up to INVERNESS COPSE.

"B" Coy. Duke of Wellington's Regt. in NEW CUT TRENCH, S. of Jasper Lane, NEW CUT between JASPER LANE AND JASPER AVENUE.

"A" Coy. Duke of Wellington's Regt. EASTERN END of JASPER AVENUE.

"D" Coy. 8TH. YORKSHIRE REGIMENT, in JASPER LANE between GRID TRENCH and NEW CUT.

"D" Coy. Duke of Wellington's Regt. in LEFT HALF of GRID TRENCH

"C" Coy. Duke of Wellington's Regt. in the REMAINDER of GRID TRENCH up to JASPER AVENUE and up JASPER AVENUE as far as "A" Coy.

O's.C. Coys. will time their departure from SANCTUARY WOOD and YEOMANRY POST so as to get into these positions as soon after ZERO + 10 minutes as possible, that being the hour when GRID and NEW CUT TRENCHES will have been evacuated by the 11TH. WEST YORKSHIRE REGIMENT and the 9TH. YORKSHIRE REGIMENT.

The Battalion plus "D" Coy. 8TH. YORKSHIRE REGIMENT will commence the advance for the attack at ZERO + 3 hours, advancing in columns of half platoons in fisk file and will deploy for the attack, "A" and "B" Coys. Duke of Wellington's Regt. and 2 platoons 8TH. YORKSHIRE REGIMENT in front of the BLUE LINE and "C" and "D" Coys. Duke of Wellington's Regiment and two platoons of "D" Coy. 8TH. YORKS. REGIMENT immediately behind the BLUE LINE and will carry on the advance immediately on the barrage going forward at ZERO + 4 hours 13 minutes.

The deployment will be delayed as far forward as possible.

"A" and "C" Coys. will take care not to move SOUTH of JASPER AVENUE in order to give room for the various companies of the 68TH. INFANTRY BRIGADE which are moving through the SOUTHERN portion of the 69TH. INFANTRY BRIGADE AREA.

The artillery and machine gun BARRAGE will be as shown on the barrage maps to all concerned.

6.   The MACHINE GUN OFFICER will arrange to place two of his machine guns at a position immediately to the EAST of STRONG POINT "P" to command the VALLEY OF THE REUTELBEEK. Two guns will be placed on the right flank of the GREEN LINE in a position to command

-3-

the egress from the SCHERRIABEEK VALLEY.

7. The O.i/c.TRENCH MORTARS will place two guns at STRONG POINT "N" and two guns near the HOUSE at J.15.d.15.45.

8. FORWARD BRIGADE SIGNAL STATION and the FORWARD BATTALION SIGNAL STATION will be at BATTALION HQ. AT STRONG POINT "I" and the SIGNAL OFFICER will proceed there immediately on the taking of the BLUE LINE and will take with him two Battalion runners and one runner of the M.G.SECTION who will return to BATTALION H.Q. at STIRLING CASTLE to act as guides.

The method of communication and dealing with prisoners, the use of flares for contact aeroplanes, and orders as to salvage have already been communicated to all concerned.

BATTALION H.Q. will be at STIRLING CASTLE until ZERO + 3 hrs. when it will move to the FORWARD HEADQUARTERS at STRONG POINT "I".

THE MEDICAL AID POST will be at J.13.d.4.0 in a dug out in STIRLING CASTLE.

BRIGADE H.Q. will be in new dug outs in STIRLING CASTLE at about J.13.c.80.10.

H.Q. of 11TH. WEST YORKSHIRE REGT. will be at CLAPHAM JUNCTION at J.13.d.70.70.

H.Q. of 9TH. YORKSHIRE REGT. will be under the MENIN ROAD near NORTHAMPTON FARM until the BLUE LINE has been captured when it will move forward to the German Aid Post at J.20.b.75.90.

H.Q. of 13TH. DURHAM LIGHT INFANTRY will be at TORR TOP SUBWAY until ZERO + 3 hours when it will move forward to the German Dug Out at J.20.b.55.25.

The position of the H.Q. 8TH. BATTALION AUSTRALIAN INFANTRY will be notified later.

9. DRESS - Fighting Order as laid down in Brigade Order No. less entrenching tool helve and carrier which have been dumped at Q.M.Stores.

10. One day's dry rations plus the emergency ration will be carried by all ranks.

The greatest care will be taken to see that all waterbottles are filled at the start from at RAILWAY DUG OUTS. "C" and "D" Coys. will each carry an extra 50 waterbottles filled.

O's.C.Coys. will be held responsible that all empty petrol tins are returned to the RATION DUMP at the earliest possible moment. Every man going back from the Line to the Ration Dump will carry at least four empty petrol tins or some salvage.

The Battalion RATION DUMP will be formed at some place on the reverse slope of the Hill in INVERNESS COPSE. Position will be notified later.

The Reserve Coy. of the 8TH. YORKSHIRE REGIMENT near BATTALION H.Q. will detail one officer and 60 O.R. on and after "F and "G" Night to carry rations from the BATTALION DUMP to Battalion H.Q. at STRONG POINT "I". Each Coy. in the line will arrange for one N.C.O. and 12 men to fetch its rations from Battalion H.Q. Each party will carry in two trips.

11. The REGIMENTAL POLICE will provide three STRAGGLERS POSTS of two men each who will be posted at intervals in front of the BLUE LINE to see that no men of this Battalion or "D" Coy. 8TH. YORKSHIRE REGIMENT turn back without authority.

12. One runner and one man per coy. will be detailed to report to Battalion H.Q. at STIRLING CASTLE when their coys. are in position at YEOMANRY POST AND SANCTUARY WOOD and will remain there.

13. All BATTLE STORES will be drawn and issued on "D" DAY before the move from MICMAC CAMP. The Qr.Master Will arrange with O's.C. Coys. the hour at which they will be drawn.

Tea will be served prior to the start from MICMAC CAMP and hot dinners prior to the start from RAILWAY DUG OUTS.

~~All ranks will take as much rest as possible during "D" Day and prior to the attack.~~

~~Great care will be taken to take all ammunition, rations,~~

-4-

14. All ranks will take as much rest as possible during "D" day and prior to the attack.

15. Great care will be taken to take all ammunition, rations, compasses, field glasses, etc. off all casualties.

16. BLUE FLAGS will be issued to Coys. to be placed at Dug-outs which have been cleared and not occupied.
RED FLAGS will be placed against dug-outs in which chemical or "P" Bombs have been used and cannot therefore be occupied for a time.

17. O's.C. Coys. will take particular care that casualty, intelligence and situation reports are in punctually to the times required.

18.9.1917.

(Signed) L.M. PHILLIPS.
Capt. and Adjutant.

Copies to
1. File.
2. O.C. "A" Coy.
3. O.C. "B" "
4. O.C. "C" "
5. O.C. "D" "
6. Medical Officer.
7. Quartermaster.
8. Transport Officer
9. Signalling Officer.
10. Intelligence Officer.
11. H.Q. 69th. Infantry Brigade.
12. 13th. Bn. Durham Light Infantry.
13. 8th. Bn. Australian Infantry.
14. 11th. Bn. West Yorkshire Regiment.
15. 8th. Bn. Yorkshire Regiment.
16. 9th. Bn. Yorkshire Regiment.
17. 69th. Machine Gun Company.
18. 194th. Machine Gun Company.
19. 69th. Trench Mortar Battery.
20. War Diary.

Army Form C. 2118.

WAR DIARY
or
INTELLIGENCE SUMMARY 10th (S) Battalion Duke of Wellington's Regt.

(Erase heading not required.)

Instructions regarding War Diaries and Intelligence Summaries are contained in F.S. Regs., Part II. and the Staff Manual respectively. Title Pages will be prepared in manuscript.

Place	Date 1917	Hour	Summary of Events and Information	Remarks and references to Appendices
BOSCHEPE AREA Camp at L.33.a.9.2	JUNE 1st 2nd 3rd		Maps 27 1/40000 28 NW 1/20000 The Battalion marched from billets in the WATOU Area to Camp at L.33.a.9.2 (Map 27 1/40000) in the BOSCHEPE Area. On the afternoon of the 2nd inst. No.13385 a/Cpl. T. THOMPSON in the 2nd Batt. was presented with the ribbon of the MEDAILLE MILITAIRE by the Divisional Commander.	
9th Camp G.18.c.9.2 Railway Dug Outs I.33.c	4th		The Battalion marched to a field at G.18.c.9.2 and were in bivouac for the night of the 3rd/4th On the afternoon of the 4th the Brigade addressed the men of the Battalion prior to this going into the line. The Battalion moved up to Railway Dug Outs I.21.c on the night of the 4th-5th. Several officers and a proportion of N.C.O's & men were left behind at the Reinforcement Camp.	
FRONT LINE T.34.b	5th 6th	3 am	The enemy shelling was very heavy on the evening of (K.5th 6th some gas shell as) were put over. The Battalion was delayed for 1½ hrs in going up into the front line on account of the very heavy shelling. The Battalion relieved the 10th NORTHUMBERLAND FUSILIERS in the right-sector of the right Brigade on the 23rd Divisional Front on the night of the 5th - 6th. At 3 am. on the 6th the enemy were reported to be forming up for an attack. The Battalion stood to. Artillery action followed. The enemy shelled the Trenches at intervals during the day but did little damage. Orders for the attack were issued as Oper A & B.	'A' 'B'
	7th	2.30am 3.10am 3.30am	At 2.30 am on the 7th the Battalion was formed up in assembly formation ready for the attack. All dug outs were cleared at 3 am, ready for the MINES going up at Zero from 3.10 am. During the half hour before Zero there was hardly any shelling on either side. At 3.10 am the Mine under HILL 60 and that under THE CATERPILLAR were exploded, all our artillery opened fire and the attack was launched. At 3.30am Battalion H.Q. moved forward from LEEK TRENCH to the GERMAN SUPPORT LINE I.35.a.35.0	
BATTLE WOOD I.35.C.6.7 I.35.d.8.7	8th	3.45am 4.45am	The Battalion had gained all its objectives by 3.45 am and began to dig themselves in. The 9th YORKSHIRE REGT passed through our line and carried on the attack according to PROGRAMME. Opers on the operation attached 'C'. The Battalion took over the line held by the 9th YORKSHIRE REGT and one Company of the 8th YORKSHIRE REGT. The Battalion was done with two Companies; the remaining two Companies in addition to the line already held, this was done with two Companies in the original line occupied by the Battalion on JUNE 7th. The new front line was at approx. I.35.d.35.0 to I.35.d.9.50. This line was held by a series of posts.	'C'
ZILLEBEKE BUND	10th 11th 12th		The Battalion remained in the position relieved by the 12th DURHAM LIGHT INFANTRY on the night of the 10th/11th. The relief was completed at 4.15 am on the 11th The Battalion proceeded to ZILLEBEKE BUND where it remained until the morning of the 12th inst.	

Army Form C. 2118.

WAR DIARY
of
INTELLIGENCE SUMMARY 10TH (S) Battalion DUKE OF WELLINGTONS' REGT.

(Erase heading not required.)

Place	Date 1917	Hour	Summary of Events and Information	Remarks and references to Appendices
HALIFAX Camp. H.14.L.1.5. MAP 28 N.W.	JUNE 12TH		The Battalion marched to HALIFAX CAMP on the morning of the 12th	
	13TH		The Battalion moved to the BERTHEN Area and was billeted round about Le Coq. de Paille R.31 and R.25.	
BERTHEN Area	14th to 28		On 16th the G.O.C. Division inspected the Battalion. Battalion continued training in accordance with daily programmes submitted to 69th Infantry Brigade	
CHIPPEWA AREA	28th		Battalion marched from BERTHEN AREA to camp at M.6.d.5.8 (Sheet 28) in CHIPPEWA AREA via GODEWAERSVELDE and RENINGHELST.	
SUPPORT TO FRONT LINE (Sheet 28 N.N.)	29th		Battalion relieves the 9th Battalion EAST SURREY REGIMENT in support to Right Sector of Divisional front on night of 29th/30th, companies being disposed as follows and Headquarters being in LARCH WOOD. — "A" Coy. LARCH WOOD, "B" Coy. THE CATERPILLAR, "C" Coy. THE DUMP, "D" Coy. IMPERIAL TRENCH (about I.34.a.7.2.). Battalion Transport arrived lines at MICMAC CAMP (H.31.b.2.3).	
			Mentioned in despatches:- 2/Lieut: C.J. Wolfe 11593 Cpl. Raffery, J. 13277 L/Cpl. Hudson, J. 12259 L/Cpl. Graty, S. } "London Gazette" Supplement 22.5.1917.	
			Awarded MILITARY MEDAL by Corps Commander:- 13768 Sergt. Ericson, W.S. — 11/12.6.17. 11839 Pte. Smith, H. — 7.6.17.	
			Casualties during month:- Killed in action 2 Officers 35 O.R. Wounded in action 6 " 159 " Died of Wounds - 16 " Wounded & Missing - 3 " Missing - 10 "	

W.W. Wilson.
Major
Commanding 10th Bn. Duke of Wellington's Regt.

SECRET.   Copy No. 7

10TH. BATTALION DUKE OF WELLINGTON'S WEST RIDING REGIMENT.

REFERENCE – 23rd. Division Map.   INSTRUCTIONS No. 1.

DISPOSITIONS OF 10TH. BATTALION DUKE OF WELLINGTON'S
WEST RIDING REGIMENT FOR ATTACK ON PORTION OF HILL 60
SUB-SECTOR.

1. The attack will be carried out by two companies; left front company and right front company.

   Both companies will advance in two waves, each with two platoons in front.

   These two companies will be supported by the third wave, consisting of two platoons – one from left rear company and one from right rear company.

   The latter companies will provide a small Battalion Reserve of two platoons, plus two Lewis Gun Sections, one platoon and one Lewis Gun Section from each of the two companies.

   This Reserve constitutes the leading line of the fourth wave.

   The second line of the fourth wave will consist of two platoons – one from left rear company and one from right rear company, less two Lewis Gun Sections.

   This line will act as carrying party.

2. "Moppers up" will consist of two platoons – one from left rear company and one from right rear company.

   These "moppers up" will move in rear of the first wave in two lines, the sections from left rear company following left front company and vice versa. Sections from right rear Coy following right front Coy.

   The leading line of "moppers up" will deal with IMPACT SUPPORT and all communication trenches leading towards IMPACT RESERVE.

   The second line of "moppers up" will deal with IMPACT TRENCH and all communication trenches leading towards IMPACT SUPPORT.

3. The first three waves will advance in extended order; the last wave moving in lines of sections in single file.

   The two Stokes Guns attached to this Unit will move in rear of the second wave; one gun behind the left front company and one behind the right front company.

   Battalion H.Q. will remain at I.34.b.50.80 until the RED LINE has been secured. H.Q. will then move forward to I.35.a.50.80.

4. Detailed instructions to leading waves, "moppers up", third wave, Battalion reserves and carrying parties will be issued later.

                                                Bathurst
                                                Major.
                              Comdg. 10th. Battn. Duke of Wellington's Regt.
May 28th., 1917.

B

SECRET.   Copy No. 10

10TH. BATTALION DUKE OF WELLINGTON'S WEST RIDING REGIMENT.

INSTRUCTION NO. 2.   REFERENCE ATTACHED SKETCH.

1. With reference to Instruction No.1 of 28.5.1917:-
   Right Front Company...."A" Coy....under LIEUT. PERKS, D.S.O.
   Right Rear Company ...."B" Coy....under Capt. REINCKE.
   Left Front Company...."D" Coy....under Capt. BULL.
   Left Rear Company......"C" Coy.... under Capt. HARRISON.

2. The first objective of the left and right front companies is the RED LINE (see attached sketch).
   The second objective of the same companies is the BLUE LINE (see attached sketch).
   Subject to the times given below in General Instruction, para.15., these companies will push straight on to their objectives.
   The objectives of the "moppers up" are given in Instructions No.1., dated 28.5.1917.
   The objective of the Third Wave is the RED LINE which they will consolidate and mop up.
   When the Left and Right Front Companies move on to the BLUE LINE the Third Wave will be responsible for "mopping up" communication trenches running from RED LINE to BLUE LINE.
   This Wave must be ready to support the leading companies in the attack if such support is required. In this case information as to action taken must be sent back to Battalion H.Q. at once.
   The objective of the leading line of the Fourth Wave is IMPACT SUPPORT.
   On arrival at the objective this line will be consolidated and strong points made. Especially are strong points to be made at the following points:-
               I.35.a.40.10
               I.35.a.50.40
   The two Lewis Gun Sections on the right of the first line of Fourth Wave will proceed at once to Strong Point at I.35.a.40.10.
   The two Lewis Gun Sections on the left of same line will proceed at once to strong point at I.35.a.50.40.
   The former of these two points will later be manned by two Machine Guns of 69th. M.G. Company, and when these arrive the two Lewis Guns must take up a defensive position on our right of IMPACT SUPPORT.
   A small garrison of riflemen will be left by the right rear company at Strong Point I.35.a.40.10 to assist the M.G.Coy. to hold same.
   Except for the Machine Guns and small garrison in S.P. at I.35.a.50.40 the troops in IMPACT SUPPORT must be prepared on receipt of orders from Battalion H.Q. to reinforce the troops in front. They will not move forward from this line without orders from Battalion H.Q.

3. The rear line of Fourth Wave consists of carrying parties.
   It is divided into five sections. They will be required to carry as follows:-
   First journey, following immediately behind the attack, as far as IMPACT SUPPORT where they will dump their loads at S.P. at I.35.a.50.40.
   On Second Journey they will carry their loads up to RED LINE and dump at the junction of the two Front Companies.
   After that they will carry from S.P. at I.35.a.50.40 to RED LINE where most required.
   As soon as BLUE LINE is secured the platoons garrisoning the

-3-

RED LINE will detail carrying parties to carry material etc. to the BLUE LINE from RED LINE. Parties will be detailed to carry also from IMPACT SUPPORT garrison. These latter parties will be detailed direct from Battalion H.Q. and will carry from GRAND FLEET STREET to S.P. at I.35.a.50.40. All carrying parties must wear yellow armlets.

Loads will be distributed as follow:-

    One Section.................Wire and stakes.
    One Section.................Sandbags.
    One Section.................Grenades.
    One Section.................S.A.A. and later water.
    One Section.................S.A.A. and later water.

Carrying parties on return journeys must bring back salvage or prisoners. If there are none of these rifles and equipment from casualties nearby must be carried back. Parties must never return empty-handed.

The N.C.O. in charge of each section must keep his men closed up and together.

4. "Moppers up" will carry with them small yellow and blue flags.

Yellow flags are to be placed on top of all dug-outs into which P. or M.S.K. bomb has been thrown.

Blue flags are to be placed on top of all dug-outs which have been cleared or satisfactorily dealt with otherwise than with P. or M.S.K. bombs.

5. The tunnellers who examine dug-outs which have been cleared will place small Red flags on top of dug-outs which are worth repairing. All available men must be set to work at once upon these dug-outs.

6. Notice boards showing the names allotted to the various enemy trenches will be carried as follows:-

    First and Second Waves........BLUE LINE.
    Third Wave....................IMPACT RESERVE
                                        RED LINE.
    MOPPERS UP.
    First Line....................IMPACT SUPPORT.
    Second Line...................IMPACT TRENCH.

These notice boards must be placed in prominent position by order of an officer or senior N.C.O. as soon as the trench has been reached. Great care must be taken that trenches are correctly marked.

7. On X/Y night and Y/Z night all present company dumps will be carried to two dumps, one on either side of GRAND FLEET STREET near the Front Line. On the same night the Battalion Dump will be moved in a similar manner to these dumps. Positions of dumps will be notified later.

Copy No........

10TH. BATTALION DUKE OF WELLINGTON'S WEST RIDING REGIMENT.
GENERAL INSTRUCTIONS.
----

1. No N.C.O. or man is allowed to move back from the front (except wounded) unless he is wearing a distinctive amulet. Any men so found are likely to be arrested by Battle Police.

2. Wounded men must not be allowed to discard their arms and equipment unless their wounds are so severe as to render the men incapable of carrying them.

-3-

Slightly wounded walking cases who have disobeyed this order will be sent back by Battle Police to fetch their rifle and equipment.

3. It must be impressed on all ranks that the word of command "RETIRE" does not exist. The enemy use it frequently as a ruse. It is only in very exceptional cases that men should be ordered to withdraw. In such cases the order will be "WITHDRAW" Anyone using the word "RETIRE" will be treated as an enemy.

4. Company and other Commanders must form dumps in captured positions. S.A.A., bombs, flares, iron rations, water should be collected from a casualty lying in the vicinity of the trench. All serviceable enemy material should be collected.

5. Strong Points should be made large enough to hold two Machine Guns and about 20 men.

6. Lewis Gun Sections should only carry forward 32 magazines. Twelve magazines should be kept at Company H.Q.

7. The S.O.S. Signal will be one RED Very Light.

8. Flares will be carried, two to every other man, and will be lighted in groups of three by troops in the front line. Signalling arrangements when called for by contact patrol by troops in whatever position they are in except when they are actually on the move.

9. ### SIGNALLERS AND RUNNERS.
Distribution.

	Signallers.	Runners.
Platoon H.Q.	-	1
Company H.Q.	2	4
Battalion H.Q.	16	32 *

* Four from each Company and with six Battalion runners.

HOW THE RUNNERS ARE TO BE USED. Companies will send runners in duplicate, one runner 50 yards in front of the other. Before the Battalion H.Q. has moved to I.35.a.30.65 the runners will hand their message in at "X" Relay Post and stop there themselves while "X" R.P.Runners take the message down to Battalion H.Q. "X" R.P.Runners wait for an answer and bring it back with them to "X" R.P., hand the message to the Company Runners and they return to their Company H.Q. with the answer. This method is used now so as to prevent any Post being left empty.

The Battalion Forward Party which consist of:-
1 officer, 1 N.C.O. signaller, 8 runners, one from each Company (from the four detached from each Company to Battalion H.Q.) 2 from Battalion H.Q., 8 signallers, 1 pigeoneer, 4 riflemen to assist in carrying stores.

This party will move up after Fourth Wave. On arrival at the C.P. runners will be sent to Brigade F.P., to H.Q. of Companies, to Battalion H.Q. on either flanks. One runner to act as guide for the Commanding Officer.

The Officer in charge of the C.P. will send back a message to the Commanding Officer when he has got all communication through.

The Forward Party must go forward to miss the enemy barrage but must not take any part in the fighting.

-4-

10. RIFLE GRENADES............"A" 125
　　　　　　　　　　　　　　"B" 75
　　　　　　　　　　　　　　"C" 75
　　　　　　　　　　　　　　"D" 125.

11. VERY LIGHTS..IV..........."A" 15
　　　　　　　　　　　　　　"D" 15
　　　　　　　　　　　　　　"C" 10
　　　　　　　　　　　　　　"B" 10

　　VERY LIGHTS RED.........."A" 12
　　　　　　　　　　　　　　"B" 12
　　　　　　　　　　　　　　"C" 10
　　　　　　　　　　　　　　"D" 10
　　　　　　　　　　　　　　H.Q. 6

12.　　　Each man to carry two bombs, one in each top pocket of his jacket.

13.　　　All messages to be carried in the top right hand pocket.
　　　　Waves will carry P. and M.S.K. bombs as follows:-

　　　　　　　　　　　　　　　　　　"P"　　M.S.K.
　　　　　　　First Wave)
　　　　　　　Second Wave)..........10　　10
　　　　　　　Third Wave.............15　　15
　　　　　　　First Line "mopping
　　　　　　　　　　　　　　up"...15　　15
　　　　　　　Second Line "mopping
　　　　　　　　　　　　　　up"...10　　10

　　　　Flares will be carried as follows:-
　　　　　　　First Wave..............................75
　　　　　　　Second Wave.............................75
　　　　　　　Third Wave..............................50
　　　　　　　Fourth Wave (first Line)................25

14.　　　ZERO - 1 ..... Bayonet fixed.

　　　　ZERO　　　..... Mines blow. Barrage commences. Infantry
　　　　　　　　　　　　　leaves trenches.

　　　　ZERO + 3 ..... Barrage lifts off enemy front line.

　　　　ZERO + 20 .... Lifts off RED LINE. Pause at 200 yards till
　　　　　　　　　　　　ZERO + 35.

　　　　ZERO + 45 .... Barrage lifts off BLUE LINE for 200 x where
　　　　　　　　　　　　it will continue till ZERO + 3 hrs.40 mins.
　　　　　　　　　　　　when advance to BLACK LINE begins.

　　　　From ZERO there will be a Machine Gun Barrage searching about BLACK LINE.

+ + + + + + + + + + + + + + + + +

In accordance with 69/L.B. Operation Order No. BMS 437/16 dated 25
the Battalion was formed up in assembly formation by 2.18 a.m.

The entire Battalion, less H.Q., was assembled between our front line
and COFFEE TRENCH. The reason for crowding the men in so much was
that it had been observed that whenever the enemy put down a barrage,
it fell in rear of COFFEE TRENCH. When the actual assaulting time
came this proved to be correct, for the entire barrage which the
enemy put up fell well in rear of the Battalion.

The difficulty of assembling without being observed by the
enemy was increased by the bright moonlight. However all ranks
got into position without mishap. A few riflemen and two Lewis
Guns continued firing as usual at gaps in enemy wire up to the
last few minutes to allay any suspicion which entire silence might
arouse.

At 3.15 a.m. the mines exploded, and at the same time our
artillery opened fire. Simultaneously our men went forward.

Our barrage was perfect, and gave the infantry a great feeling
of security. Men were heard to observe afterwards that they could
have gone any distance behind that barrage.

Our men advanced over "No Man's Land" and into the enemy's
front line with very few casualties.

The leading waves pushed ahead towards the RED LINE, leaving
the front line and support line to the "Moppers up".

In one place I.36.a.35.9 an enemy machine gun held up a small
portion of our line. The troops on either side however pushed
on, and the machine gun was dealt with by rifle grenadiers and a
few bold riflemen.

In the meantime Battalion H.Q. remained in GRAND FLEET STREET
hoping for some information to come back from Companies in front.
By 3.30 a.m. no information having arrived, Battalion H.Q. moved
forward to ascertain the position.

By this time the line to Brigade H.Q. had broken, so that
the only means of communication to Brigade was by runner.

The enemy barrage was by now considerably decreased and soon
became almost negligable.

Crossing "No man's Land" it was very noticable how few
casualties our Battalion had incurred in the initial stages of
the attack.

Upon the arrival of Battalion H.Q. at IMPACT SUPPORT,
information was received that the RED LINE and BLUE LINE had been
secured.

I at once sent this information back to Brigade.

Owing to the fact that our P.B. and Amplifier were damaged
early on there was no communication with Brigade H.Q. except by
runner.

Touch with the 8/Yorkshire Regt. was at once obtained. It was
different however on the right, and it took some 20 minutes to
obtain touch with the 22/London Regt. on my right.

In the meantime the enemy's shelling was gradually increasing
in intensity and accuracy and it is to be feared that we suffered
several casualties at this period.

Work was at once commenced on consolidation, and patrols
were pushed out beyond the BLUE LINE.

At this period one of our heavy guns commenced firing very
short, and caused us to evacuate one strong point, in which we
had commenced work.

The Artillery Liason Officer was with me, but he was unable
to assist in any way. It seemed to me that throughout this officer
was wasted. He had no means of communication with the Artillery, and
we had no means of communicating with Brigade except by runner.

Now followed the pause of over three hours before the 2nd.
Phase of the attack commenced.

We were now in touch with troops on our right and left.

In my opinion had we not had to pause in the BLUE LINE, we
could have secured the BLACK LINE comparatively easily. The enemy
was observed to be running away fast and was now putting up no

opposition at all. Rifle fire and Lewis Gun fire were opened on him as he retired, and it was thought many casualties were inflicted on him.

At Zero + 3hours.40 mins the 9/Yorkshire Regiment passed through the BLUE LINE.

In the meantime our men continued the work of consolidation and carrying up material and water.

The hostile artillery fire now became much heavier, but it was not very effective.

About this time I received a message from O.C. 9/Yorkshire Regiment to the effect that his right flank was held up. He asked for one platoon to be sent up forward to reinforce him.

I ordered one platoon to be sent forward, but it is regretted that they went astray, and did not arrive until very much too late.

I futher sent up 1 Stokes Mortar to assist the 9/Yorkshires. This arrived but was not able to be made use of owing to lack of ammunition.

By now the 9/Yorkshire Regiment informed me that they had not quite reached their objective, but were holding a position about fifty 50 yards short of the BLACK LINE.

On our front the situation remained unchanged for the remainder of the day.

In the evening, in consultation with O.C. 9/Yorkshire Regt. I took up a line running roughly along BLUE LINE and dug in there. Orders were issued to Companies that this line was to be held at all costs in the event of the 9/Yorkshires being forced back.

The line taken up by me commanded all the low ground as far as and beyond the BLACK LINE.

In addition to this defensive line taken up by my Battalion, I garrisoned three strong points in IMPACT SUPPORT. The 2 M-G's attached to my Battalion and a section of riflemen occupied one of these strong points. The other two were held by Lewis Guns and a small garrison of riflemen.

Of the two Stokes Mortars attached to my Battalion, one was now forward with the 9/Yorkshire Regt., and one was in position in IMPACT RESERVE whence it could open fire to cover any part of the line held by me.

The position remained unchanged on our front throughout the night and the following day.

On the evening of 8th June, I received orders from Brigade H.Q. to take over the line held by 9/Yorkshire Regt. and one Coy. of 8/Yorkshire Regt. in addition to the line at present held by me.

This relief was satisfactorily carried out without any casualties. Our dispositions were then as follows:-

Two Companies holding front line by a series of strong points small posts well dug in.

Two Companies less 2 sections holding second line (the line previously held by my Battalion during the day of 8th, June).

Two sections and 1 Lewis Gun holding strong point at Battalion H.Q. at I.35.a.35.0 .

Position remained unchanged and quiet until night 10/11th. when we were relieved by 12th /D.L.I. Regiment.

The effect of our Thermite Guns could not really be traced. One German wounded, who was found in IMPACT RESERVE, was terribly burnt, and it is supposed that it was the result of Thermite.

I attach notes drawing attention to short-comings which I observed in my own Battalion during the attack, and copies of which I have issued to Company Commanders. These points are perhaps somewhat exaggerated but I feel that all of them should be

(3)

be given more consideration in future training.

I have no futher notes or suggestions to offer on the preparations for the attack. Everything as far as I was concerned was most satisfactory.

I wish to state how excellent was our Artillery and M-G. barrage throughout the attack. It inspired our men with a great feeling of security and confidence and certainly demoralized the enemy who ran away hard, and who with the exception of one or two points, put up a very feeble resistance.

The value of the Yukon Pack carriers was very great, and should go a long way to solving the problem of carrying parties in future offensives.

In my opinion the supply of Stretcher Bearers was exceedingly inadequate. Taking my own Battalion as an example. I had no less than 24 extra stretcher bearers in addition to the 16 allowed in Establishment, making a total of 40. Even with these numbers, the wounded both of the enemy and our own troops had to go through much additional suffering through exposure.

If the R.A.M.C. bearers cannot come up to the battlefield until the battle is over, it seems that additional men should be supplied from other units not actually employed in the attack.

Though the stretcher bearers were working hard all day long and during the night, some of the wounded were not removed until 24 hours after they had received their wounds.

As an alternative to this, if the Regimental Aid Posts could move forward it would save the stretcher bearers long carries which would greatly save the delay in collecting all the wounded.

The signalling arrangements struck me as being the most difficult problem to solve. The P.B. and Amplifier seem to be far too delicate for the purpose.

Even three days after the attack, we were only in telephonic communication with Brigade H.Q. by an ordinary D.3. telephone and wire. This wire was of course continually broken, and for the most part we had to rely on runners as one sole means of communication.

No less than two P.Bs. were tried and neither of them was a success.

I am certainly of opinion that lines should be run out from Battalion H.Q. to Companies as soon as possible after an attack. The system of runners is slow and almost exhausting to the men. If lines were run out and linesmen properly organised into groups, each group being responsible for a certain length of line, it seems to me it would be more satisfactory. In the recent attack we had no wire to run out to Companies, and had to rely absolutely on runners.

WAR DIARY
or
INTELLIGENCE SUMMARY 10th (S) Battalion DUKE OF WELLINGTON'S Regt

Army Form C. 2118.

Place	Date July 1917	Hour	Summary of Events and Information	Remarks and references to Appendices
YPRES SALIENT TRENCH MAP HILL 60 front of Sheet 28 1/5000	1st		The Battalion was in support Battalion in the Right sector of the Divisional front. One Company and Battalion Headquarters at LARCH WOOD I.29.c.2.9. One Company at the DUMP I.29.c.25.35. One Company at the CATERPILLAR I.35.a.9.6. One Company at I.34.a.7.2.	
Camp H.31.6.N.T MAP 28 N.W 1/20000	2nd		On the night of the 1st/2nd the Battalion relieved the 8th YORKSHIRE Regt in the front line of the right sector of the Divisional front. Battalion Headquarters at I.35.a.35.20. One Company at the CATERPILLAR at I.33.a.95.20. and one Company believed O.6.a.25.10. and I.36.b.2.5. The line was held by a force of two more Companys.	
STEENVOORDE AREA	3rd		On the night of 3rd/4th the Battalion was relieved by the 17th LONDON Regt. and moved back to a Camp about H.31.b.2.2. MAP 28 N.W. 1/20000	
	4th 4-11th		On the afternoon of the 4th the Battalion moved to the STEENVOORDE AREA. By train from OUDERDOM to GODEWAELWELDE and thence by road to billets about J.22.; 23.a.; and 34.b. MAP 27 1/40000 The Battalion received several big drafts of men and carried out the usual training programme.	
Camp H.31.6.N.2 MAP 28 N.W 1/20000	12th		The Battalion moved to Camp about H.31.6.22. MAP 28 N.W. 1/20000 by road to GODEWAELWELDE STATION thence by train to OUDERDOM.	
YPRES Salient TRENCH MAP HILL 60 front of Sheet 28 1/5000	13th		On the night of the 13th/14th the Battalion moved into support in the left sector of the 23rd Divisional front relieving two Companys of the 8th YORKSHIRE Regt and two Companys of the 9th YORKSHIRE Regt. Battalion Headquarters and one Company in HEDGE ST TUNNELS about I.24.d.5.1. One Company in CANADA dug outs about I.30.a.9.4. One Company at RUDKIN HOUSE TUNNELS about I.24.a.05.10. and one Company in METROPOLITAN LEFT about I.29.a.8.2.	
	16th		On the night of the 16th/17th the Battalion relieved the 9th YORKSHIRE Regt in the front line. The front line was held by a force of four Companys in the front line between I.30.6.9.8 and I.30.c.8.4. One Company and Battalion Headquarters about I.24.d.5.1 and One Company in CANADA TUNNELS about I.30.a.9.4.	
	18th		Here was a good deal of rain and the ground became almost impassable. A fighting patrol went out on the night of the 18th/19th but failed to find any enemy.	
	19th 19th/20th		On the night of the 19th/20th the Battalion was relieved by the 8th YORKSHIRE Regt. and moved back into reserve. Battalion Headquarters and LARCH WOOD at I.29.6.25.90. One Company in the DUMP I.29.c.2.4. One Company at BATTERSEA FARM I.23.c.75.25. Two Companys at SCOTTISH WOOD near DICKEBUSCH H.34.a. MAP 28 NW 1/20000	
Camp H.31.6.N.T MAP 27 N.W 1/40000	22nd		On the night of the 22nd/23rd the Battalion was relieved by the 8th Royal West Kents and moved back to Camp about H.32.c.5.7.	
BERTHEN Area R.23.C MAP 27 1/40000	23rd		On the 23rd the Battalion marched to the BERTHEN Area billets about R.23.C MAP 27 1/40000	

Army Form C. 2118.

WAR DIARY

INTELLIGENCE SUMMARY 10TH (S) Battalion DUKE OF WELLINGTON'S Regt.

(Erase heading not required.)

Place	Date	Hour	Summary of Events and Information	Remarks and references to Appendices
BERTHEN AREA	July 1917 25th		The G.O.C. Division inspected the Battalion.	
BOISDINGHEM	26th		The Battalion moved to the BOISDINGHEM area, billets about W.1 & N.2 and Q.31.6 and of MAP 27A S.E. 1/20000. The Battalion marched to CAESTRE and entrained for ST OMER thence by road route to billets.	
St R. at 27A S.E. thence	to 31st		The Battalion was occupied in training and musketry.	
			Casualties :- Lieut. D.L. Evans - wounded in action.	
			1 O.R. killed in action.	
			25 " wounded in action.	

Ruchman Sharper
LIEUT: COLONEL
Commanding 10TH DUKE OF WELLINGTON'S Regt.

Army Form C. 2118.

WAR DIARY
of
INTELLIGENCE SUMMARY. 10th (S) Battalion Duke of WELLINGTON'S Rgt.

(Erase heading not required.)

Instructions regarding War Diaries and Intelligence Summaries are contained in F. S. Regs., Part II. and the Staff Manual respectively. Title pages will be prepared in manuscript.

Place	Date	Hour	Summary of Events and Information	Remarks and references to Appendices
BOISDINGHEM AREA MAP Sheet 27 NE 1/20,000	August 1917 1st.		The Battalion was in billets in the BOISDINGHEM AREA about Q.31.6.5 W.1.5.9.d W.2.W.3.a W.8.a V.22.b	
	7th		The Battalion was inspected by General Sir H.C.O PLUMER, 2nd Army Commander, at ACQUIN V.22.6.	
			During the whole time in the BOISDINGHEM AREA the Battalion was occupied in Musketry and Field Training.	
MOULLE MAP Sheet 27 NE 1/20,000	9th.		The Battalion marched to fields at MOULLE about Q.11.C , Q.10.C.9.d	
	19th.		Colonel R.F. RAYMER D.S.O left the Battalion and Major F.W. LETHBRIDGE, from the 8th DUKE OF WELLINGTON'S Rgt, took over the command of the Battalion.	
			The Battalion was occupied in Musketry, Company and Field Training while in the area.	
PATRICIA Camp K.29.b.1.8 Map Sheet 27 I/40000	24th.		The Battalion moved to PATRICIA CAMP K.29.6.1.8 by train from WATTEN to ABEELE, the Transport moved by Road all the way.	
Camp H.33.a.8.3 MAP Sheet 28NW 1/20000	25th		The Battalion moved to Camp near DICKEBUSCH H.33.a.8.3 by train from ABEELE.	
			The 26th and 27th were very quiet.	
CHATEAU SEGARD H.30 central	27th to 31st		The Battalion marched to Camp (bivouacs and dug-outs), at CHATEAU SEGARD H.30 central.	
			Casualties during month :- 1 Officer slightly wounded; 1 OR through; 1 OR accidentally wounded in action; 1 OR wounded	

J.W. Lethbridge
Lieut Colonel
Commanding 10th Bn Duke of Wellington's Rgt.

"A"

REPORT ON ATTACK OF VILLAGE OF VELDHOEK AND GERMAN LINES IMMEDIATELY EAST OF IT AND THE SUBSEQUENT HOLDING OF THE GREEN LINE BY THE 10TH DUKE OF WELLINGTON'S REGIMENT AND 8TH YORKSHIRE REGIMENT.

++

In the afternoon of 19th August the Battalion plus "D" and "A" Companies 8th Yorkshire Regiment moved from Micmac Camp to Railway Dugouts and thence after 9.30 pm to the trenches and dugouts in the Sanctuary Wood area. This was effected without loss but the move into Sanctuary Wood was carried out under most trying conditions in pitch darkness and heavy rain which made the ground very muddy and slippery and with the area not thoroughly reconnoitred owing to the two parties that had been sent out to reconnoitre the two previous days both having been knocked out by Shell fire. The way in which the Companies were handled by their Commanders and the behaviour of the men under the circumstances was most admirable. At about 3 a.m. the Companies began to move up to their assembly positions in Jasper Avenue, Jasper Lane and Grid and New Cut trenches. "A" Company 8th Yorkshire Regiment which was acting as part of Brigade Reserve having been directed by the Brigade to go to   The Companies had been ordered to be in positions so as to be able to get straight into their respective trenches immediately on these being vacated by the 9th Yorkshire and 11th West Yorkshire Regiments at or as soon after Zero as possible and this was duly carried out within about five minutes of Zero, but owing to a party of the 9th Yorkshire Regiment without an Officer, remaining in Jasper Avenue, Major Borrow who was temporarily commanding "A" Company for the battle was unable to get into it for a considerable time and the Company suffered severe casualties in consequence at this stage. A platoon under 2/Lieut Hulburd too was late in getting into position owing to its Commander, and platoon Sergeant both being badly wounded and this Platoon suffered considerable casualties.

(2)

At 8.40 a.m. The Companies moved forward in columns of half platoons in file with "A" Company followed by "C" Company on the right - "B" Company followed by "D" Company in the centre, and "D" Company 8th Yorkshires on the extreme left. The latter Company moved up on the northern side of Inverness Copse and got through to their jumping off point in front of and behind the Blue line in good order having the good fortune to get very little barrage on them. The four Companies of this Battalion who had to go through Inverness Copse had a pretty heavy barrage put on to them and suffered considerable casualties, and arrived at the blue line about 9.10 am.
"B" Company having lost all its Officers, except Lieut Anderson who with his platoon had lost direction somewhat and got on the right of "A" Company, arrived in a somewhat disorganised state, but was pulled together by Capt. Payne and the whole line advanced punctually to time at about 9.53 am, about 10 minutes after I had arrived with my Headquarters party at the Tower in S.P.I, and from this time the advance could be watched from the Tower up to the time when our men disappeared over the ridge just behind the Green line, though the smoke and dust of the shells made it difficult to see details but it was obvious all was going well.

Northampton Farm itself on the left proved no obstacle to speak of, but just beyond it a line of over a dozen concrete dugouts and pill-boxes were heavily manned and armed with Machine guns which together with the enemy shells caused a great many casualties to our "B" and "D" Companies.
"D" Company 8th Yorkshire Regt. was more fortunate though it too at this stage appears to have had a good many casualties

in crossing from the same causes. These dug-outs were eventually cleared of the enemy by "B" and "D" Companies of this Battalion, whilst others still further to the left were dealt with by the 8th Yorkshires, and these Companies took up a line in the dug-outs with posts from 75 to 150 yards in front which were well dug in within an hour. At the same time Capt. Payne finding no one on his right flank formed a defensive flank with 1 platoon of "B" Company reinforced by 2 Lewis Gun Sections. Meanwhile "A" and "B" Companies on the right had had stiff fighting for some of the concrete dug-outs in the village of VELDHOEK and a strongly held hedge in front of it, but these were cleared by the fine manoeuvering of Major Borrow, 2/Lieut Sparling and 2/Lieut Anderson, whose platoon of "B" Company had rather lost direction, but came on the scene just in time to outflank the dug-outs at S.P.M. and rendered valuable service to "A" and "C" Companies in the taking of these strong dug-outs. Meanwhile 2/Lieut Wilson with a platoon of "C" Company seeing that there was no touch with "D" and "B" Companies on the left took his platoon most opportunely into the gap and enabled Capt. Payne to send the men he had on his defensive flank forward. As "A" and "C" Companies attacked the last line of concrete dug-outs in the Green Line C.S.M. Parker observing that the dug-out on the left front of the 13th Battn. Durham Light Infantry was rather holding them up promptly attacked it from the flank and rear and captured it. This completed the capture of all our objectives and everywhere the troops dug in energetically, and by noon our new line was secure. Meanwhile about 10.30 am. Capt. Miller "B" Company 8th Yorkshire Regt. reported his arrival at the dug-outs about 150 yards N.N.W. of S.P.I. with part of his Company which had been very heavily shelled on their way bringing up wire and other materials, had suffered considerable casualties and were rather scattered and started reorganising and salving material which had been dropped.

At about 11 a.m. having received a message from Capt. Payne that he was in his objective but not in touch with anyone on his left and that he was too weak to cover the gap himself I ordered Capt, Miller to at once send up 2 platoons of his Company to report to Capt. Payne and fill the gap obtaining touch with "C" Company on the right and to hold himself and his other two platoons in readiness to go up at a moments notice, and I asked for one of the Brigade Reserve Companies of the 8th Battn.Yorkshire Regt. to be sent up at once to take his place and for the others to be sent up at dusk. Capt, Miller's first 2 platoons arrived at their destination just about noon in small parties without much loss and took up a position in the front line between my "B" and "C" Companies considerably strengthening the line which was then rather thin.

As soon as I learnt the Brigade Reserve Company was coming up, I sent up Capt.Miller with the rest of his Company to take up as much S.A.A. as he could collect to Capt.Tilley and then report to Capt. Payne with a view to going where he was was most wanted and thus make as sure as possible of the line.

At 12.45 pm. being still uncertain of the exact dispositions in the front line I sent 2/Lieut Edwards my Intelligence Officer to reconnoitre and report on it, a duty he carried out most thoroughly with the utmost gallantry in the face of considerable fire of every description, and was able to tell me on his return the exact dispositions and the fact that the 2 Vickers Guns which I had ordered to take up a position on the right flank did not appear to be there. I did not in fact succeed in getting them taken there until the night of the 21st inst. notwithstanding my urgent orders.

At 2.45 p.m. we observed from the Tower considerable bodies of the enemy massing for counter-attack on a line J16 C entral to J16.c95.05 and in front of it. I at once let Brigade and Artillery know and sent out urgent warnings to all concerned and deployed my reserve

Company of the 8th Battn. Yorkshire Regt. which had just arrived on a line right and left of S.P.I., Our artillery opened on the enemy at once and with evident effect for the attack did not materialize, and when the dust and smoke of our barrage cleared no-one was to be seen. At dusk I moved my Battalion Headquarters from the Tower in S.P.I. to a more commodious concrete dugout which had evidently been a German Headquarters, about 50 yards south of the Tower, keeping the Tower as an Observation Post and Signal station connected with me by 'phone.

The night was very quiet with the exception of some heavy shelling of my Headquarters and the Tower about midnight and I was able to spend about 3 hours in going round and examining the posts and dispositions behind in comparative peace before the opening of our trial barrage, during which time I thoroughly satisfied myself that our position was secure everywhere.

Early on the morning of 21st August "A" Company 8th Battn. Yorkshire Regt. relieved my "B" and "D" Companies in the centre of the left of the line – "C" Company 8th Battn. Yorkshire Regt. having been sent up to support my right on the previous afternoon.

The day of the 21st August was fairly quiet with the exception of some shelling of my Headquarters and the Tower about 1 p.m. and again during our trial barrage – when the various dug-outs in the Green line were also shelled, and a faint hearted attempt to form up for a small local attack on our front at about 1 p.m. which was nipped in the bud by our rifle and Machine gun fire, in which we used a Bosche gun with great effect in the neighbourhood of the

Chateau. At 6.30 pm. I noticed from the Observation Post a f[ai]r[ly] heavy mixed shrapnel and H.E. enemy barrage in the neighbourhoo[d] of our front lines and at 6.40 pm. I received a message from Major Grellet that the enemy could be seen massing for attack at J 16 a 7.6. I also noticed at this time the enemy barrage beginning to advance. I at once let Brigade and Artillery and my companies in front know, and at 6.47 our barrage came down, actually 3 minutes before our S.O.S. went up from the front line where about 150 of the enemy appeared in front of my "A" and "C" Companies, and were promptly wiped out by rifle and Lewis Gun fire. There is little doubt this was meant to be a strong counter-attack and the enemy must have lost very heavily in our barrage.

Large numbers of enemy wounded and dead were seen being still taken away early next morning under cover of the red flag.

The remainder of our time in the line was perfectly quiet with the exception of bursts of shelling on all dug-outs and intermittent searching shell fire., Snipers from the direction of Tower Hamlets or thereabouts/ and also from the Chateau in front and from the Red House to the left front of it were always more or less active. A Machine gun was located in the latter and movement in the open by daylight in front of my Headquarters was always a risky proceeding., Our relief by the 11th Battn. Sherwood Foresters and and 9th Battn. Yorkshire Regt. were carried out with the utmost smoothness and practically without casualties.

Whilst holding the line the two Vickers guns on my left were very well handled by the Officer in charge of them and did several executions on several occasions.

During the operations we captured 3 Trench Howitzars/, 4 Machine Guns and a very large amount of trench materials of every description including many flammenwafer, many thousands of rounds of M.G. ammunition etc. We captured about 190 prisoners of whom the first 47 were sent back in one batch under an escort, but the rest could not be escorted owing to the thinness of our line, and went back to rear units by themselves covered by a Lewis Gun until they were seen to be taken over.

We buried 146 dead Germans, including several Officers, and sent back about 70 badly wounded Germans. A necessarily very rough estimate of casualties inflicted by our Machine Guns, Lewis Guns and rifles on the enemy in front of line places the number of his casualties at about 450 for the 36 hours we were in the line. In addition to this our artillery barrage must have accounted for large numbers of the enemy during the attack and each of his counterattacks. Our own casualties during the course of the fight were 3 Officers, 40 O.R. killed, 6 Officers 244 O.R. wounded and 50 missing, of whom the majority will I fear be found to be killed or wounded and certainly none are prisoners.

Army Form C. 2118.

WAR DIARY
or
INTELLIGENCE SUMMARY.
10th (S) Battalion Duke of Wellington's Regt

(Erase heading not required.)

69/23

M 26

Place	Date 1917	Hour	Summary of Events and Information	Remarks and references to Appendices
CHATEAU SEGARD AREA Sept 28th TON	Sept 1st		The Battalion was in reserve	
STEENVOORDE AREA April K33 Central	2nd		The Battalion passed through Kindred Huts to Steenvoorde and via Dickebush, Reninghelst & Abeele, Rent and K33 Central	
LEDERZEELE G7d & G27d68	3rd		The Battalion moved by Route March to Lederzeele area via Steenvoorde, Cassel, Bavinchove, Zuytpeene, Noordpeene, Lederzeele Battalion HQ at G27 d 68	
LEDERZEELE G7d & G27d68	4/4/12		The Battalion was training for open warfare at Lederzeele. Musketry S.S. 121 etc a Rifle Platoon Course etc etc	
STEENVOORDE AREA Sept 13th K25 d43 Central	13th		The Battalion was billeted by Sunday March to Steenvoorde area via Noordpeene, Zuytpeene, Bavinchove, Cassel, Steenvoorde Bn HQ at K25 c 93 Bn 27 Bnlfs. 1 Branch	
WOOD CAMP M5d63 Sheet 28	14th		The Battalion moved to Wood Camp via Abeele & Reninghelst Bivouac HQ M5.d55 Sheet 28 I 10 Wood Camp was occupied by the Battalion for the 14th & 15th	
MIDDLE EAST CAMP N a 3.5 Sheet 28 SW	16th		The Battalion moved to Mail Reds & Middle East (Camp N a 3.5 Sheet 28 SW) relinquishing Wood Camp for the 19th	
YPRES SALIENT	19th		The Battalion moved up to Railway Dugouts at I 21 c + I 21 d Sheet 28 NW upon Theater Menzies & Their Dugouts	
At Ap 2nd Lieutenants Ourter 28 March Ord R + Lt K + Lt 3	20th		The Battalion attacked the German Line (as per Appendix A) Kells Main for the night 22/23	APPENDIX A
	21/23		The Battalion came back to Reserve & Railway Dugouts at I 21 C Central	
WOOD CAMP N a d 63	24th		The Battalion moved back to Wood Camp (M5.d.55) in reserve and to reorganise June 22nd 29th	
	25th		The Battalion was inspected attacked for the band by Brigadier General 23rd Brigade Div. Comdr 29th Ymsh Div. Major Gen Babington	
CANAL BANK DUG OUTS Sept 28 NW	27th		The Battalion moved up by night lorries to Canal Bank Dugouts about I 25 & 77 Ref Sheet 28 NW when they arrived in rounds 16.30 a.m.	
Aug I25 & 77	30th		D Coy plus 1 Platoon of B Coy took over the front line from A Coy 8th Yorkshire Regt about J 16 a 10 15 & J 16 a 55 (Zillebeke Sheet 28 NW + NE) in the night Sept 30/1st October	

MM4/10

WAR DIARY
or
INTELLIGENCE SUMMARY

Army Form C. 2118.

Place	Date	Hour	Summary of Events and Information	Remarks and references to Appendices
			Casualties:- Killed in action - Capt. A.C.B Reuss, Lt J.Brooker, 2/Lieuts. Taylor	
			D.H.P. Yates & J.A. Brooks and 57 O.R.	
			Wounded in action:- Maj. E. Borrow, A/Capt. R.E. Watts, Lieut. A.H.	
			Garratt, 2/Lieuts. G.A. Hubbard, G.A. Lotherington, L.W. Walker, J.R. Cass and	
			275 O.R.	
			Missing - 21 O.R.	
			J.W. Lethbridge	
			Lt. Col.	
			Comdg 10th Bn Duke of Wellington's Regt	

Army Form C. 2118.

WAR DIARY
or
INTELLIGENCE SUMMARY.
(Erase heading not required.)

10th (S) Battn Duke of Wellington Regt.

Vol 27

69/23

Instructions regarding War Diaries and Intelligence Summaries are contained in F.S. Regs., Part II. and the Staff Manual respectively. Title pages will be prepared in manuscript.

Place	Date	Hour	Summary of Events and Information	Remarks and references to Appendices
RIDGEWOOD CAMP Sheet 28 about H.35.c. N.5.b.1.4.	October 1917 1st.		The Battalion less D. Company & one platoon of B. Cy. moved by March Route to RIDGEWOOD CAMP about N.5.6.1.4 Sheet 28 from CANAL BANK DUGOUTS. On the way D of the 1st D.Cy. plus 1 platoon of B.Cy. found a critical situation at about J.13.d.2.6. by repelling a strong German Counter attack when the flank of the Corps on their left had been turned.	
BERTHEN AREA Sheet 27 about R.21.c.& d	2nd.		The Battalion less D Company were embussed at RIDGEWOOD CAMP to BERTHEN AREA via VIERSTRAAT – KEMMEL – LOCRE – BAILLEUL. D.Cy. plus one platoon of B.Cy. left the front line on the night 1/2nd Oct. & after assembly at RIDGEWOOD CAMP entrained later for BERTHEN AREA	
do	3rd		Companies partially reorganised after being in the line	
do	4th		D.Cy. plus one platoon of B.Cy. were attached to 8th YORKSHIRE REGT & the remainder of the Battalion moved by March route to CAESTRE where they entrained for YPRES	
YPRES Sheet 28 H.6.c central	5/6th		at about H.6.c central Sheet 28. D.Cy. plus one platoon of B.Cy. remained in train at BERTHEN AREA. The remainder of the Battalion were attached to 2nd Battn. CANADIAN RAILWAY TROOPS for work in the construction of a light Railway. These were under the orders of the Second ANZAC CORPS.	
Camp Sheet 28 H.35.c central	11th		The Battalion less D.Cy. & one platoon of B.Cy. moved by march route from H.6.c Central to Camp about H.35.c Central (Sheet 28)	
BREWERY CAMP H.28.d.4.2.	12th		The Battalion moved from Camp about H.35.c central to BREWERY CAMP at H.28.d.4.2. (Sheet 28) and were joined there by B.Cy. & one platoon of B.Cy. from BERTHEN	
do	13/14		The Battalion remained at BREWERY CAMP & came under the orders of the 68th Brigade.	2
do	15th		The Battn moved to RAILWAY DUGOUTS & ZILLEBEKE BUND	
RAILWAY DUGOUTS ZILLEBEKE BUND	16th		The Battalion moved to the front line & relieved the 12th DURHAM LIGHT INFANTRY on the night 15/17. HQ was at THE BUTTE J.10.a.7.9. A & B Cys. occupied the front line from J.10.70.50 & J.10.a.5.5 C & D Cys. occupied the support line	
		CHELWEINE 28NE	On the night 17th/18th B.Cy. repulsed a GERMAN RAID	
THE BUTTE J.10.a.7.9	17/19th		The Battalion was in the line	2

2 Luck

WAR DIARY
INTELLIGENCE SUMMARY

Army Form C. 2118.

10th (S) Battn. Duke of Wellington Regt.

Place	Date	Hour	Summary of Events and Information	Remarks and references to Appendices
THE BUTTE J10 a 70.90 (GHELUVELT J.12.a.N.W)	19th		The Battalion was relieved in the night 8-19/20th by the 12th D.L.I. & moved to ZILLEBEKE BUND & RAILWAY DUGOUTS	
C CAMP A30 c.4.2 (Ref Sheet 28 Zoom)	20th		The Battalion moved by march route to C. CAMP A 30 C 4 2 (Sheet 28 Zoom)	
MICMAC CAMP	21st		The Battalion moved by march route to MICMAC CAMP No 15	
ZUDAUSQUES AREA Sheet 27A S.E.	22nd		The Battalion Entrained at H 30 d 4. 2 & proceeded to ZUDAUSQUES via VIERSTRAAT - KEMMEL - LOCRE - BAILLEUL - HAZEBROUCK - ST OMER. Battn Hqrs at NOIR GARME W 1 d 5.6 (Sheet 27A S.E.) & came under orders of 69th Brigade	
do	23/3/st		The Battalion carried out Drawing & Range Practice G. 31st the Battalion was inspected with other battalions of the Brigade by Field Marshal Sir Douglas Haig	
			Companies carrying on training. Reorganisation & Refitting. PC. terminate on 15.10.17	
			27 OR joined the Battn	
			48 OR were sent on Course to Infantry School Arques	

Honours awarded during October:-
Distinguished Service Order - Lt Col P H Falkridge
Military Cross - Capt & Bt Major B. Bonsius
           " Capt. R. Harrison
Bar to Military Cross - Lieut. E.A. Loveless M.C.
Distinguished Conduct Medal - Coms Sarl n. Cb. 13769
                       Pte Kelly J.J. 18903.
Bar to Military Medal - Pte. Joyce W.T. 136615.
Military Medal - 32 other ranks.

J. W. Jackson Lt-Col
Comdg 10th (S) Bn Duke of Wellington's Regt

www.ingramcontent.com/pod-product-compliance
Lightning Source LLC
Chambersburg PA
CBHW080917230426

43668CB00014B/2148